BEGINNING
BLACKSMITHING
WITH PROJECTS

A very special thanks to my wife, Pat. All I did was put the information down in nearly illegible longhand. She translated those scratch marks into the words and sentences and organization that accurately reflected my thoughts. Then she typed the manuscript over and over again.

Her artistic skills gave meaning to my illustrations.

Most of all her encouragement and strength gave me the strength to say what I had to say.

As always I love and thank her, and to her this book is dedicated.

No. 2651
$18.95

BEGINNING
BLACKSMITHING
WITH PROJECTS

JIM CONVERSE

TAB BOOKS Inc.
Blue Ridge Summit, PA 17214

FIRST EDITION
FIRST PRINTING

Copyright © 1986 by Jim Converse
Printed in the United States of America

Reproduction or publication of the content in any manner, without express
permission of the publisher, is prohibited. No liability is assumed with respect to
the use of the information herein.

Library of Congress Cataloging in Publication Data

Converse, Jim, 1919—
Beginning blacksmithing, with projects.

Includes index.
1. Blacksmithing—Amateurs' manuals. I. Title.
TT221.C66   1986   682'.4   85-27743
ISBN 0-8306-0351-4
ISBN 0-8306-0451-0 (pbk.)

Cover photograph courtesy of Pat Converse.

Contents

Preface

I WAS REARED AND WORKED AS A YOUNG FEL-low on several of the large cattle ranches of southern Arizona during the 1920s and 1930s.

It is hard now to visualize ranch life in southern Arizona in those times. In 1920 Arizona had been a state for only eight years. Cattle was our product. Big ranches ran from 100 to 150 square miles or more, and it was common to live 50 miles from town. A trip to town might be made once or twice a month over primitive roads that would challenge today's four-wheel drive vehicles. We used to amuse ourselves on those trips by shooting at jack rabbits along the sides of the road.

Because of this isolation, a typical large cattle ranch maintained its own complete shop. The ranch hands did all the repair work on wagons, agricultural machinery, harness, and tools. The ranch blacksmith made most of the parts and tools needed to keep the ranch going. The blacksmith in south-ern Arizona in those days was the last remnant of the trade as it was practiced in the pioneer days.

On the ranches where I worked, we had no power hammers or gas or electric welding equipment. It was necessary to develop "hand power" with hand hammer and sledge hammer.

I learned blacksmithing in this atmosphere and under these demanding conditions. My first teacher was old Tio, a tall Mexican with white hair and moustache whose straight back and stout muscles belied his 80 years. He taught me to plan ahead, to think a problem through, and to make every move count. There was little room for mistakes. The nearest supply center was a long way away.

My background is deeply ingrained in this book and is the basic of my methods and teachings. Blacksmithing is a thinking game. If you can't think it out, you can't hammer it out. In this book, I will show you how to think it out and hammer it out.

Acknowledgments

I WANT TO THANK THE MANY SMITHS, YOUNG and old, whose enthusiasm for blacksmithing has made the writing of this book seem worthwhile.

Four of us smiths have been gathering at my shop every Saturday afternoon for several years now. We light our fires, heat up some iron, work out blacksmithing problems together, exchange ideas, and sometimes even do a little work. Bob Brunjes, Kirk Jenner, and Roy Whisenant have been unfailingly enthusiastic and encouraging about this book. I thank them particularly.

My students have been a constant source of encouragement and have taught me much about teaching smithing. They have also taught me that not all blacksmiths are brawny folk who have spent their lives at hard physical work; women and office workers can be blacksmiths, too.

I thank all the supply houses in Grants Pass, Medford, and Portland that have been patient and helpful in locating scarce tools and materials. I also want to thank organizations that have invited me to demonstrate traditional blacksmithing to their members. And special thanks to the blacksmiths' organizations—national, regional, and local—that are spreading the knowledge of traditional blacksmithing to a new generation.

Introduction

MANY BOOKS TELL THE HISTORY OF THE blacksmith and describe all manner of historic tools and lore. Some of the writings are very good; some leave much to be desired. A large portion of the available printed material has been collected from libraries and old books and makes fascinating reading. A great deal can be learned from them. But remember as you study these works that most are copies or variations, in part or completely made from other copies, and that this process has continued until, in many cases, the articles and information often are nothing more than fiction. Some of the information is very good, but the beginner has no basis on which to make judgments. Few of the books on blacksmithing are suitable as a beginner's text.

The information and the instructions in this book are used and have been proven in my shop and school. Every exercise has been tested. Beginners are advised to take each step in the order it appears and master it well before going on. Skipping sections will surely confuse you and might block your progress. When you have mastered this book, you will have a fine foundation on which to pursue your special interest, be it farm machinery, cutlery, railings, builders' hardware, or traditional blacksmithing. The foundation for all your future blacksmithing will be no better than your mastery of the following exercises.

No doubt you will find some methods here that are contrary to what you have heard, but go along with them with an open mind. You will be very glad you did.

The book is designed to lead you step by step through each succeeding exercise. Take each one in order; note that some will not be completed until you have also worked on a subsequent exercise. Sometimes two or more things must be learned together before you can complete an exercise. Read completely through the steps in each exercise before you begin work. Some of the exercises will be challenging. Stay with them, and your anvil will ring a song into your heart.

PART 1

Getting Started

Chapter 1

What You Will Need

T HE SIZE, QUANTITY, AND TYPE OF PRODUCT you wish to produce determines the tools and equipment needed. A shop for one man working alone will be compact. However, if you plan to have someone working with you, a larger and more fully equipped shop might be desirable.

I assume that you are planning to establish a small one-man shop on a low budget. I also assume that the largest item you plan to build will be the size of an average fireplace screen, garden gate, or window grill. Figure 1-1 shows the layout of a typical one-man shop.

TOOLS

Following is a list of the basic tools you need to start:

- A good hickory handled 2 1/2-pound hammer, preferably a cross peen.
- A 1-pound ball peen hammer with a hickory handle.
- A large pair of straight jawed, vise-grip pliers or the equivalent.

- A simple 12-inch hacksaw frame and two 18-tooth blades of the best quality.
- A forge.
- An anvil.
- A vise.
- Safety equipment.

You will need other tools as you progress through the book. Many of them you can make; others you may prefer to buy.

SAFETY

Of first concern is safety equipment. Take a look at yourself. You are made of flesh and bone, and you are very easy to burn, damage, and break. You will never have any more parts than you do right now. Don't spoil any of them; there are no replacements.

In blacksmithing lots of sparks, chips, dust—all hot— and, frequently, large pieces of hot iron fly around at a remarkably high rate of speed. Get some good protective eye gear that fits and that you

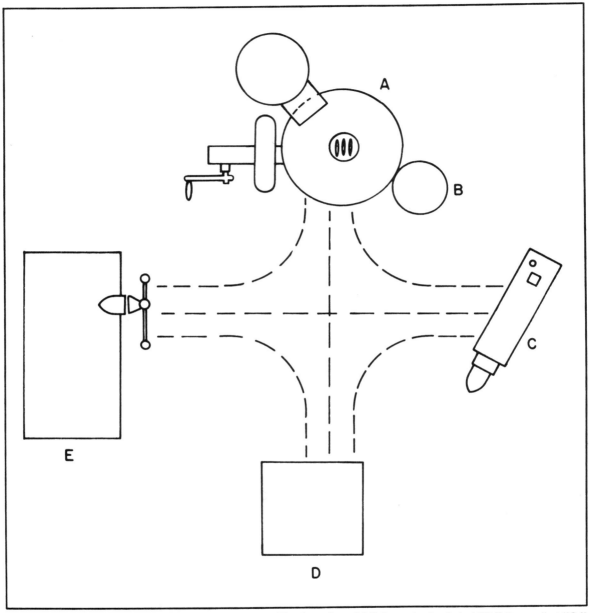

Fig. 1-1. A suggested layout for a small one-man shop. The forge is at "A," the water bucket at "B," the anvil at "C," the tool table at "D," and the workbench at "E." The dotted lines show the easy traffic flow between all the pieces of equipment.

can wear all day. If you already wear glasses, make sure the lenses are not plastic and are shatter proof or safety type. If you are not sure about your lenses, discuss them with your optician.

Wear some kind of head cover to keep dust and sparks off your hair and scalp. Some smiths wear a bandana; others, a tight fitting cap. If you wear a beard, crop it short and neat. Big bushes make big fires. If you wear long hair, do it up tightly in a braid or bandana and don't let it dangle over the front of your shoulder.

Wear an apron to protect your clothing and to give you protection around groin, hips, thighs, and knees. A denim shop apron is all right, but denim won't stop hot iron or offer much protection against a hard blow. If you use denim, be sure to remove the pockets at waist level because they will become traps for hot sparks. A leather apron is better, but it is more expensive. I have included instructions for making your own leather apron in Chapter 16. Any apron should come up above the shirt pocket and tie snugly around the body.

Wear good leather work shoes. These will protect you from falling pieces of hot iron and when you step on a hot piece. Remember that in good daylight (not direct sunlight), iron that appears black may yet be over 1,000 degrees Fahrenheit. Don't forget.

Get a good pair of heavy leather gloves and develop the habit of using them, especially on holding hand, the hand that holds your work. I do not recommend the welder's gauntlet type of glove because of its bulk. A leather glove with partial cloth backing on the fingers and a short gauntlet works well for me.

Buy a good general purpose fire extinguisher and mount it in a convenient and conspicuous place. Get the type that has a gauge. Take the time to check it periodically and recharge it if necessary.

Keep children out of the shop whenever any blacksmithing is going on. Their faces are at the level of the anvil and are in the line of fire when sparks, chips, and hot pieces of metal fly around unpredictably. When you are forge welding, there is always a heavy spray of sparks in every direction, and the danger of fire and injury is great, particularly to someone at a child's level. Children often move quickly and unexpectedly, and you may bump

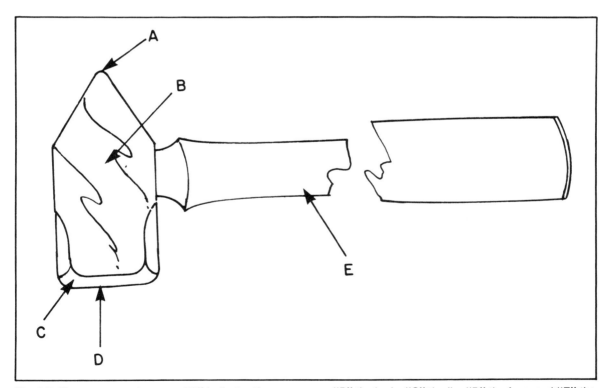

Fig. 1-2. The cross peen hammer. "A" indicates the cross peen, "B" the body, "C" the lip, "D" the face, and "E" the handle of the hammer. The handle is made of hickory or ash. Notice that the peen is rounded like the side of a round rod.

into them with a piece of hot iron. Also, it is hard to convince a child that a piece of scrap iron that looks black may still be hot enough to cause severe burns. Damage to a child received in the blacksmith shop may well be permanent. Don't chance it.

HAMMERS

There are many types of hammers, and you may add some as you go along, but for now the two listed will do.

The cross peen with a 2 1/2-pound head weight is a very good general purpose hammer. The face is usually round and has a slight crown (Fig. 1-2). The edge of the face is softened; it is given a radius so that it will not mar the work. Remember that every mark, scratch, chip, or flaw in the face of the hammer will leave its imprint in the hot iron. The peen must be in good shape with a smooth crown and rounded corners.

Your 1-pound ball peen hammer will be used a great deal in light work and in small forgings, as well as for finishing. Again, it is important that the face, as well as the ball, is nearly perfect. The ball should be a portion of a sphere and not have any suggestion of a point (Fig. 1-3).

In all cases every hammer should have a high-quality, straight-grain, hickory or ash handle. The handle should never be plastic or any synthetic material because the heat will soon ruin it. Also a synthetic handle will not transmit the feel of the blow truly enough to "read" it. A metal handle is the worst of all. It will work you to death and hurt your hand even if it has a rubber grip. Stay with the wood handle.

To read a hammer handle means to interpret the feel of the handle in your hand at the instant of impact. This feel will direct your next blow as much or more than your eyesight. A good wooden handle will always read the same for any given blow, right or wrong, at any temperature. Plastic, fiberglass, and metal handles all read differently as

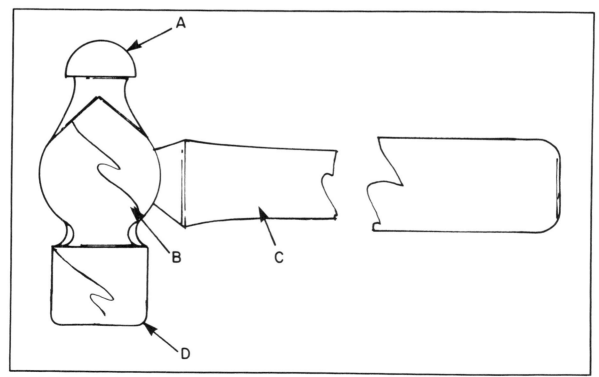

Fig. 1-3. The ball peen hammer. "A" shows the ball, "B" the body, and "C" the handle, which is made of hickory or ash.

the heat changes. These different readings occur frequently in a single heat and could spoil your blow.

You will usually use your 2 1/2-pound cross peen to start your work, to rough it out, and, in many cases, to finish it. It is the hammer you will most commonly use, regardless of what you are making. Other hammers will be introduced as you need them.

VISE-GRIP PLIERS

You will use vise-grip pliers as a substitute for tongs. You will be building your own tongs, but in the meantime the vise-grip pliers are good around the forge and anvil because they have a very positive grip over a wide range of sizes. Their drawback is that if they are overheated the jaws will be softened. If the handles are plastic plated or coated, they will surely burn up at the worst possible time. Try to find a large pair that is all metal. Some of the vise-grip or locking type pliers have an easy-release catch. Watch out for this catch because it might release when you least want it to. However, these locking type pliers are more than worth their few drawbacks.

HACKSAW

You will need a hacksaw from the start. It is a useful, easy-to-use tool that you will need often. Be sure you get the best quality blades available. These cost about $1 each at the time of this writing. Chapter 4 presents the best way to use the hacksaw.

THE FORGE

As you are aware, the forge is a central piece of your equipment. Much mystery and romance can be wrapped around it because the smith's fire and his control of it are vital to his success.

The forge consists of a hearth, on which to build a fire, and a blower to feed more than natural amounts of air to the fire in order to increase the intensity of heat in the heart of the fire. A forge may be stationary or portable, but a stationary forge is not practical for most small shops.

The part of the forge in which the fire is built is simply an open hearth with an opening in the middle of the bottom. The opening is placed so that a blast of air can be forced up under a fire built on the hearth.

A few patented forges are manufactured. See Figs. 1-4 and 1-5. They come in various shapes, sizes, and weights. Nearly all used forges will be old and badly rusted. You can make a good forge out of scrap. I have two homemade forges in my shop that are as satisfactory as any manufactured forge. Each cost about $10 at the time of writing.

Materials

To make your own forge hearth you will need a used hot water tank 19 inches to 24 inches in diameter and at least 3 feet high. You can obtain a used, rusted-out hot water tank from a plumbing supply house or a plumber. All you want is the inside of the tank, which has a dished head. The tank, when removed from its insulating jacket, should stand about 3 1/2 feet high. It should be no less than 19 inches in diameter, but it can be as much as 24 inches in diameter and still be practical. If it is any larger, it may be cumbersome,and weight becomes a factor. The condition of the threads in the pipe hook-up holes is unimportant. You won't be using those threads.

You will need used pipe fittings that can be screwed together a few turns by hand. They need not be water-tight quality. They can be galvanized, black iron, or other metal. In all cases 2-inch standard pipe size is needed. None of these pipe fittings should be put together "wrench tight." It is not necessary, and you might want to dismantle them to change things around at a later date. A list of fittings follows:

- One bell reducer between 3 and 2 inches long.
- One 2-inch standard T.
- One 2-inch malleable pipe coupling.
- One 2-inch pipe nipple between 4 and 5 inches long, with threads at both ends.
- One 2-inch pipe nipple between 8 and 10 inches long with threads at both ends.
- One 2-inch pipe nipple between 4 and 6 inches long with threads at one end.

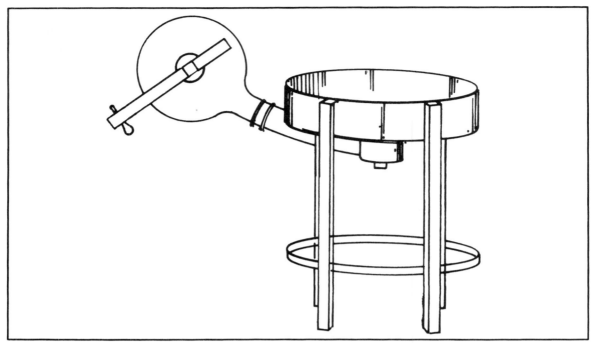

Fig. 1-4. A small round hearth forge, including a blower. A forge of this type is being manufactured at the time of writing.

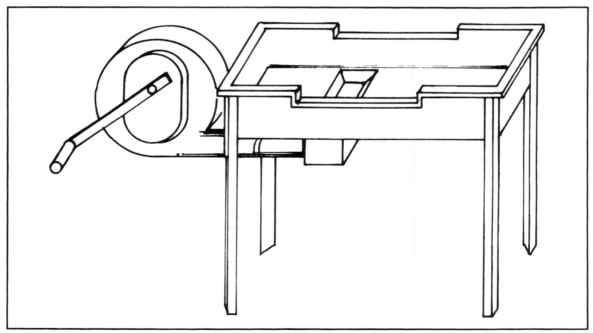

Fig. 1-5. A rather large rectangular forge available from the manufacturer at time of writing. It may be purchased with an electric or a hand blower.

8

- Four 3/8-inch-by-1 1/2-inch carriage bolts with nuts.
- One 1/2-inch steel plate, round, 6 inches in diameter.
- One 1/4-inch- or 5/16-inch-by-1-inch standard bolt with nut and flat washer.
- One 1/8-inch steel plate about 4 inches square.
- Four 1/8-inch- or 3/16-inch-by-3/4-inch-angle iron or 3/4-inch water pipe. Used is acceptable.

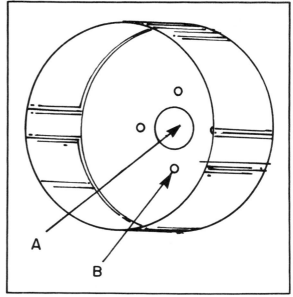

Fig. 1-7. In this illustration you are looking down into the crown of the tank. "A" shows the circle to cut for the grate; "B" shows the four bolt holes.

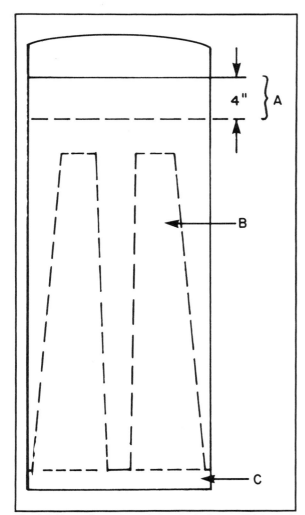

Fig. 1-6. How to lay out your hot water tank to cut it into parts for a forge. The dotted line at "A" is the point where you will cut for the hearth. Dotted lines at "B" show cuts for the legs. The material below "C" is discarded.

Figure 1-8 shows a forge with legs cut from the water tank. Figure 1-9 shows one with angle iron legs. Figure 1-6 shows how to mark off a tank to be cut up with an acetylene torch. When the tank is cut as marked, a portion of it becomes the legs. The lower end (marked "C" in Fig. 1-6) is cut away and discarded. The top of the tank is cut off 4 inches below the crown of the tank as shown in Fig. 1-6. It is then turned over. After cutting a 4-inch center hole and four bolt holes for the grate (Fig. 1-7), it can be welded or strapped to the legs as shown in Fig. 1-8. The top has become the hearth. The sides have been cut into legs, and you are ready for the fittings, which will permit the forge to receive air from the blower.

Figure 1-9 shows how to use angle iron or pipe legs. In the supply list above I have included the angle iron leg stock. You may choose to use these legs because your assembled unit will be considerably lighter. Also, the splayed-out feet of the angle iron legs add a little more stability to the forge.

The grate is made from 1/2-inch thick common steel plate (Fig. 1-10). Your auto salvage dealer will know what this is. The grate is 6 inches in diameter.

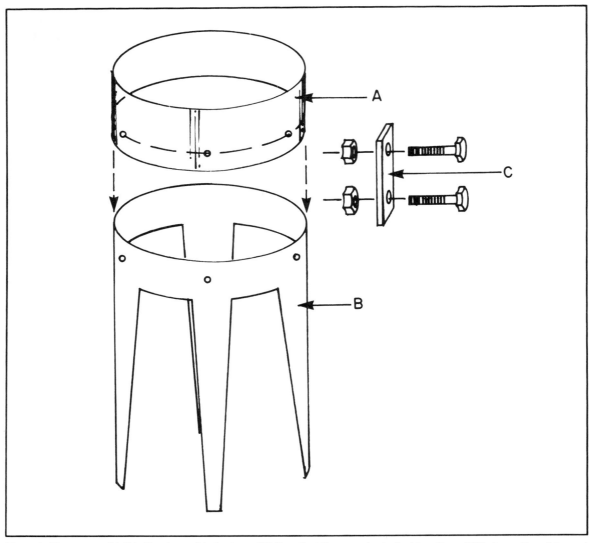

Fig. 1-8. The crown, "A," is lined up with the legs, "B," so that they can be bolted together. "C" shows the plate and the nuts and bolts used to join the crown and the legs.

The slots are 2 1/2 inches long by 3/8 inch wide. They are spaced 1/2-inch apart. These slots must be carefully cut for size and neatness. If the slots are not correct, the grate will not function properly, and air blast and fire control will be troublesome. Drill four, 7/16-inch holes at 90 degrees apart, located on a 5 1/4-inch bolt circle. Use the completed grate as a pattern for the four bolt holes in the bottom of the hearth around the 4-inch round hole.

Assembling Jim's Forge

Follow these instructions to assemble your forge, referring to Fig. 1-11 as you work.

Place the hearth upside down on the workbench.

Place the bell reducer so that it is centered around the 4-inch hole and is inside the 5 1/4-inch bolt circle.

Place the "HR" brackets (Fig. 1-12) over the

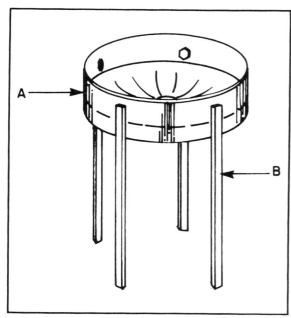

Fig. 1-9. Angle iron legs, "B," may also be used for the forge, "A."

3/8-inch hole in the hearth bottom and up against the side of the bell reducer. Mark the brackets for the 3/8-inch hole and for a 1/4-inch or 5/16-inch hole in the other leg. This will line up with a hole you will be making in the bell reducer. Drill the two holes in the bracket. Place them again over the 3/8-inch holes and mark the bell reducer for companion holes. Drill them as shown in the exploded view in Fig. 1-11.

Assemble the hearth, grate, and bell reducer, making sure the reducer is firm against the hearth bottom to avoid air leaks. Place bolt heads inside the reducer as shown (Fig. 1-11).

Fasten the legs to the hearth. Lay out the legs so that the slots in the grate point between any pair of legs. This is important because this line-up of the grate slots indicates the front of the forge, where no leg should be. Drill the legs and hearth and assemble them as shown in Fig. 1-11. Fasten them together with the bolt heads inside the hearth.

Drill the ash door and handle (Fig. 1-11) and assemble them with the end bolt only. Drill bracket "BR," as shown (Fig. 1-12). Lay this out so that the ash door, the door bracket (which becomes a

hinge), and the unthreaded end of the bottom pipe nipple can be worked from the front of the forge. When all these are assembled, there must be room for the door to swing clear of the pipe in order to dump the ash out. Study Fig. 1-11 carefully. Double nut the hinge bolt as shown. This will maintain the proper adjustment. Stove bolts or 1/4-inch bolts will be heavy enough for all the ash door assembly. Be sure all bolt heads are inside the pipe.

Before drilling for the ash door in the bottom pipe, screw the short nipple into the bell reducer, which is mounted onto the hearth, "one hand tight." Next screw the 2-inch T onto the nipple. Bring it up snug. Now with both hands turn the T until it points to the left as you look at the front of the forge. Make this "make-up" hand tight so that it is rigid. Screw the long nipple into the side outlet of the T; screw the coupling onto this and make the two up hand tight.

Screw the nipple with threads on one end only into the bottom end of the T. Make it hand tight because it must resist the twisting action of swinging the ash door open and closed. Mark the front of this nipple. This mark is for the line-up of your ash door hinge. Remove this nipple and drill and mount your ash door assembly. Make sure in this

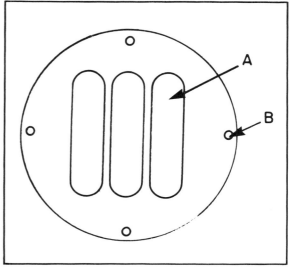

Fig. 1-10. Grate openings for the forge are shown at "A." Bolt holes to attach the grate to the bottom of the hearth are shown at "B."

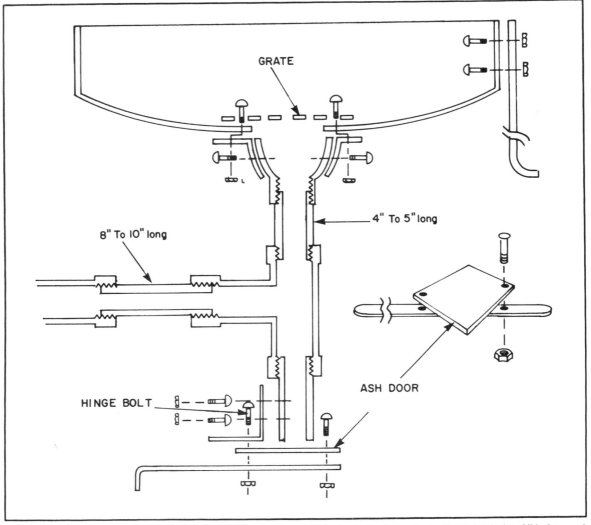

GRATE

8" To 10" long

4" To 5" long

ASH DOOR

HINGE BOLT

Fig. 1-11. A cross section view of the forge assembly. Dotted lines indicate the holes that will receive bolts. All bolts used in the hearth or the air pipe must have their heads inside the hearth or pipe.

make-up that the ash door will shut off the air flow so that you will not lose air blast at the grate.

A careful study of Figs. 1-11 and 1-12 should answer all your questions. Figure 1-11 is a cross section as seen from the front of the forge. Notice that the ash door in Fig. 1-11 is out of alignment for illustration purposes. Normally the door handle will be pointing toward the front of the forge when the door is closed.

Install the ash door and nipple into the bottom

of the T and align it for forge operation, and your hearth unit is complete.

I do not recommend any cement, clay, concrete, or other filler in the bottom of this forge. If you build and maintain your fire as I teach in this book, your forge will work extremely well. Any permanent lining on the bottom of this or any iron face will speed up the rusting out of the unit because it will collect and hold moisture.

A 3-inch sheet metal pipe will fit, with a little

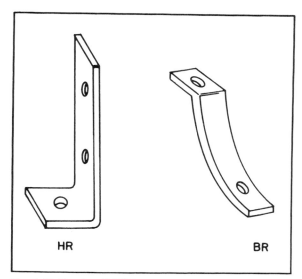

Fig. 1-12. Bracket "HR" is used in assembling the hearth grate and the bell reducer. Bracket "BR" is used to assemble the ash door. Note that the long leg on bracket "BR" is curved.

coaxing, over the 2-inch coupling. Use this to hook up your blower to the forge tuyere, which you have just completed.

Assembling Your Hot Water Tank Chimney

You can make a very satisfactory chimney for your forge by welding together used hot water tanks. If you cut the heads out carefully so that good contact is made from tank to tank, you will need only enough welding to stick the tanks together into a straight pipe. You will use wire and narrow strips of sheet metal to seal up the seams in order to reduce draft loss. Study Fig. 1-13 for details. The person who sells you your tank can probably direct you to supplies for the fittings. Even if you buy some new fittings, their cost will be much less than the cost of a new outfit.

Study Figs. 1-13 through 1-16 carefully before you begin the assembly.

Use used water tanks that are from between 12 and 16 inches in diameter. These will run up to about 40 inches of wall length. Five sections of 40 inches, more or less, will give you about 16 1/2 feet of height from the ground. This chimney will be quite heavy, so you will need a base that can carry

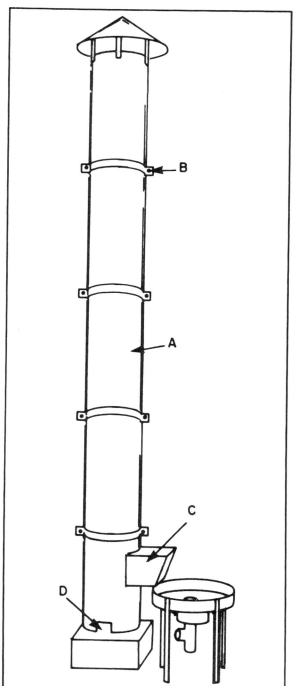

Fig. 1-13. View shows the Chimney, "A," the bands, "B," the hood, "C," and the clean-out, "D," as well as the forge. They are shown in the proper relationship to each other.

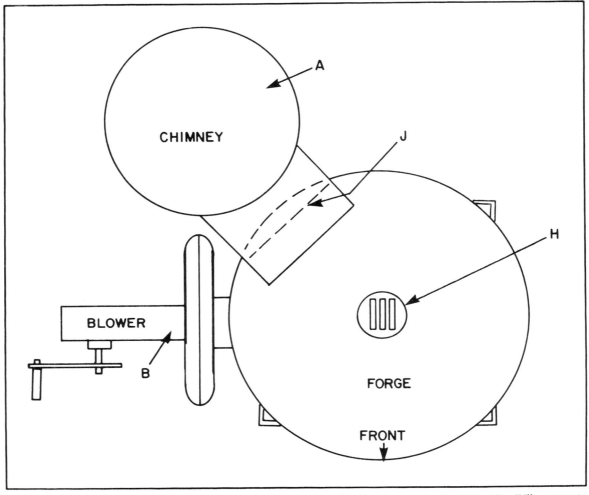

Fig. 1-14. Arrange your hearth, blower, and stack so that long work can be placed across the fire. Dotted line "J" represents the bottom lip of the hood. The chimney is at "A," the blower at "B," the hearth at "H."

several hundred pounds. I suggest that you weigh your tanks so that you know their total weight. The base for the chimney can be built up to get more height from the hearth level to the top of the stack. However, allow 12 inches or more of stack below the bottom of the smoke intake (Fig. 1-16). This space forms the ash and turbulence chamber. Make every effort to locate the stack to avoid any bends or turns. Keep in mind that the forge must be close to the stack to ensure good operation and smoke removal.

Cut an opening 3 inches high by 4 inches wide

in the bottom of the stack (Fig. 1-13). This will be used as an ash clean-out. It should be closed when the stack is in operation to eliminate draft loss.

Carefully cut the head and base from each tank. This should be a clean, neat radial cut. This will enable you to make a better joint when you join the tanks. Line them up end to end and fasten them together. If you weld them together, a continuous weld all around is unnecessary. Several 1 1/2-inch welds will be adequate. In lieu of welding you may use six 1/8-inch by 1-inch iron straps 4 inches long, spaced equally around. Fasten these with four num-

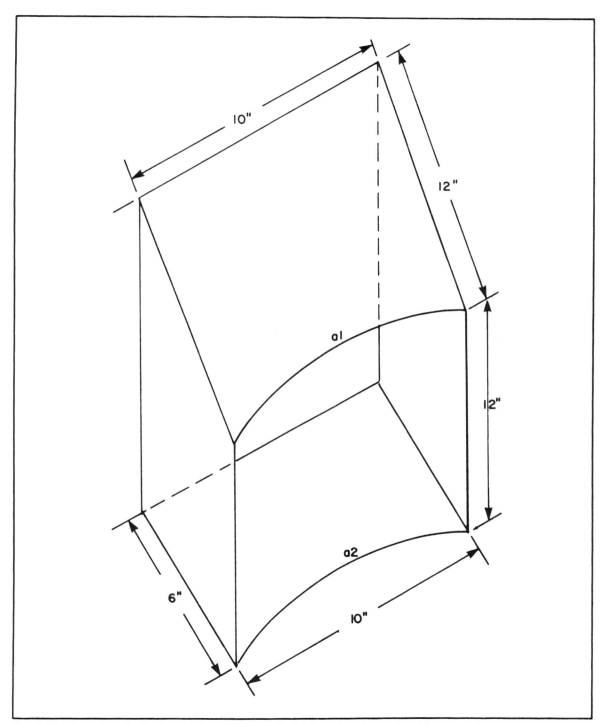

Fig. 1-15. Dimensions for the hood. The cutout must fit tightly to the side of the chimney stack.

15

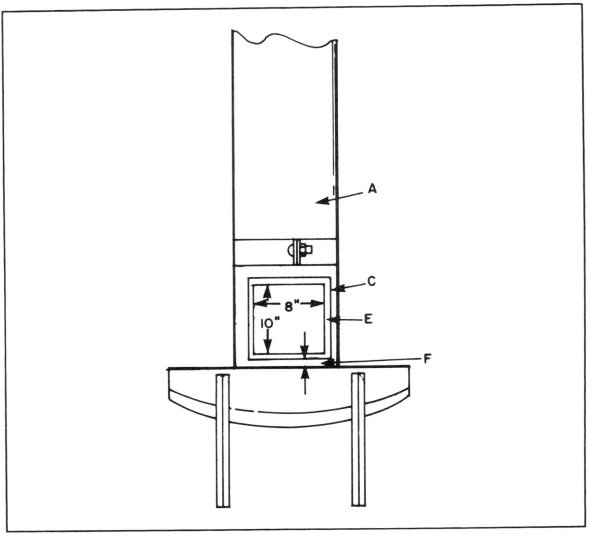

Fig. 1-16. The line-up of the stack, "A," the hood, "C," and the hearth should look when you are looking straight into the hood. "E" shows the opening in the chimney. At point "F" you should allow about 1/4-inch clearance between the hood and the hearth.

ber 14, or 1/4-inch by 3/4-inch long, thread cutting, self-tapping metal screws. Use four screws to each strap, and four straps to each tank. This should do the job.

Make 4-inch-wide strips of light galvanized sheet metal, which will go around the assembly at the joint to form a band (Fig.1-13). Pack some fiberglass insulation under the band against the seam to seal it against draft leaks.

Determine the height of your stack base. Then cut a rectangular hole 8 inches wide and 10 inches high (Fig. 1-16). Locate the bottom of the opening 2 inches above the hearth top edge.

Make a hood of scrap sheet aluminum. Old roofing aluminum will work well. Galvanized sheet metal would be your second choice. The hood will corrode quickly if it is made of iron-base sheet metal, and it will have to be replaced sooner than one made from aluminum. Make the hood to the dimensions shown in Fig. 1-15. Cut the arc as shown so that it fits the wall of your stack.

Move the hearth up to the stack directly in line with the opening "E" in Fig. 1-16. Install the stack, hearth, and blower as shown in Fig. 1-14. This arrangement allows long work to be placed across the fire.

Place the hood on the edge of the hearth. Adjust the hearth so that the bottom of the hood is just fully inside the hearth edge. See dotted line "J" in Fig.1-14 and sideview "C" in Fig. 1-13. Line up the hood as in Fig. 1-16 so it is centered around the opening. Then raise the hood just enough to give clearance between it and the hearth edge; 1/4-inch should be plenty. This will eliminate squeaking and will prevent the jiggling of the forge from shaking the stack.

Mark the location and fasten the hood to the chimney with angle clips and sheet metal screws. The head should fit well against the stack.

Use guy wires to lock the chimney into position. It is heavy, and if it falls it will break something. If you live in a rainy area, install a cap twice the diameter of the stack. Put it three-fourths the diameter of the stack above the top.

You now have an excellent forge with very good draft. When it is completed, this forge is light enough to be carried by one man. It will last for years and handle the largest work in this book and the heaviest and the most delicate that you are likely to encounter for many years. Hook up your blower and enjoy your forge.

The Blower for Your Forge

Manufactured forges have various styles of blower. Some have an electrically driven blower; some have a hand-cranked, belt driven blower; some have a hand-cranked, gear type blower. None will have bellows. Bellows are fine to look at for the romanticist, but they are not practical for the modern twentieth century early American smith. You can see from the illustrations in history books that a great deal of room in the shop is given over to the bellows and the framework to manage it.

I strongly recommend that you don't buy any form of electric blower. The beginning smith (and some intermediate level smith) finds that he cannot concentrate on the control of a power blower and manage the fire and the work at the same time.

The hand-cranked, gear type blower is the most common and perhaps the most practical type. I recommend it for your first forge. This blower uses the gears to step up the speed of a rotary flat-blade centrifugal fan. The fan is in a housing with an outlet convenient for installing a tube or pipe to direct the air blast under the forge hearth into the "tuyere."

Tuyere is the name given to the nozzle, or airbox and grate, or sometimes simply to the end of a tube or pipe that controls the shape and direction of the air blast from the blower into the base or side of the fire. It is arranged so that the fuel does not easily block the flow of air. The amount of air delivered to the fire is controlled by a valve in the pipe, by the speed of the blower, or by both. For the purpose of this text, I will be concerned with a bottom blast, hand-cranked, gear type blower used with a portable hearth. Air flow will be controlled by cranking speed.

Often a suitable used blower can be found for a reasonable price. There are several makes of used blowers available, all old. The Champion 400 is the one shown in the illustration on making your own forge. One that is in fair, or better, shape is an excellent blower. Its handle may be turned in either direction. The Buffalo is another excellent blower. Its handle must be turned in one direction only. There are other good makes too numerous to name individually. Whichever you get, try it first and feel for a good blast of wind with little handle pressure. Listen for scraping and rattling noises. If you hear either, look further.

YOUR ANVIL

You can use nearly any piece of iron for an anvil if it is solid and heavy and has a flat surface. A piece of I-beam or a piece of railroad track has served in an emergency. However, the better your anvil, the better your work. A good anvil will be a major expense in your shop whether you decide on a new or a used one. Its quality will determine what you can do on it and how well you can do it. As is the case with your hammer face, every mark, scratch, chip, or flaw in the face of the anvil will leave its imprint in the hot iron.

Figure 1-17 shows the parts of the anvil. Commit them to memory. I will refer to them often. Every part is useful. You will be forging on all parts—the face, the table, the horn, the body, the heel.

Anvils come in a variety of shapes and weights. For your purpose and also for more advanced work, I recommend the London pattern at about 150 pounds. A 100-pound anvil is a little light for general work. A 200-pounder is quite large and more than you will need unless you plan to go into heavy work.

You need to look for several things in a used anvil. Your first consideration will be weight; you will want the 150-pound average. Then look at the face. It should be flat and free of dings and cracks. Some small pits and scars may be tolerable, but every mark on the anvil will show up on the anvil side of your work. Remember that you will be working all over the face.

The edges around the face should be firm with very few chips or chunks broken out. There should be several inches with a fairly good corner along both sides near the center so that when you bend a piece of iron over it, you can shape a precise inside corner or shoulder. It should have about 3 or 4 inches of each edge ground to a 1/8 inch to 3/16 inch radius. This should start at the step and run toward the heel. It should fade back into a square-

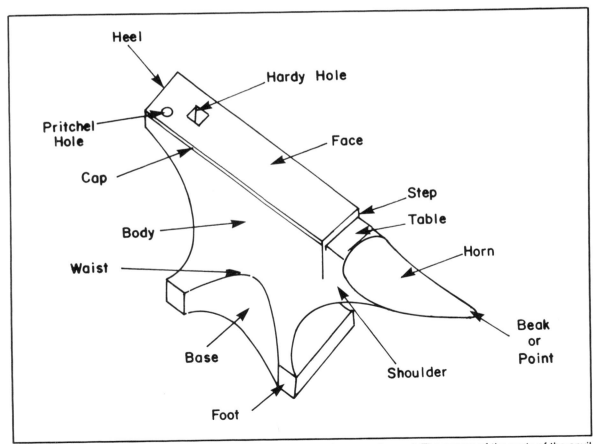

Fig. 1-17. This anvil is the London style pattern. It is the type most commonly used. The names of the parts of the anvil are shown on the drawing.

cornered edge by the time it is 5 or 5 1/2 inches away from the table.

The corners of the heel should be well formed and not beaten out of shape. The hardy hole should not have its edges too badly scarred or the hardies won't set right. The pritchel hole should be round and straight through.

The horn is a very important part of the anvil. About 30 percent of your work will be done on it. It must have an even taper and be free of big scars and dings. The point should be rounded, not all beaten back so that it forms a wart. Because you will do finish work on the horn, the top of the horn should be smooth with no cuts in it.

The table on most used anvils will be in bad condition. Sometimes experienced smiths use the table for a cold or hot cutting place, which chews it up. However, if the rest of the anvil seems good, don't reject it because of the table condition. It is the least important part of your anvil.

In general the anvil should have a pleasing appearance. It should not look abused. Never buy a broken anvil. It is very difficult to repair, and the repair seldom holds.

Most of the used anvils you see will have a forged body, base, and horn all in one piece. On top of the body there will be a welded-on hard face. This cap is very easy to spot as no effort is made to hide the weld. These caps will be from 3/8 inch to 1/2 inch thick. See Fig. 1-17.

The anvil should have a good firm ring when you strike it a light blow. The hammer should bounce on the face in a lively manner. If the anvil is tied down securely, the bonds will dull the ring, so get the anvil loose, put it on the floor, and then test for the ring. If it has no ring or only rings in some spots, look for cracks or loosening of the hard face, or for cracks in the body or the horn.

Since World War II most anvils have been made from solid tool steel, cast in one piece then machined and heat treated. They have a beautiful ring and are very good anvils.

You should know that one maker built his anvils in such a way that they did not ring. In fact they sounded as if one were hitting a stump. However, they were well made and of good quality. I under-

stand they are no longer available new. This style can be identified by looking closely at the waist and the edge of the face. The waist looks as if the top and bottom halves were either welded together or cast one into the other. The top half seems to be a finer grain material, and it does not have a welded-on hard face. The entire top half is made of cast tool steel; the bottom half was regular cast iron. After assembly the anvil was machined to the desired state, and the whole unit was then heat treated. The face of these old anvils is extremely hard. This anvil is good and is an exception to the rule that anvils that do not ring are suspect.

If you can afford a new anvil, get it. There are some very fine heat-treated, cast tool steel anvils on the market. Some are imported, and some are made in the United States. They are very well made and finished. The corners and edges of the face will all be sharp, and the whole face and most of the horn will be polished. In time you will grind the edges of the face to suit your needs. If you are new to blacksmithing, don't grind on your anvil until you have worked on it long enough to have a good idea of what you want. You cannot replace any metal you have removed. You will find instructions on how to grind an anvil in Chapter 16.

Don't be misled by fast talking, know-it-all types who will tell you just what to do out of a vast fund of misinformation. It is also wise to be skeptical of so-called "old masters." These people can sometimes romance you into making changes to your anvil or other equipment that you will regret later.

When you get your anvil, new or used, take good care of it. It is, in a sense, the other side of your hammer.

Beware of new anvils that are priced unusually low or that do not have a look of good workmanship. Many cheap, soft cast iron anvils were shipped into the United States in the late 1960s and through the 1970s. They are absolutely no good to blacksmiths. Some interesting anvils are made for the horseshoeing trade. These are fairly good anvils, but most of them will not stand up to general blacksmithing because they are too soft. They were not intended for general blacksmithing.

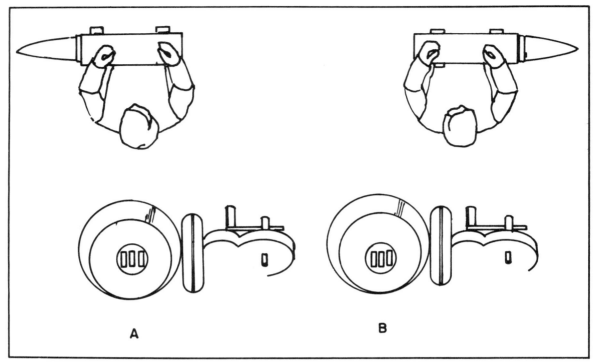

Fig. 1-18. Illustration shows the hand of the anvil. "A" is a left-hand anvil. "B" is a right-hand anvil.

In the exercises in this book, I refer to the *hand* of the anvil. There may be other ways to describe the hand of an anvil, but for this book and in all my classes I follow this rule: the hand of the anvil is always determined in reference to the forge. When the smith stands between the forge and the anvil, facing the anvil with his back to the fire, the end to his left is the left end, whether it be the horn or the heel. The side nearest him is always the front. The side away from him is always the back. So if he walks around to the side away from the forge, he has walked around to the back of his anvil. If he positions his anvil so that the horn is to his left when his back is to the forge, then the anvil has a left-hand horn. If the anvil is set the other way, he has a right-hand horn.

No rule dictates the way the horn should be. My experience shows that whether an anvil is positioned with a right-hand or a left-hand horn is largely a matter of the preference of the blacksmith working on it (Fig. 1-18).

All the work and illustrations in this book are based on a right-hand anvil unless otherwise specified.

Chapter 2

Setting Up Shop

NOW THAT YOU HAVE YOUR EQUIPMENT TOgether, you need to set it up for efficiency and safety. When it is properly set up, you will want to build your first fire and begin heating some iron.

SETTING UP

You need to consider three things when you locate your shop. The first is lighting. You want good light, but no direct sunlight should enter the shop or fall on the work. You do not want a window or a bright light that will shine in your face when you are at the forge. You do want a light that remains much the same all day. If you work at night, arrange your lights so the shop is well lighted but without glare. When you bring a piece of mild steel to 1,700 degrees Fahrenheit, it will have a very bright color in subdued light. As the light gets brighter, the color of the steel will fall off or darken. If you place the steel in full sunlight, it will appear to be dark red. You will be estimating heat by color, so the consistency and intensity of your light should be uniform and practical. Do not allow sunlight to hit the forge because it will make the heat of the fire invisible. You can set up under a big shade tree and get along fine as long as the sun does not get through the leaves, or you can work on the shady side of a building.

The second consideration is the weather. Keep rain and wind out of your shop. Rain will rust your equipment, ruin your handles and measuring devices, and make mud of the dust and ash. Wind blows dust and sparks around. It chills your hot iron too fast. Wind will make fire welding nearly impossible, and your fire will not perform well.

The third consideration is adequate space. Give yourself room to move about and handle long pieces. Pick a place that has enough clearance overhead so that you can swing long-handled hammers (Fig. 2-1).

The drawing on shop layout (Fig. 1-1) is to be used as a guide. It represents the ideal situation, but much fine work has been done under a shade tree. Set up your equipment as well as you can to begin. You can always move the gear around to suit your needs as you gain experience.

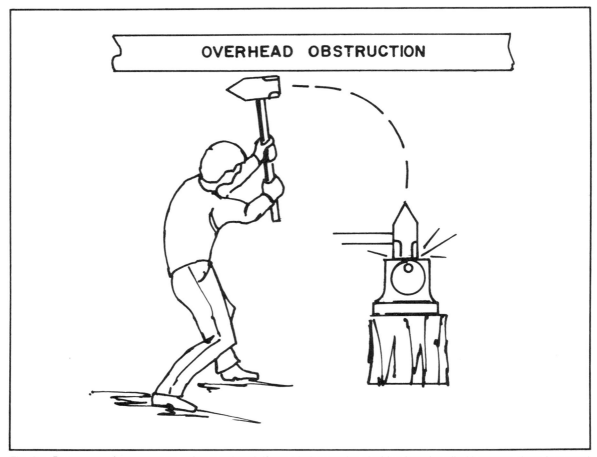

OVERHEAD OBSTRUCTION

Fig. 2-1. Be sure you have room to swing overhead. If you hit the overhead with a long-handled hammer, there is a good chance you will do serious damage to yourself or the work.

Ventilation of the work area is extremely important. Remember that your fire is producing carbon monoxide and carbon dioxide, and is consuming oxygen. If you notice that you are sleepy, headachy, or feeling a general malaise after working in your shop, look to your ventilation. Smoke does not need to be present for you to have symptoms.

In an indoor shop remember these rules:

• Ventilating fans should push fresh air into the shop (Fig. 2-2). If your fan removes air from the shop, it will stop or impede the draft of the chimney and may even bring outside air down the smokestack onto your fire. This would make your shop impossible to stay in (Fig. 2-3).

• Keep a vent open to the outside close to the forge at a low level. It should have an air passage area not less than twice that of the stack. A rule of thumb is 2 square feet of air intake for 1 square foot of stack (Fig. 2-4).

• To work well, a smokestack should have at least a 12-inch inside diameter and be as straight as possible. Avoid turns if you can.

YOUR FIRST FIRE

Various fuels are used for blacksmithing in your type of forge. Coal, coke, charcoal, and wood blocks are common. You will be using a 14,000 to 15,000 BTU semibituminous coal low in ash and sulphur,

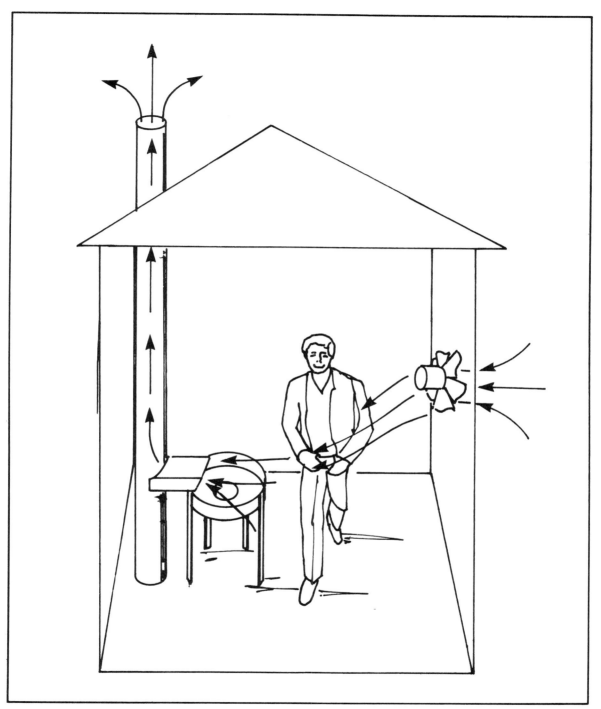

Fig. 2-2. Ventilating fans must bring fresh air into the shop so that you do not smoke yourself out. This also increases the draft up the chimney. Notice the direction of air flow.

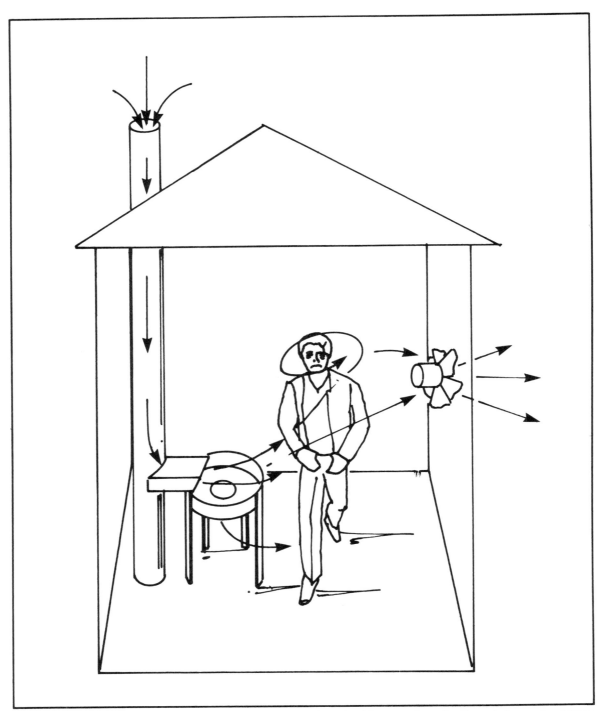

Fig. 2-3. A fan that pulls air out of the shop will frequently pull air down the chimney and over the fire and give you headaches and nausea.

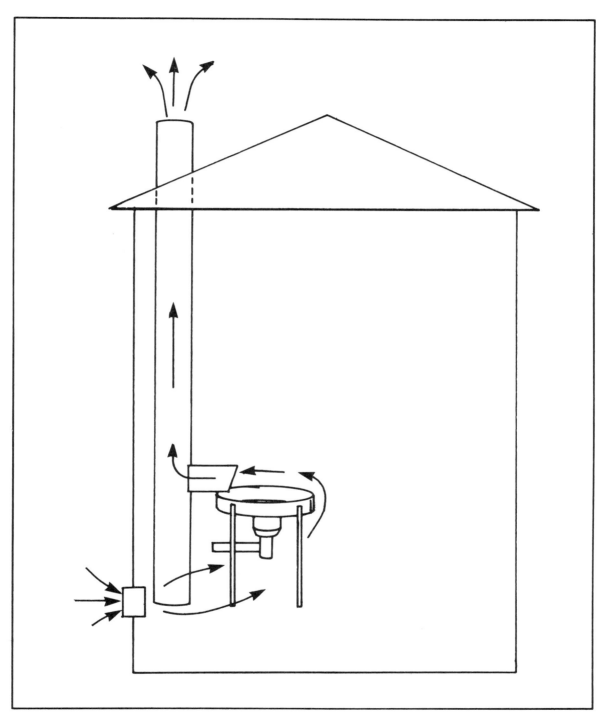

Fig. 2-4. Any partially enclosed or fully enclosed shop, should be equipped with a low-level air inlet close to the forge because the forge requires an enormous amount of air.

high in carbon, and low in water and dirt. This coal can be in big lumps or dust, or any size or mixture of sizes in between. I like coal that has about one-half to two-thirds of its volume in about 1/2-inch-to-1 1/2-inch lumps. The balance of the volume will be small grains and dust.

Buy semibituminous or bituminous coal. If an analysis is available, look for 70 percent or higher of fixed carbon. It should be a coking coal that sticks together when burned. This forms chunks of coke—a desirable feature. If the coal does not stick together well, large lumps of coal are needed to form coke and many of the small particles of coal will be lost.

Don't get too involved in coal types until you are much farther along. You will return to coal as the need arises.

To handle your fire for the first few days, you will need a coal or stove ash shovel from the hardware store (Fig. 2-5). You will need a poker made from a piece of 3/8-inch rod about 20 inches long with about 2 1/2 inches of the end bent over to 90 degrees. Find two tin cans, about a pint size, such as canned vegetables come in. Using an 8-penny nail, punch about five holes around the bottom of one can near the sides. This is your sprinkle can. Punch one hole at the edge of the bottom of the second can. This is your dribble can. Finally find a metal bucket that holds several gallons of water. Set your bucket close to the forge on a support high enough that the top of the bucket and the top of the forge are at about the same level (Fig. 2-6). Keep the bucket full.

I will assume that this is the first coal fire you have ever lighted. You can follow this procedure to light a fire in any style forge, but for now you will use your homemade forge.

First, fill the forge with coal about half full and level across. Cover the grate and all. Sprinkle the coal all over with water, using two cans of water. Let this stand while you get some small kindling. Use chips or short, thin sticks of wood. None should be more than 6 inches long, some can be shorter. Take a whole sheet of newspaper and work it into a tight ball. Get a few kitchen matches, the "strike anywhere" kind. By now the water has been on the

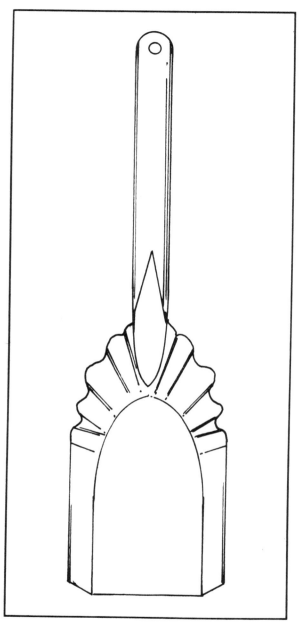

Fig. 2-5. This style sheet-metal shovel will serve well for starting your blacksmithing.

coal for about 5 minutes, and the coal is ready. Second, dig a crater in the middle of the coal pile down to the grate so that air can get through. Pat the sides of the crater so that they will stay straight and

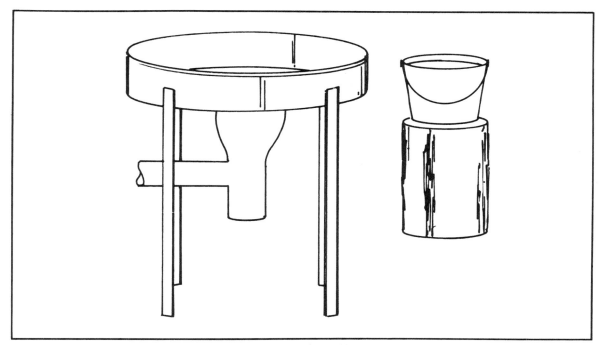

Fig. 2-6. Always keep a bucket full of water alongside your forge. Have it about level with the top of the forge.

steep. The pile should look like a little volcano. See Fig. 2-7.

Light the newspaper ball, and when it is burning well, place it on the grate with the flame down. Turn the blower crank slowly, just fast enough to keep the paper burning well. Cover the paper with a tight pile of kindling. Keep all this inside the crater you built. Now keep the blower going and pick up coal lumps from the sides of the forge and place them on the fire. Start at the edge of the crater and fill toward the center. Use only one layer of lumps (Fig. 2-8). If you stop the blower, your fire may go out almost instantly. The flame from the paper and kindling will light the lumps of coal. As the kindling pile burns away, it will sink down to the grate. As this hole develops in the center of your lumps, drop in two or three more lumps. Don't tease your fire with a poker. Let it develop a nice, glowing heart.

After a few minutes the sides of the crater will begin to burn down near the grate. When this happens, your fire should be pulled together in the center, and some more cool coal should be put around it against the crater wall (Fig. 2-9). If large amounts

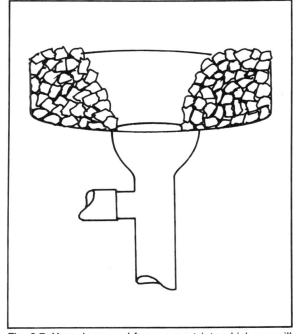

Fig. 2-7. Your damp coal forms a nest into which you will put your kindling.

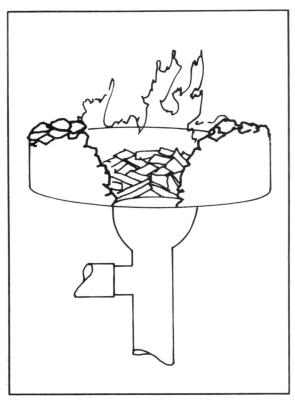

Fig. 2-8. The kindling and paper core for your first coal fire.

of *green coal*, new, unburned coal, are put into and onto the fire, excess smoke will be a big problem. If you have excess smoke, speed up the air blast and get the fire hot. Blow by mouth on the smoke toward the center of the fire, and usually the smoke will ignite.

All subsequent fires you build will be done a little differently unless they are built entirely from new coal as this one was.

HEATING THE IRON

The first time you heat iron, you will use a practice piece. It should be put into the fire with care. Don't just jam it into the heart of the fire. Rather look to see that the burning heart of the fire is about 4 inches deep and full of chunks and bits of coke. Coke is what is left of the coal after the volatiles burn out. Nearly 100 percent carbon, coke will burn a long time and deliver a tremendous amount of

heat, even in a fire no bigger than a small cantaloupe.

With your fire gathered thus, take a bar of 1/2-inch square or round stock, about 15 inches long. Lay it on the fire so that the end is about halfway across the center of the fire (Fig. 2-10). Don't dig it into the fire. Some of the volatiles will have burned off the coal on the sides of the crater, and the coal will be partially coked. With your improvised poker, pull a layer of this partially burned coal onto the top of your work. Be sure that you do not pack it. Leave it loose, but cover the end of the bar and the heart of the fire. This becomes insulation.

The bar should be horizontal, or nearly so, and the cold end—the handle end—should be out in the clear. Put your glove on the hand that will be holding the work, your holding hand. Get in the habit of wearing your glove whenever you are working. Now, with your shovel, move some new coal onto the sides of the fire and built up your crater a little. Sprinkle a small amount of water on this fresh

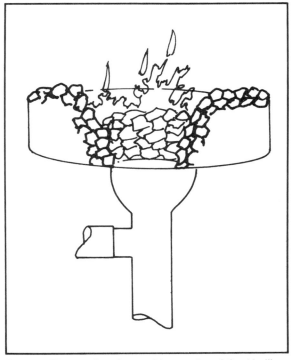

Fig. 2-9. The new burning coal has replaced the kindling. Don't overload a new fire with green coal.

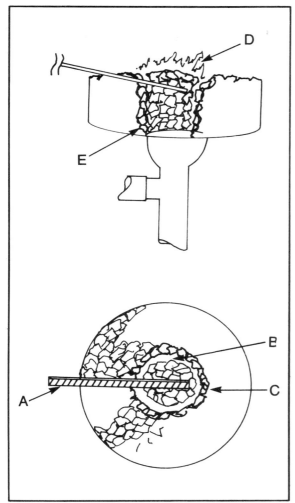

Fig. 2-10. Place your work on top of the fire and pile some coke over it as at "D." The area around the fire is forming coke all the time at "E." "B" is the burning core of the fire. "C" is a green coal. "A" is the work piece ready to cover.

coal to help it "coke up" and, as the fire heart is consumed, push the sides of the crater toward the center (Fig. 2-11). Use your poker to get down near the bottom of the forge and push the new coke in from that low level.

Turn the blower crank in order to keep the fire hot, but don't blow hard. If too much heat develops, it will burn out your fire and burn up your work. The rule for air blast is: the less air, the better—until you reach the point where the air blast does

not do the job. You can determine adequate air blast easily. If the heart of your fire is white hot or if it is throwing off sparks and roaring at you, back off the air blast.

Put a little water in your dribble can and drop some on the handle of the practice piece. If it steams, drip some more water until the handle is cool enough to pick up comfortably (Fig. 2-12).

If bright, exploding starlets start coming out of your fire, your iron is burning, literally burning, like a stick of wood. Jerk it out of the fire. If it is

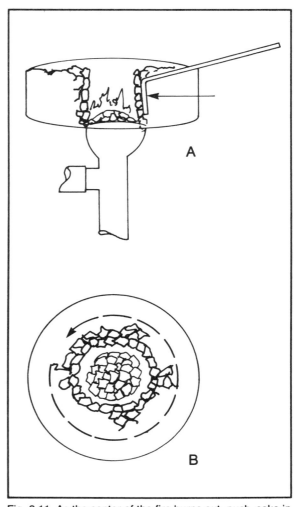

Fig. 2-11. As the center of the fire burns out, push coke in from the sides with the poker as shown in "A." The dotted line at "B" shows where this water should go.

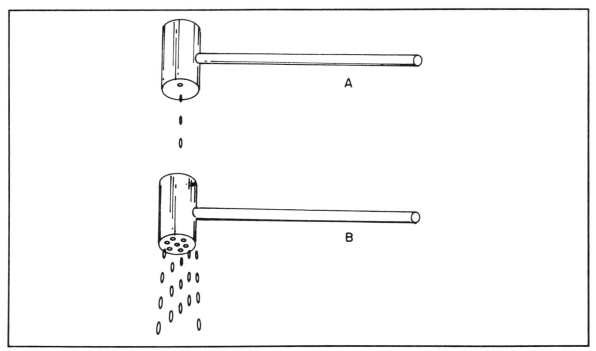

Fig. 2-12. "A" shows the dribble can and "B" the sprinkle can. You do not need a large sprinkler; six holes are enough. Notice the layout of the holes in both cans.

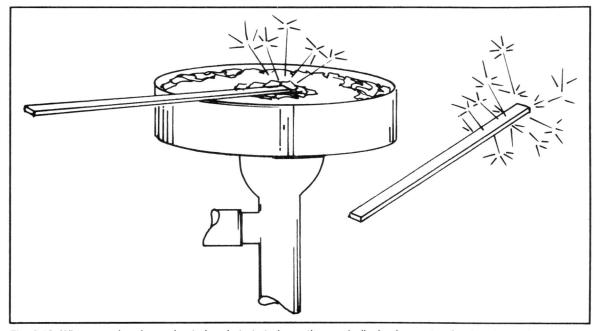

Fig. 2-13. When your iron is overheated and starts to burn, the spark display is spectacular, but the work is ruined.

sparking, the sparking portion is already burned and ruined. You will have to cut it off and discard it (Fig. 2-13). When you have a piece of work in the fire, don't neglect it, because it can be ruined in less than 15 seconds. The time will depend on its size and shape.

Keep an eye on the center, or heart, of your fire. Don't let it get hollow. As it needs fuel, push it in from deep on the side with your poker. Be gentle and study your fire carefully. See and hear what it is saying to you. Without a good fire you won't do much successful smithing. Much poor work comes from mishandling the fire so that the iron does not heat properly. The fire in your forge can be considered your primary tool.

Before you start forging or hammering on hot iron, you need to learn how to use the blacksmith's hammer. Let your practice piece of iron cool while you master the skills presented in Chapter 3. When you have learned them, you will be able to hit the iron correctly. You will understand how and why you should use a particular part of your anvil, and you will be ready to start your first blacksmithing project.

Chapter 3

The Hammer

YOU HAVE NOW SET UP YOUR SHOP, GATH-ered your tools, and built a fire. You probably experimented by beating on that hot piece of iron you heated. Before you try to make that piece into something, you should learn how to be accurate and effective with your hammer.

Your hammer is the only hand tool in your shop that you can't get along without. With it you can make (or destroy) almost anything, and at times it will seem to have a mind of its own. Thoroughly understand and practice the information offered in this chapter before you begin the exercises and projects. You will be glad you did. My students have to be persuaded to do the exercises. They often do them sheepishly in the beginning, but they soon understand their effectiveness. I practice them frequently in my own shop to keep my hand and eye in tune.

A FEAR OF THE HAMMER

As I watch most of the people who are interested in learning blacksmithing, I notice the same thing repeatedly. Something holds them back. It slows them down and, in a very real way, it frightens them. What do you do with all that power, that creative force, that terrible destructive energy that is in a moving hammer? It might help the beginner to know that those of us who started "way back when" had the same problems he is having now. The old man says, "Use the 2 1/2-pound hammer. Don't choke up on the handle. Get a hold way out on the end and lift the hammer up by your head. Come down hard and square."

So the beginner does as he is told, but somehow while that hammer is coming down like a thunderbolt, he panics. He thinks, "My God, how do I stop this thing? It's going to wreck everything!"

The beginner is afraid of that hammer, and he should be. By the time he has it going fast enough to do any good, he has lost control of it. He does not have any real idea of where it is going to land or what it is going to do when it gets there.

We experienced blacksmiths usually start our demonstrations in the middle instead of at the beginning. Most of us assume a beginner knows how to use his hammer as well as if he had been using it for 20 years. We are comfortable with the tool, and it seems like a waste of time to talk about it. But talking about the hammer and how to make it work is necessary.

LEARNING TO STRIKE

One of the first things you need to do is to change your way of thinking about the hammer in your hand. When you hold the hammer, adjust it, finger it, roll it, until it feels just right, until it feels like a new part of you that is an extension of your arm and hand. Allow yourself to think that you can feel the heat and cold coming right up your arm out of that wooden handle. I have had a hammer in my hand for over 40 years, and sometimes I think I can feel the work with my hammer as well as I can with my fingers. My hammer does what I tell it to—most of the time. So will yours, and here is how you use it.

You will need a 10-inch or a 12-inch bastard-cut half-round file and an armload of 1/2-inch or 3/4-inch scrap plywood pieces about 2 inches wide and 8 inches long or longer. Be serious about the following instructions because what you are about to do will have a profound effect on all your future blacksmithing.

Start with your 1-pound hammer. Take hold of the hammer handle so that about 2 inches stick out beyond your little finger. Shake the hammer around in the air. Talk to it. Tell it, "Hammer, you and I are about to have an affair." Lay the end of one of your plywood sticks flat on the anvil. Keeping your hammer grip, hit the stick with a fairly light but firm blow, just once. Now look at the stick. What kind of a mark did it make? Was it a perfect imprint of the face? Was it even all around? Or did it tip a bit this way or that? Try again, and each time observe what has moved or changed. These must be made to produce a perfect mark. Now hit harder. Study out each strike until you have a good idea of what you have to do and how you must hold the handle. Now hit several times without stopping, putting each blow in a new spot. What do all those marks tell you now? Practice this for about 20 minutes while you try to achieve the perfect mark.

Your wrist is probably tired now, but do this next. Raise your hammer until the head is 18 inches to 20 inches above your stick. Observe the feel of this. Now mark out a circle about the size of a nickel on a new spot on your stick. Raise your hammer again and hit that stick very hard right in the middle of that circle seven times, just as fast as you can. I mean, hit it! Hit it fast and hard! Study your marks and your reaction to this sudden attack. What you see and what you felt will tell you how much practice you need.

The perfect blow is one that, just before hitting the work, is traveling straight down a plumb line. The hammer center line from face center through peen center is perpendicular to the anvil face. There is no sideways or front-to-back movement. All the energy must be in one line of travel. Practice until you have it. Diligently practicing 20 or 30 minutes a day will pay off.

ADJUSTING YOUR HAMMER

Today's hammers will be exactly alike within any given high-quality brand. But no two human hands are alike. That is why gloves come in different sizes. By now you probably have found that the hammer is all right, you guess, but your grip seems strained. Well, it probably is. So think about it a bit. Where would you take off a little wood? This is why you have a file, but don't file yet.

Go to a standard table, 30 inches high, and mark a spot on it. Take a working hold of the handle in your regular grip. Step back from the table just a little so that you rather have to reach out to strike that spot. Use only the amount of force you would need to crack an egg and stop the blow just as it touches the table. When the hammer comes to a stop on the table, hold it there. Don't move. Does the head lay a little to one side, or tip back, or forward? You may want to repeat this several times until you can begin to feel where that hump in the handle is.

Now use the file. Be brave. Take after it. A six-pack costs more than that handle did. Dress the handle here and there until there is no tip from side to side when you swing. Polish it a bit with the sandpaper. Sand off all the painted finish in the areas of your grip.

Look to the fore and back tip. If the tip is forward and the handle is high, put some books under the table to bring it up an inch or two. If the tip is back and the handle is down, put some books or something under your feet. When you strike, you want the handle to be just tipping up. The center line of the handle should be from 1/2-inch to 3/4-inch above horizontal at the butt end. Remember you are supposed to be reaching out just a little with this exercise. When you move in toward your work, your handle will dip down some. Measure the heights you have settled on. This is the correct height for your anvil. It probably will not fit anyone else just right. Now adjust the anvil to this height.

Keep practicing on your sticks. Get some more if you need them. They are your imaginary hot iron, and they receive a mark, good or bad, just as hot iron does, when you hit them. You are teaching your muscles to place the hammer face exactly where you want it, and this is why you practice on

the sticks. The wood yields to the blow surprisingly like the hot iron does. The stick of wood I describe is big enough to protect the anvil face from being marked up by wild blows. Strike easy, medium, hard, and really hard. Practice for perfection. What you are learning here you will keep for the rest of your life.

CONTROLLING THE BLOW

Every blow, regardless of its type or style, is good if it did the work you intended it to do in the manner you wanted. What you are after in blacksmithing is to have each hammer blow do its share of the work. All the energy used in doing that work is coming right out of you, so spend it wisely.

Figure 3-1 illustrates a problem. Note that the hammer is hitting the work in the middle of the anvil. It is tipped and coming from the side. Everything that will happen here is bad for the beginner. The hammer's edge digs a hole and piles up some misplaced metal along the side of the hole. You probably will not be able to save the piece. If this blow is intended, that is fine, but plan it carefully.

In Fig. 3-2, the line of force shown by line "B" is straight down. The metal is thinned in the cen-

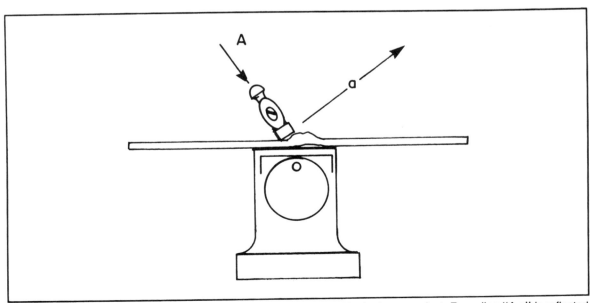

Fig. 3-1. Hammer blow digs holes in the metal and piles it up alongside the hammer dent. Force line "A-a" is reflected up through the iron and takes the metal with it.

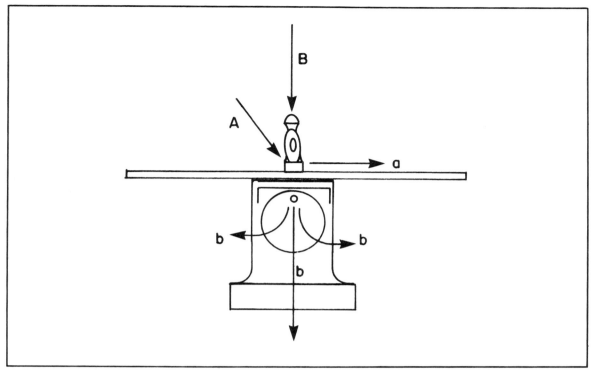

Fig. 3-2. Hammer blows along force line "A" will drag the metal along line "a." Note that the hammer angle is different from the angle in Fig. 3-1. If the blow is made on force line "B," it will move the metal out from under the hammer, but it will move evenly all around the face forming a crater, shaped like the hammer face. The energy is dissipated along line "b."

ter of contact and then pushed out evenly all around the center. Remember that every time you hit, some metal is moved somewhere. It never goes away unless you cut it away.

In a *wiping* blow, shown by line "A" in Fig. 3-2, the hammer will crush the metal thinner, but it will also drag some of the displaced metal along the direction of the force line, as toward "a." These wiping blows are frowned upon by some people. I have no idea why, unless they could not master them. The wiping blow is one you should master. In this blow you can control the line of force in two directions and two strengths at once. The wiping blow tends to slide the top of the metal only and leaves the bottom unchanged.

In *chamfering* you are doing many things at once, as is shown by force line "A" in Fig. 3-3. This action is crushing the end and pushing some of the iron back into itself as shown by dotted line "x-y."

It also is ramming the work back into your hand. The blow in force line "B" will crush the end, but in the process it drags the iron toward "x." Note the relationship of the tip of the hammer to the line of force. It will help to reduce most of the jamming of the work back into your hand, and the drag of the anvil will soak up the rest of the shock. Master this blow. Remember to keep the end of the work exactly at the back edge of the anvil. When the work or metal is located just right and the hammer control is right, all the energy of the blow will be soaked up just before the hammer strikes the edge of the anvil. Practice this blow because it is one of the more important ones. Practice with your sticks. It is good to wear a glove on your holding hand.

When you practice, smear a little grease on the top and bottom face of your stick where the hammer blows will be landing. This will allow the wood to move out from between the face of the hammer

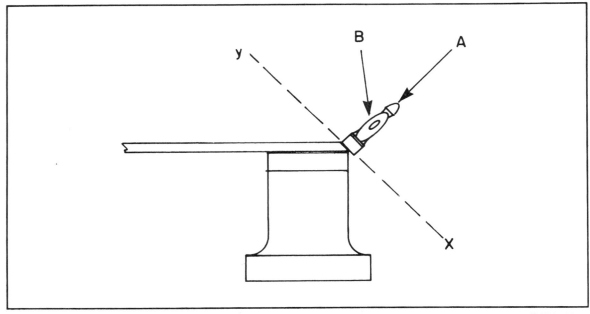

Fig. 3-3. Force line "B" is the correct blow to use here. Notice the angle of the hammer to force line "B." This blow tends to reduce the degree to which the work slides away across the anvil face. The line "x-y" shows the angle desired in the finished work. The finish surface and the hammer face must be in the same plane. Along force line "B" the hammer is putting a little extra pressure downward, which will cause a braking action on the anvil face while maintaining the desired contact of the face with the work piece. If you had struck so that the force was along force line "A," you would have found that the work tended to slide away from the hammer and jam into the holding hand. As the work slid away, the anvil edge would have been exposed to the blow of the hammer.

and the face of the anvil when you hit the stick. It will also allow the hammer to slip along the stick in various blows. Try wiping blows toward the right and the left, toward you and away from you. In all cases keep the hammer face flat to the impact spot on the wood. If you watch the slipping carefully, it will tell you a great deal about where the lines of force are developed. These lines of force are what move the hot iron around and determine its shape.

You need to know how to cock your hammer. Choose a clean stick. Put a circle the size of a dime about 3 inches from the end of the stick. Place the hammer face flat and centered over that circle. Draw around the hammer face. You should now have two concentric circles. Now cock your hammer to the left about 15 degrees. Slide it over until the *lip* or edge is resting between the two circles. Holding the hammer in that cocked position, raise it for a full swing and hit exactly where it was rest-

ing. You are trying for a clean dent in the wood between the circles. No marks or denting should appear inside the small circle or outside the large one.

Cock your hammer to the right and back and forward. Practice hitting with the edges of the face on the exact spot you want to hit. You will have to move the wood around on the anvil to achieve these blows.

In Fig. 3-4, force line "A," three things are happening. These results depend on how hard you hit and where you have located the work on the edge of the anvil. First is a *bottom fullering* blow, second is an *offsetting* blow, and third is a *cutting* blow. Be very sure of your move before you strike any over-the-edge blow. In Fig. 3-4, line "B," you see a wiping blow that is very useful. You are turning your iron down, reducing thickness, and elongating the turned-down portion, but the portion of the work on top of the anvil face will not be affected.

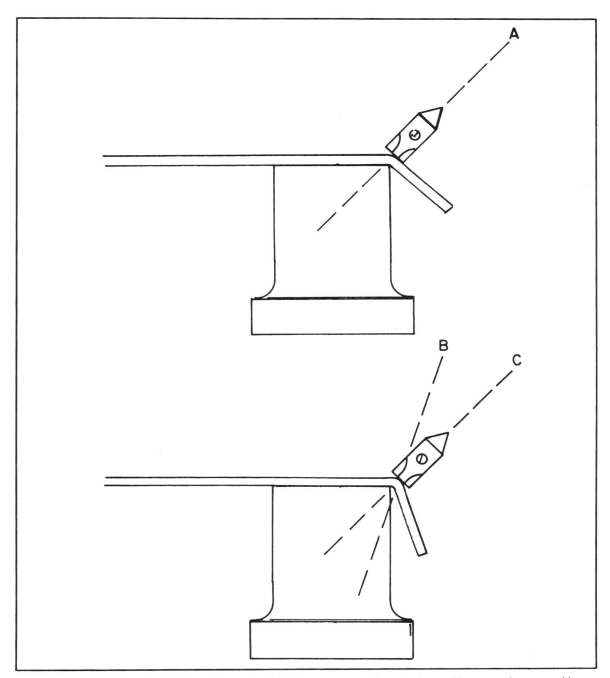

Fig. 3-4. In general, force line "A" and the angle of the hammer are such as to give nothing more than a crushing or bottom fullering action. Very little bending will take place. With force line "B" and the angle of the hammer at line "C," the lower lip of the hammer hits first and starts the bend. Force line "B" tends to hold the work tightly against the anvil edge. The combined action of "B" and "C" will make a finish bend with few flaws and little effort. Adjust angle "C" appropriately as you finish the bend.

• Never swing a hammer and bang on anything without aiming at an exact spot you intend to center with the face or chosen lip of your hammer.

• Never swing a hammer until you have made up your mind what you want the stroke to do; then follow through.

• Never try to change the direction of hammer travel once you have started to swing. If you realize that the swing may be faulty, stop the hammer and start over again.

The edge of the hammer is called the lip. If you are holding the hammer with your right hand on the face of the anvil in a strike position, the lip to your left is called the *inner lip*. Along the right side is the *outer lip*. The lip away from you is the *toe*; the lip closest to you is the *heel*. If you strike left-handed, the names of the sides are reversed. Add these names to your vocabulary. The names of the parts of the hammer are always as seen by the hand holding the hammer, not by an observer or helper.

The number of ways to strike the work is limitless. Any move or blow can be good or bad. Think out what you want to do, which way you want the metal to move. Decide on the direction of the force line, the tip or cock of the hammer if needed, and whether there will be any reflected energy to ruin something. All these things must be thought out before your iron comes out of the fire.

By now you have used up most of your sticks, and my guess is that you have learned a great deal. Now it is time to get out your 2 1/2-pound cross peen hammer with its wooden handle. Go back and get some more sticks and start all over again with your 2 1/2 pounder. Do every step. Study yourself and learn to marry yourself to the hammer when you pick it up. It must be an extension of you and your thoughts.

Take this rule to heart and do not let any Johnny-come-lately steer you from it: if the last blow did what you wanted it to do, it was right. If it did not do want you wanted, it was wrong.

Chapter 4

The Hacksaw

R ARELY HAVE I SEEN ANYONE USE A HAND hacksaw properly. He usually goes at it as if he were trying to kill the hacksaw blade (which he is doing in many cases), and he makes enough friction to melt the piece in two. When I ask him, "What kind of blade are you using on that piece?" he says glumly, "I don't know. Why? Does it make any difference?"

You need to understand this very useful hand tool and discover its true value. I will tell you how to choose your blade and how to use it. If you have not liked using a hacksaw, it is probably because you do not know how to use it properly and efficiently. I will discuss the common 12-inch hacksaw frame with a pistol grip handle or its equivalent, and the thin, 12-inch-long blade with a hole in each end. The blade is about 1/2 inch or 9/16 inch wide. You can buy one almost anywhere in a wide range of prices.

THE FRAME

Look at the hacksaw frame as shown in Fig. 4-1.

It may be fixed or adjustable to take various blade lengths, but it must be ridged. When a blade is installed in the frame and adjusted to tension, you should not be able to wind the frame or twist it from end to end. The handle should be comfortable with a rather broad surface against the palm of your hand. Notice that the grip is completely enclosed. This is ideal. It will help prevent injury to your fingers should you push the saw too hard and cause it to jump out of the cut, thus causing the hand and grip to slam into the work. Serious injury can occur if the grip is not enclosed as shown in Fig. 4-1.

The frame should be in line with itself when you sight down it from either end. It should have some weight of its own. It should be made of good-quality, rather thick, solid tool steel—not of light, flimsy tubing. The frame should be fixed with a wing nut for adjusting. The knurled type of adjusting nut is not much good because you cannot turn it tight enough. The front and back blade-anchor shanks should be square so that they can be turned to the left or right and locked in position in order

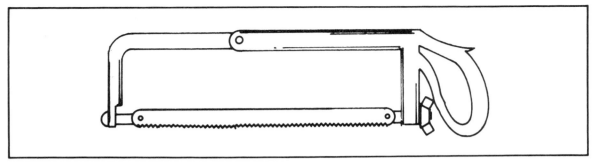

Fig. 4-1. Hacksaw frame with an enclosed grip is a desirable style.

to reach into the cut. To get a really solid hacksaw frame, you may have to find a used one.

THE BLADE

The hacksaw blade comes in many different *tooth counts*. The tooth count refers to the number of teeth per inch (Fig. 4-2). For your purposes you are interested in three different counts: 18 tooth, 24 tooth, and 32 tooth. You are also interested in the steel from which the blades were made. Some are of plain high-carbon steel; some are of high-speed steel; some of tungsten alloys. Some will have printed on them their alloy, their tooth count, and the maker. Some blades will be sold as "hot-cutting" or "super-hard" or with similar claims. I do not recommend that you buy any blades called hot-cutting or any that are made to cut hot steel. These specialty items will not work well for your projects.

Selecting the correct blade is important. You should have a stock on hand of the 18-, 24-, and 32-tooth blades. If you are going to cut a piece 3/16 inch thick or thicker, you will want an 18-tooth, high-speed steel blade. Put it in the frame so that the teeth point forward (Fig. 4-1). Make sure that the eyes are tight against the shank and that the pins point a little away from the center of the blade so that it cannot slip off at the eye. Slightly tighten the screw and thumb-nut and wriggle the frame and the blade to be sure everything is seated. Now tighten, grasping the blade between the fingers, until the blade is quite difficult to spring out of line. Bump the frame on the bench. It should sound like one solid piece. Hold the saw over the vise jaws and bounce it like a fiddle bow using about a 2-inch to 3-inch bounce. Have the center of the blade strike (Fig. 4-3). It should rebound with good life and sound. It should have a melodious bell or chime-like sound.

CUTTING

Decide whether you are going to cut to the right

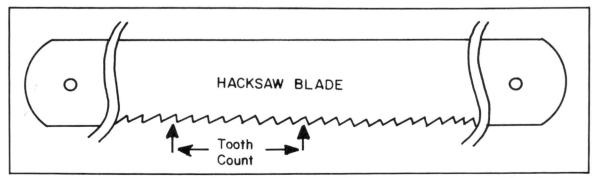

Fig. 4-2. The method of counting teeth per inch on hacksaw blades. The teeth must point forward, away from the handle.

40

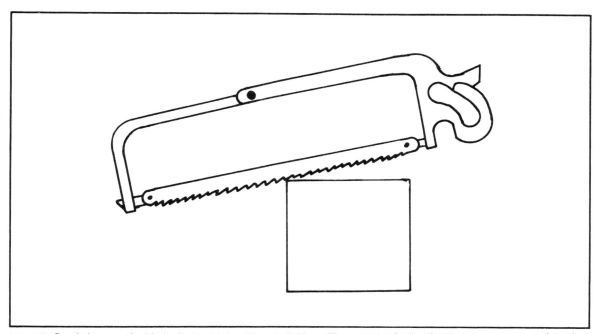

Fig. 4-3. Gently bounce the blade. It should ring like a bell. You will soon get a feeling for the proper amount of tension.

or left of the mark on your work or whether you will cut the mark out. The following discussion assumes that your right hand will hold the handle. If the left hand holds the handle, the process is reversed.

Cutting Flat Stock

If the stock to be cut is flat under the cut, tip the handle up about 2 or 3 degrees. This rests the blade on the far edge of the stock (Fig. 4-4). With your left thumb locating the blade, put a little downward pressure on the blade and push it forward using the far half of the blade. Make a few such strokes slowly, lifting some of the saw's weight on the return stroke, until you have a defined cut started.

Now smear a drop or two of old engine oil on each side of the blade. Grip the front of the frame with your left hand, with the thumb hooked into the crook. Pull the saw all the way back until the front pin nearly hits the far side of the piece. Hold the saw at the same angle to the work as it was when you started. Use very little downward pressure. Let the left hand only drag the saw forward—exert no downward pressure. You want just enough pres-

sure to keep the blade from bouncing. Let the right hand push the saw forward in unison with the left. Let it add a little pressure by wrist action only. Don't lean on the blade. As the left hand is dragging, give a rocking action about 2 inches up and down with the right hand while going back and forth (Fig. 4-4).

When you return the saw for a new cutting stroke, take most of the weight off the saw. This is most important. Leave just part of the weight of the saw on the work as you drag it back. This cleans the chips out of the teeth but does not bend the teeth down. Keep up this process through the entire cut. Watch the blade to see if it needs more lubrication. It will if you are cutting through anything larger than a pencil. Be sure you put no side pressure on the blade because this will wear the teeth on one side and ruin your blade. It will also cause the cut to wander off the mark.

A study of the drawings will show you how the hacksaw works. The hacksaw is a series of chisels called teeth (Fig. 4-5). Half of the teeth will be a bit to the right of center; the other half, a bit to the left. This makes the cut a little wider than the back

41

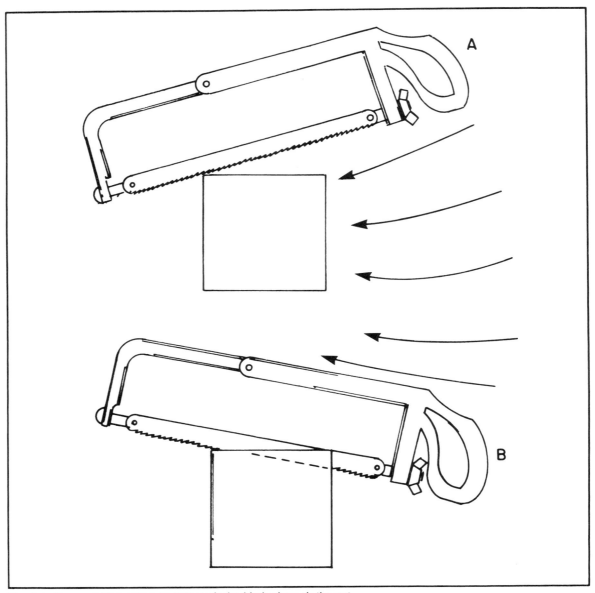

Fig. 4-4. Use a rocking action as you push the blade through the cut.

of the saw so that the body of the saw will not bind. Each tooth chisels out some metal as it is pushed along its way, and the only place this metal can go is into the gullet (Fig. 4-6). When the gullet is full, the tooth can no longer reach down to cut, so the whole blade just slides along on the chips the rest of the way through the work. The gullet can fill very quickly. When you apply the rocking action, the tooth behind has moved downward in relation to the tooth ahead, and its full gullet has risen a little. Thus the tooth behind can take a bite, and so it goes with each following tooth.

Move the blade slowly and rythmically at about one stroke per second. Use the full length of the

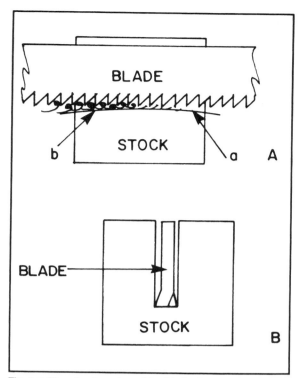

Fig. 4-5. The phantom view of the blade shown at "A" shows the chip falling away from departing teeth while the entering teeth are cutting out new chips. At "B" you see the cutting clearance given to the teeth so that the blade does not drag along the sides of the cut and jam up.

blade at each stroke. When you near the end of the cut, carry the saw a bit so that the pressure is light. If you lighten the pressure, the saw will not skip out or wedge in when the cut-off begins to bend down. Many blades are ruined or even broken as a result of forcing that last little bit.

The same rules apply when you are cutting any shape of stock. Get a cut started and follow through.

Cutting Thin Metal

Cutting thin metal with a hacksaw presents some problems that must be considered before the cut is started. The number of teeth per inch determines the space between them, and the tooth spacing or pitch largely determines the way you saw sheet metal. As a general rule, at least two teeth should be completely within the cut at all times (Fig. 4-6).

If the thickness of the metal is less than the distance between the teeth, the whole of the metal thickness will try to enter the gullet. When this happens the blade grabs or locks up. Force applied to overcome this lockup usually breaks the blade or tears out some teeth (Fig. 4-6).

Study the following chart and use it as a guide to determine which blade to use. The values given are good for all practical purposes. The figures are close approximations.

Space Between Tooth Points
18 tooth points—1/18 (.0555) inch apart, U.S. Standard (USS) 18 gauge
24 tooth points—1/24 (.0416) inch apart, USS 20 gauge
32 tooth points—1/32 (.03125) inch apart, USS 22 gauge

The actual decimal thickness of any given gauge for sheet metal will vary according to the company producing the sheet metal. When you use charts, be sure they correspond to the date of manufacture of the metal.

Sawing sheet metal is entirely practical. Under some conditions you may saw metal as thin as 28-gauge steel (.01563 inch thick). You may be able to saw an even thinner gauge if you are patient and practiced. I teach the following methods in my shop and use them regularly with good results. Most smiths saw iron water pipe the same way they saw sheet metal, so I will start with it.

Cutting

To saw off a piece of 3/4-inch standard iron pipe, use a 24-tooth saw blade. The pipe has a wall thickness of .113 inch, and halfway through the cut the blade is looking squarely at this thickness. The blade will have two teeth in the cut at all times. (Refer to the preceding chart and do the arithmetic to verify this.) When you saw standard iron pipe, black or galvanized, use the same action explained in this chapter under "Cutting Flat Stock." The whole process will be short and satisfying and will use little effort.

Thin wall tubing such as electrical conduit and

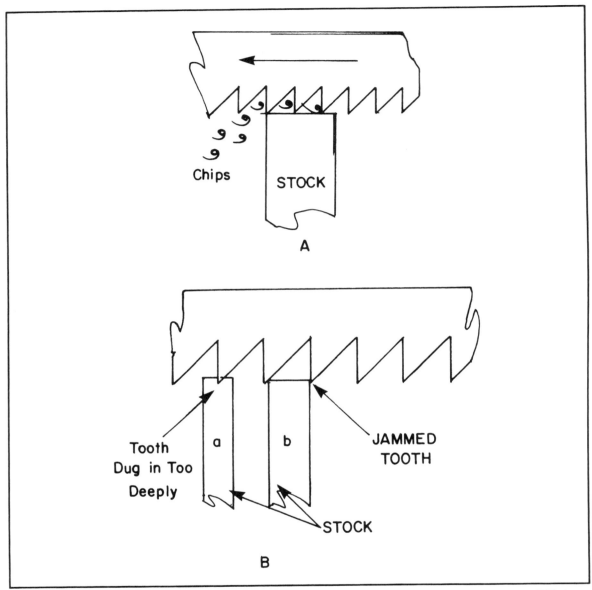

Fig. 4-6. "A" illustrates the rule that there should be at least two teeth actually cutting in the cut at all times. "B" shows what happens when metal is so thin that two teeth are not cutting: the tooth will break as at "a" or jam as at "b."

steel tubing are slightly different. Study the wall thickness and you may find that even a 32-tooth blade may have trouble. For example, a 3/4-inch outside diameter wall tubing will usually have a thin wall, about .050 to .060 inch thick. A 32-tooth blade has .03125 inch between points. The cut will go along fine until the blade is looking at the edge of the tubing wall where there isn't room for two teeth within the cut (Fig. 4-7). To correct this problem, roll the pipe a little as you cut so that the saw is always looking at the metal at an angle, just as it was when you started the cut (Fig. 4-8). By rolling the tube a bit as the cutting proceeds, the saw can have two, three, or even four teeth within the cut. Up to a point, in thin metal the more teeth within the cut, the better. Great care must be taken to carry the saw. Any downward pressure might force the saw to tear through the metal and jam up in the cut. Sometimes it will cave in the wall of the tubing around the blade and cause a misshapen end on your tube. With practice you will find that by using this method you can cut thin wall tubing very easily. Keep your stroke slow and even and the downward pressure very light.

It might occur to you at first thought that cutting thin sheet metal pipe, like the air pipe for your forge, would be impossible with a hacksaw. If you will use the following method you will have no problem.

Most pipe that connects the forge blower to the tuyere has a 3-inch diameter, and most 3-inch diameter sheet metal pipe is between 24 gauge (.02010 inch) and 27 gauge (.0142 inch). This is getting quite thin. Mark your pipe for your cut and place it in your vise so that it rests on the rail or thread boxing. Close the vise until the pipe won't

fall out and you have a three-point contact. Do not crush the pipe. Start your cut on top of the pipe. Use light, easy strokes with a 32-tooth blade. You could use a 24-tooth blade, but it would be very difficult. Apply very little downward force and make long, even strokes. Do not use a rocking action. Use no lubricant. When the saw breaks through, lower the handle a bit and make a few more strokes. As the near side of the cut carries away, keep tipping your handle toward the entry of the cut (downward) thus following the marking line around the pipe. Let the blade see enough metal in the cut to have three or four teeth within the cut at all times. When it becomes awkward to make the stroke, loosen the vise grip on the pipe and roll the pipe around. In this process your saw is always approaching the metal at a very acute angle, and it will not grab or bind.

Take care, however, because after you have sawed into the pipe, the blade is looking at an edge of very thin metal in the far wall. If it strikes that edge, it will jam or cave in the pipe, or some other problem will occur. To avoid any problem, keep the blade carried in such a manner that the back edge

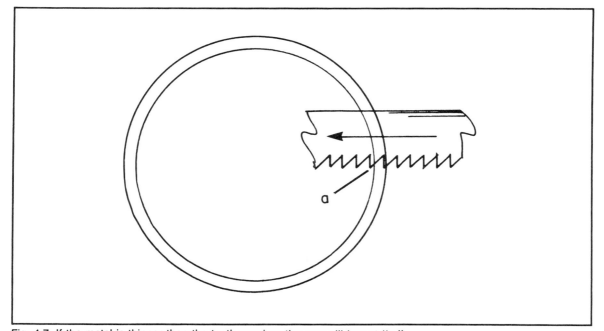

Fig. 4-7. If the metal is thinner than the tooth spacing, the saw will jam at "a."

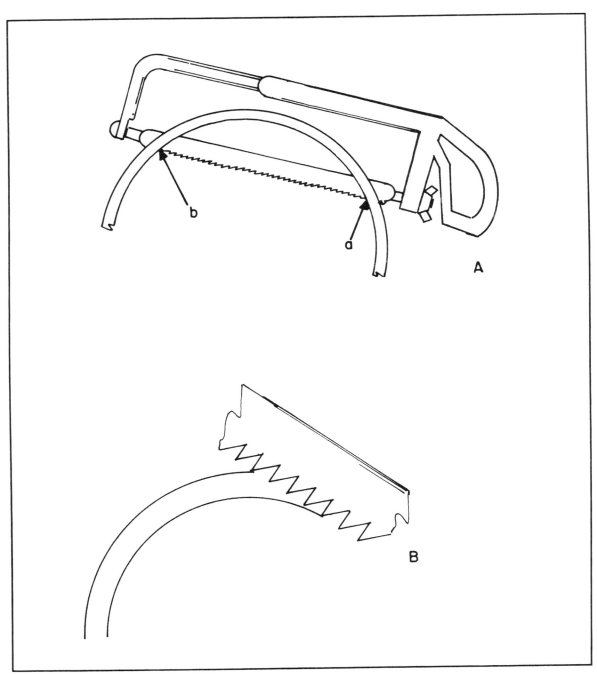

Fig. 4-8. Roll thin wall tubing so that the saw always has two, three, or more teeth in the cut at one time. When you are sawing sheet-metal tubing, do not rock the saw. While the saw is cutting through the wall of the tubing as shown in "A," cutting action occurs at "a" and "b." At about the point shown in the figure, "b" will usually jam the saw, so cut at "a" only when you have reached this point. Roll the tube as you go along. "B" is an enlargement of "b" and shows how the saw will tend to jam at this point.

of the blade is always outside the pipe no matter how far around you are with the cut (Fig. 4-8). Again, take it slow and easy.

ADDITIONAL POINTS TO REMEMBER

When you consider the cut to be made, you should always think of the relationship of the cut to the blade and the problems the tooth will be facing in following your command. It will try to do exactly what you have ordered. If it cannot, it will bind, jam, over-fill its gullets, or all of these things, and it may break.

Never buy a cheap blade. They are of poor steel and poor tempering. At this writing I pay $1 apiece for my hacksaw blades. I consider this to be the minimum quality blade.

I never use a hacksaw blade for hot cutting. A blade that claims to do hot cutting may be able to make a few cuts, but according to my experience making a hot cut with a hacksaw is not necessary in this work. I cannot imagine an instance in black-smithing when a hot cut with a hacksaw would be better than a cold cut.

As you work with the hacksaw in the way I have described, you will find the principles apply in all cases. When you saw a thin piece of flat sheet metal, the saw must be set to the work so that two or more teeth are always within the cut. Simply imagine cutting it as if it were the side of a thin-walled tube.

When you work with pipe or tubing, your hacksaw is looking at two pieces of metal. Each piece of wall is at a different angle to the blade. Each wall cut must be considered a separate cut (Fig. 4-8).

After a little practice, and with the use of some lubricants, you will consider the hacksaw one of your favorite tools. As you learn to use these methods your blades should last 10 times longer than before, your work will improve, and your frustrations with the saw should nearly disappear.

Some final suggestions: write to a blade manufacturer for information about his blades; don't let anyone use your hacksaw.

PART 2

Learning the Basic Processes

Chapter 5

The Working Fire
and Fundamental Shapes

Y OUR SECOND FIRE WILL BE BUILT DIFFER-
ently from the first one, which was made entirely with green coal. Look around the old, dead
fire, and you will find pieces of burned coal, called
coke. This coke is nearly pure carbon. It will light
more easily than most green coal and will make
very little smoke.

Build your fire as you did your first one, but
place the coke instead of the green coal over the
kindling to light it. Add new coal as needed around
the outside of the fire. To avoid excess smoke, work
toward a fire that flames up rapidly at first. As the
heat builds up in your fire, it tends to coke the new
coal around the fire. This new coke is fed into the
fire from the sides and is replaced with more green
coal for more coke and so on. Sprinkle water on the
green coal as you pile it around the fire. During your
working period remember to pick out some of the
coke from your fire by raking it to one side. Use
this reserved coke to cover your fire when you have
iron in it.

As you learn to feed your fire, try to achieve
the proper fire, one nearly free of flames and

smoke. It takes very little air blast to become white
hot. White hot is too hot for most purposes. Your
proper fire will be light pink, like a light pink night-
gown with a small light behind it. It will give off
a rather intense light and be odorless. It will look
like a pile of light yellow-pinkish rocks.

A proper fire for all forging purposes will have
a total volume of burning coke about the size of half
a large cantaloupe. It will heat any of your metal
to the desired heat. You will not need to increase
the size of the fire until you do work much larger
than that covered in this book. In the few instances
when reshaping the fire would be an advantage, I
will describe the procedure.

When you lay a bar of iron over the heart of
the fire, do not dig it in. Mound up some coke over
the iron so that it is well covered. This does three
things. The coke ignites and builds heat on top of
your iron. It insulates it from the rush of cold air
coming in from the sides of the fire. It burns oxygen from this cold air and keeps it from reaching
the iron, thus greatly reducing scale and burning.

To put it another way, the portion of your iron

that is to be heated should be in a package of burning coke to get the best results. You may drop some lumps of green coal on top of the cover of coke if you need more cover, but try to keep the pieces from touching the iron. The lumps on top will become coke in a short time.

In the projects that follow, start with a good fire and maintain it as you proceed.

You are ready now to tackle making some fundamental shapes. Dive into this lesson with a notebook, a pencil or pen, and a measuring tape that won't burn. Record every measurement as you go along so that you can see what effect each shape change has on the overall length, width, and thickness of the bar. You will want to refer to these notes to repeat a project. You will find them particularly helpful when several days have elapsed between workdays. Your notebook becomes a shop tool. I keep records on every new project and enter each into my workbook.

Learning to work to dimension is extremely important. Picture a door fitted with hinges that are not the same size or a fireplace set with the shovel an inch of so shorter than the poker. If you are doing commercial work your customer is going to want the piece exactly as he ordered it. In replacement and repair pieces, approximately isn't good enough.

A LONG SQUARE TAPER

The purpose of this exercise is to draw out a 6-inch-long square taper with a 1/16-inch square point on a square bar. *Draw out* or *draw* in this case means to lengthen or widen a portion of the metal in one direction only without changing the balance. To draw out a taper means to make or form a taper on a portion of a piece of stock, that is, to stretch out a portion.

Stock Required

One bar of 1/2-inch square mild steel (M.S.) exactly 18 inches long.

Procedure

Heat about 2 inches of one end of the stock to a

yellow-orange heat. I have found that a very good way to recognize heat colors is to use Crayola crayons. The waxy surface of the crayon looks almost like the hot iron before you take it out of the fire. Use the 24-crayon box; it will contain all the colors you need. For this yellow-orange heat, compare the yellow-orange crayon, not the wrapper, with your iron. When the iron matches that color, the iron will be about 1,900 degrees Fahrenheit.

When your iron has reached this heat, place the hot end of the square bar just inside the back radius edge of the anvil, holding the cool end slightly elevated. Using your 2 1/2-pound hammer, hit hard and true inside the end. That is, hit so that the hammer face neither hangs over the end nor is up on the stock away from the end. Strike thus twice on each face (Fig. 5-1). This will drive the iron out of the center of the bar and form a round nose on the

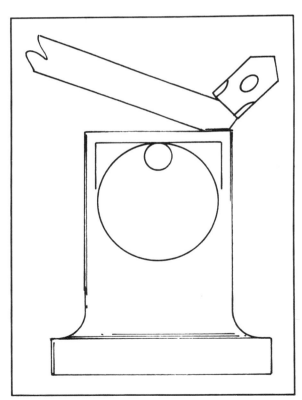

Fig. 5-1. When you make the first hammer blow, be sure the lip of the hammer, the end of the bar, and the edge of the anvil are touching.

end. If you strike lightly, it will slide the surface of the bar out over the end of itself and form a hollow nose. You don't want this.

Taper the point for about 2 inches to about a 1/4-inch square, keeping the bar four-sided. Move up the stock some and increase the length of the taper. Keep your stock at a very slight angle to the face of the anvil because a 6-inch pointed taper in a 1/2-inch square bar has very little angle to the center line or axis. Bring the point down to about 1/8 inch and line up the work.

Measure your bar. How much did it grow? Judge from this how much farther up the stock you need to go to complete the 6-inch taper.

Work to make the tapered point exactly 6 inches long. It should have four true faces. Now, how long is your bar overall? If you have not lost too much metal to scale, it should be about 20 1/2 inches long.

If we had brought the taper to a sharp point and it remained true, the bar would be 4 1/4 inches longer overall, or an increase of three-fourths the length of the taper. Because of loss to scale and because you did not sharpen your point, the mathematical theoretical growth will be greater than the actual growth. Record this growth; it should be about 2 3/4 inches.

You will observe that you lose dimension to scale in each heat. Scale, or oxide, is the black, scaly material that forms on your hot iron. It results from the chemical combination of oxygen with the surface molecules of iron. When it occurs at room temperature or under weather conditions, it is called rust. When iron is heated to forging temperatures, the combination of the oxygen with the iron is rapid and can be very deep. It is possible to lose as much as 1 percent of your heated iron to oxidation in one poorly managed heat. Maintain your fire so that it uses up all the oxygen that enters the fire before it gets to the iron. Don't work where there is a breeze on your anvil or hot iron.

When the hot iron is removed from the fire, there is a corona of heat so great that it can burn some of the oxygen away before it gets to the iron. Even so it is important to work your iron immediately when it is removed from the fire. This means

you must think ahead and plan your moves in order to use all the heat in your iron and lose as little of the iron as possible to oxidation. Don't wait until the iron is out of the fire to decide what size hammer you will use, or just where you will lay the piece on the anvil, or what blow you will use to strike it. These and similar decisions should be made while the iron is still in the fire.

In blacksmithing we usually refer to oxide as scale because the iron looks and acts somewhat like fish scales. When the oxide is being formed in the fire, it is in a plastic state at the high forging temperature. The dust and ash and bits of clinker in the fire stick to it so that what you knock off your iron is more than pure iron oxide. This scale should be rubbed or brushed off your iron using a wire brush or a wooden stick. Otherwise, it will be driven into the surface of the iron when it is forged. This will cause roughness and sometimes a weakness in the finished product.

A ROUND TAPER

In this exercise you will draw out a round taper 6 inches long with a 1/16-inch point.

Stock Required

Use the same square stock you used to make the long square taper.

Procedure

With your hacksaw, cut off the square taper you just made. Record the length of the remaining bar. Begin to taper the bar, keeping the point square, just as you did before. When drawing out a round taper, always draw it out square first; then round it.

When the taper is about 2 1/2 inches long, make your taper eight-sided, then sixteen-sided.

Add more length from the stock. Work it square first, then eight-sided, then sixteen-sided (Fig. 5-2).

It is time to round the taper. True it up by hammering in all the edges and eliminating the flats. This will lengthen the taper still more. Check the length of your taper and your stock and record the measurements. During the last little bit of drawing out, work the last inch or so to the size desired, a 1/16-inch round point. Then with light blows work out the rest of the taper. If you hit too hard and reduce the cross section of the taper too much during the process, there is no way to correct it. Just start over.

In forming this round taper, you will have some loss of iron to scale just as you did in the square taper. This loss must be entered into all your calculations when forging hot iron to dimension.

THE SHOULDERED TONGUE

Now you will draw out a shouldered tongue 2 1/2 inches long, 1/8 inch thick, and 1/2 inch wide, us-ing round stock. The tongue is to be offset so that the outer surface of the tongue and the surface of the bar are in the same plane (Fig. 5-3).

Stock Required

One 1/2-inch round bar, 18 inches long, M.S.

Procedure

Mark off 3/4 inch from one end of the bar. Mark it with a center-punch. Bring this to a light yellow-orange heat.

Lay the marked-off end to be shaped onto the face of the anvil and put the mark directly over a

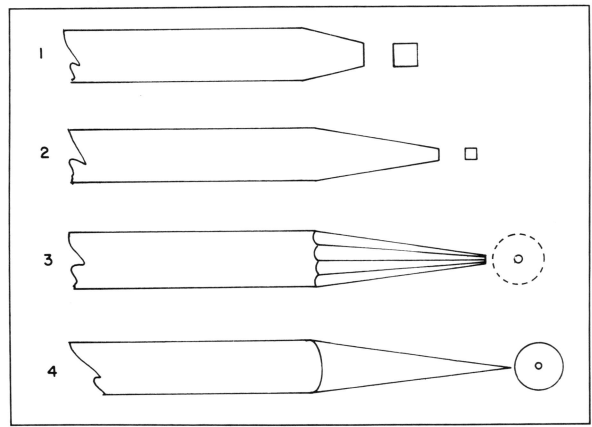

Fig. 5-2. The taper should progress from square to rounded as shown here. At "1" it is still square; the tapering process has begun. At "2" it remains square, but the taper is longer. At "3" it has become octagonal and proceeds to 16-sided (not shown). At "4" it becomes rounded.

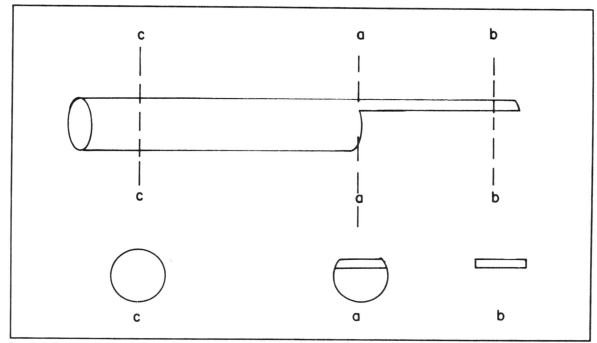

Fig. 5-3. You are forging a bar with a tongue on it. Lines "aa," "bb," and "cc" give a cross section view of the work.

sharp edge (Fig. 5-4). Strike with half the face over the edge. This blow will drive the shank down along the side of the anvil while the measured section is flattened on the face of the anvil. As soon as a shoulder is well started, press the shoulder very hard against the anvil, holding the bar level (Fig. 5-4). This step helps to prevent a slanting shoulder.

Continue to strike until the shoulder is about half-formed. Start the work at a yellow-orange heat.

Lay the forged part edgeways on the anvil face and shape it up to 1/2 inch wide (Fig. 5-4).

Place the shoulder up to the edge again and, with half a hammer over, increase the shoulder depth. Trim up again and repeat these steps until the part, now called a tongue, is the desired width and thickness. Hold the shoulder against the edge of the anvil and hit the end of the bar to help shape the shoulder (Fig. 5-5).

If all went well and nothing was lost to scale, the tongue will be very close to 2 1/2 inches long, and the end view will look like Fig. 5-3.

Repeat this exercise using the 1/2-inch square

bar. Mark off 5/8 inch with the center-punch. Lay the marked-off end over the edge of the anvil with only the measured end fully on the face. Strike with half a hammer over. You want the same 1/8-inch by 1/2-inch by 2 1/2-inch tongue on the square bar.

How much did your bar grow? How long did the tongue become? Did the shoulder come clean, or did it have a slant (Fig. 5-5)? How many heats did you use to make this? How much was the length affected by scale? In general you will lose a small percentage of the iron each time you heat it. How much was lost in a poor shoulder? All these questions must be answered. You will soon learn how much to add to or subtract from any rule to fit your individual work. In all cases be as careful and accurate as you can. Remember an old saying of mine: "The customer is paying you to make it the way he wants it, and it's up to you to do so or turn the job down."

Now that you have worked with some fundamental shapes, you are ready to tackle a more exciting project: making a hearth set.

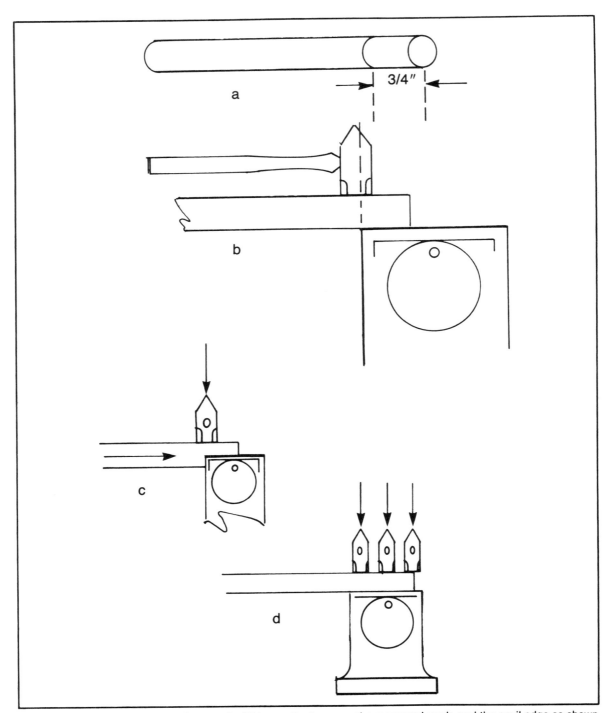

Fig. 5-4. Measure off 3/4 inch as shown at "a." Line up the hammer, the measured mark, and the anvil edge as shown at "b." The tongue shape is starting at "c." As you work along, turn the work to keep the sideways spread under control ("d").

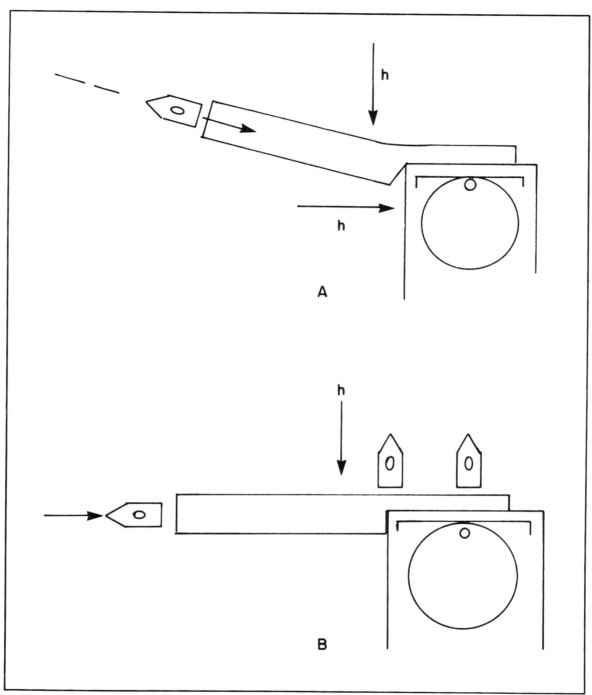

Fig. 5-5. The square shoulder can be controlled by bumping it against a sharp anvil edge. "A" shows the shank bending up a little as you hold the work down hard against the edge of the anvil at "h." "B" shows the steps in final dressing of the work.

Chapter 6

A Three-Piece Matching Hearth Set

I N THIS LESSON YOU WILL MAKE A THREE-piece hearth set for working around the forge. The set will include a hearth poker, a shovel for working with coal and ash, and a lance poker. This is a long lesson. It is designed to cover many important steps you will need to know in order to work independently on other projects. Read completely through each exercise before you begin any work. Do each exercise in its order, carefully and studiously. The completed units will make a good working forge hearth set of which you can be very proud.

Work all parts at a yellow-orange heat, unless noted otherwise. You will again be working to dimension. As you did in Chapter 5, cut your stock carefully to size and measure it after each step. Then record the measurements for later study. I know of no better way to learn when where and how the metal goes. By recording your variances from a rule, you will learn rapidly what your individual work will do.

A HEARTH POKER

The purpose of this exercise is to make a well de-signed hearth poker. It is illustrated in Fig. 6-1.

Stock Required

Square stock, 3/8 inch × 20 inches, M.S.

Procedure

You will divide this exercise into three steps: making a small eye, making the large eye, and making the blade of the poker.

Making a Small Scroll Eye

Cut the stock with a hacksaw using the method you learned in Chapter 4.

Draw out a 4-inch round taper to a 1/16-inch point.

Turn a small scroll with a 1/16-inch eye (Fig. 6-2). To do this, heat your taper to a yellow-orange heat. Watch the point carefully as it will burn up easily. Use a very light air blast. Pass the point over the sharp edge of the back face of the anvil about 3/16 inch and turn it down with a 1-pound hammer

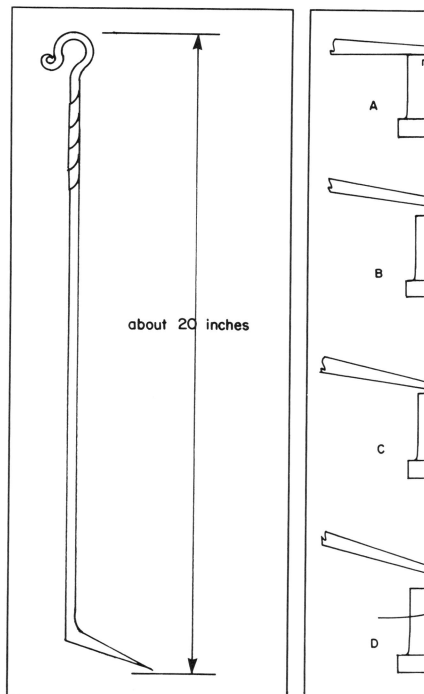

about 20 inches

Fig. 6-1. Your completed poker will look like this. Notice that the tongue is bent about 75 degrees.

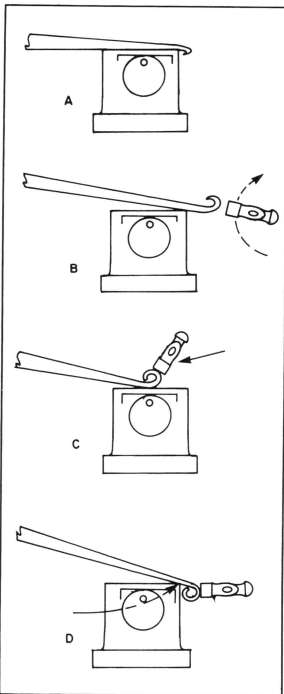

A

B

C

D

Fig. 6-2. Develop your small eye as shown here. In "D" the arrow points to the square edge of the anvil.

using a light wiping blow. Do not crush or cut the point on the edge of the anvil.

When the point is bent down about 60 degrees, rotate the stock until the turn points up. Then press down on the stock with the turn about 1/2 inch over the back edge. Do this with your holding hand so that the work won't bounce while you work it. Use the 1-pound hammer. Hold the handle of the hammer parallel to the back edge of the anvil face and make an upward wiping blow that forces the outside of the curl to stretch (Fig. 6-2). Hit lightly. Hold the work down firmly on the anvil face so that it does not bounce. Feed it into the hammer as needed. During this step the part you are actually working is sticking out in midair beyond the anvil face. Continue this procedure until the point is returning and goes into a curl as much as it will, before you return to using regular blows. Reheat as needed. Do not work this type of detail cooler than a low red heat; which will be Crayola color violet-red. It may break off later if it is worked too cool.

You may strike as needed to close up the scroll for final closing (Fig. 6-2). Hook the scroll over a sharp edge of the anvil and bump it closed very gently, if necessary (Fig. 6-2). This type of turn is called an *eye*. The hole in the eye should be quite small, from 1/16 inch to 1/8 inch in diameter.

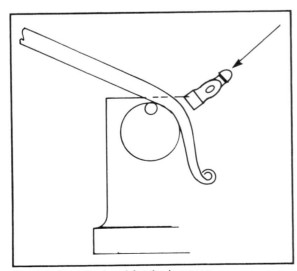

Fig. 6-3. Start the bend for the large eye.

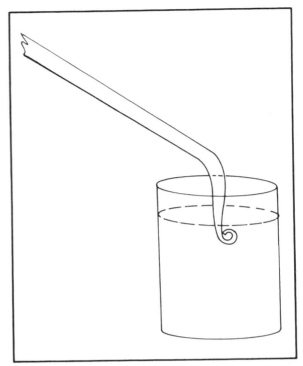

Fig. 6-4. Chill the small eye.

Making the Large Eye

Find a tin can that will hold about a pint of water. Fill the can with water and set it on or very near the anvil block. This water will be used for local cooling.

Place your work in the fire so that the small eye is passed through the fire and extends partially out of it. Heat the entire taper and about 1/2 inch of the stock to a yellow-orange heat. Place the narrow end of the taper close to the point of the anvil horn with the eye down. Strike the taper over the side of the horn to start the large eye. Make a short bend at the taper base (Fig. 6-3). If the small eye tends to whip up, don't correct it. Go on to the next step.

Dip just the small eye in water and chill it until it is black (Fig. 6-4). Hook the bend under the point of the horn and close up the large eye (Fig. 6-5). If you need a second heat, take it, but chill the small eye before striking so you do not spoil it. Dress the work smoothly and let it cool to full black. Then

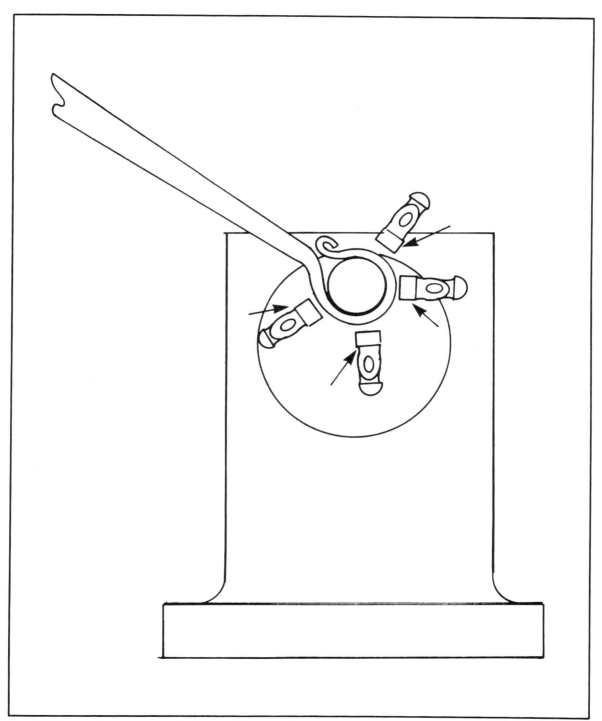

Fig. 6-5. Close up the large eye with hammer blows as shown here.

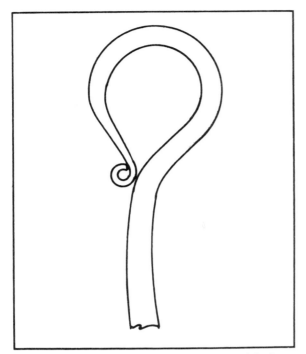

Fig. 6-6. You have completed both the small and the large eye on the end of the poker handle.

Making the Blade of the Poker

The blade of the poker goes on the opposite end of the bar from the eyes. Draw out a tongue 4 1/2 inches long by 1/2 inch wide by 1/8 inch thick. Use about 2 1/4 inches of your bar to form this tongue (Fig. 6-7). Don't shoulder it on the sharp edge of your anvil. Use your largest radius instead. The flat of the tongue is to be perpendicular to the plane of the large eye and to come out of the center of the stock (Fig. 6-8).

Starting 3/4 inch behind the tongue, develop a waist in the stock 4 inches long by 5/16 inch by 1/4 inch at the smallest part (Fig. 6-9). Work this out over the base of the horn with the 1-pound ball peen hammer. Let the waist develop from the estimated center to both ends. This waist will cause the bar to grow from 1/2 inch to 3/4 inch depending on the flow you develop.

In the shank size portion of the bar between the waist and the tongue, start a 75-degree bend with about a 1/4-inch radius. This lies just above the tongue so that it is in the plane of the large eye. Avoid damaging the waist (Fig. 6-10).

Lay off a 3-inch section starting 3 inches below the eye. Bring this 3-inch section to a red heat, between Crayola color red and orange-red. This is not very hot. Grip one end in the vise 1/4 inch outside the mark; grab the other end with your turning wrench 1/4 inch outside the mark. A 10-inch

quench it in water to barehand heat. When you are finished, it should look like Fig. 6-6.

Measure your work and see how much change in length has occurred in your 20-inch bar. Record this.

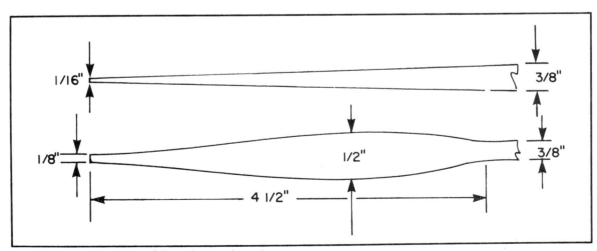

Fig. 6-7. Lay out the blade of the poker as shown here.

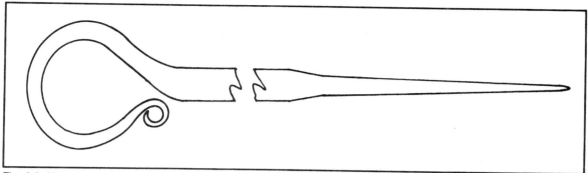

Fig. 6-8. Keep the flat of the blade opposite to the plane of the eye.

or 12-inch adjustable end wrench or Crescent wrench will suffice as a turning wrench. Then, with an even turning speed, not fast, make one complete revolution (Fig. 6-11). If the work looks out of line as in Fig. 6-12, use two hammers, one a 2 1/2 pound and one a little lighter, to straighten the work. Hold the heavier hammer away from the jaws of the vise and against the shank on the side you want the work to move to. Strike near the jaw on the oppo-

site side. This will move the center of the stock as desired (Fig. 6-12). Straighten the bend by bending, not striking, to line up the work after centering the twist. Sometimes the bend in the twist can be removed in the vise by squeezing the bend between the jaws (Fig. 6-12).

Brush it with a hand wire brush and lay it aside to cool. Do not quench. The poker should be 20 inches long. You now have a good-looking, well-

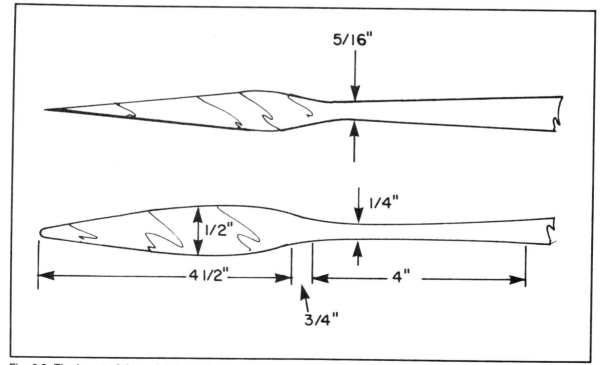

Fig. 6-9. The layout of the waist above the poker blade.

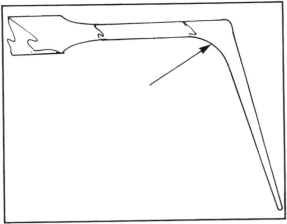

Fig. 6-10. The completed blade, waist, and tongue should look like this. The arrow points to the 75-degree bend.

balanced, and useful poker to use at your forge. You should also have a complete record with sketches of every dimension change.

A HEARTH SHOVEL

In this exercise you will make your hearth shovel.

Stock Required

Square stock 3/8 inch × 15 inches, M.S.

Hot-rolled, black 16-gauge sheet metal, 5 1/4 inches × 5 3/4 inches. If you buy this stock, be sure you ask for it by name, "hot-rolled, black 16-gauge sheet metal."

Two 3/16-inch by 1/2-inch roundhead rivets.

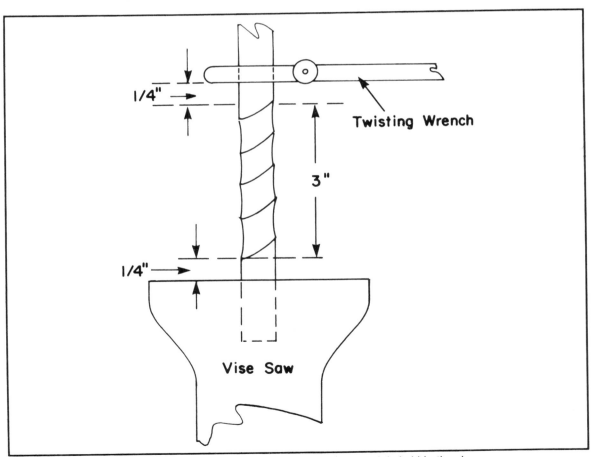

Fig. 6-11. Use a twisting wrench to make a decorative spiral while the work is held in the vise.

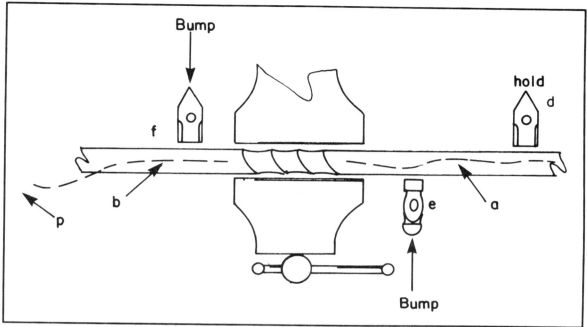

Fig. 6-12. The dotted line represents some of the bends that might occur as you proceed with the work. To straighten the bend at "e," hold a heavy hammer at "d" to serve as a bucker and strike with light hammer blows at "e." To straighten the bend at "a," work it out over the anvil. To straighten the bend at "b," bump the bar gently between "f" and the vise jaws while you put bending pressure on the bar. If the bend is at the twist, work out the same back up method, being careful to avoid flattening any part of the twist.

Additional Tools Required

A cold chisel with a 7/8-inch or 1-inch bit or cutting edge. Buy the best quality available. Try a quality auto supply store for this tool.

A 3/16-inch or number 11 metal drill, a twist drill.

A 12-inch or 14-inch bastard-cut flat file. Look for this in an industry-oriented hardware store. Get a Lenox or Nicholson or similar quality brand, again the best available.

A 1 1/2-pound ball peen hammer (optional). Best results will be had with this hammer, but you can do the exercise with the 1-pound ball peen.

A cutting plate to protect your anvil face. It can be made of any piece of soft metal such as hard brass, bronze, or mild steel. It should be as wide as the face of your anvil and at least 6 inches long. See Chapter 16 for directions on how to make a fitted cutting plate.

Your forging heat for this project will be a yellow-orange heat unless otherwise noted.

Procedure

The procedure for making the hearth shovel is divided into four steps: making the handle, preparing the blade of the shovel, working the blade of the shovel, and riveting the shovel blade to the handle.

Making the Handle

Repeat the steps for making the poker handle and eye end, trying to match the size and shape of the eyes for the shovel handle with those of the eyes for the poker. Refer to "Making a Small Scroll Eye" and "Making the Large Eye" in Exercise 1 of this chapter. Don't twist yet.

On the other end of your bar, draw out a flat, bull-nosed tongue 1/8 inch by 1/2 inch by 1 3/8 inches long. Now work up a waist behind the tongue just as you did with the poker. You will eventually attach the blade of the shovel to this tongue (Fig. 6-13). The flat of the tongue must be perpendicular to the plane of the completed eye.

Lay the tongue beyond the back edge of the anvil. Draw the shoulder in the plane of the tongue down to 5/16 inch and taper up the shank for about an inch.

Rotate the work a quarter turn and draw the shank down to 1/4 inch wide. Taper it on back to full size stock in about 3 inches (Fig. 6-13). Extend the 5/16-inch taper up the shank to match up with the 1/4-inch taper (Fig. 6-13).

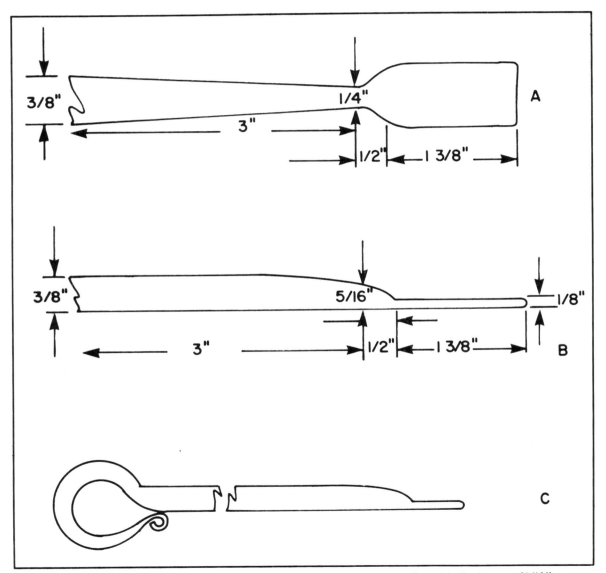

Fig. 6-13. Three views of the flat tongue and the 3 inches of the handle that are adjacent to the tongue. At "A" you see the development of the shoulders on the blade. "B" shows development of shoulders on the shank. "C" shows how the two ends will line up.

Measure your work thus far to see what length you have overall. Record it.

Bend a curve in the area just above the shoulders. Then curve the tongue back up. It should look like Fig. 6-14. This tongue will eventually fit into your shovel blade as shown in Fig. 6-31.

Put in your 3-inch twist as you did with the poker. Locate it 3 inches below the eye (Fig. 6-1). Clean completely with a wire brush and lay it aside. Do not quench. If you were to quench the tongue to harden it, you would have trouble in drilling it later and might break your drill.

Now hold the poker and the shovel handles together. The planes of the eyes and the flats should be the same.

Preparing the Blade of the Shovel

This step includes laying out, cutting, and filing. See Fig. 6-15 for the layout for cutting your metal.

Cut away the shaded area. Until you are well practiced at this, use a cutting plate to avoid injury to your anvil and your cutting tool. Cut with a sharp cold chisel that has a 7/8-inch or 1-inch bit. Lay your piece of sheet metal on the face of the anvil and cut into your layout lines just enough to mark the metal. Use your 2 1/2-pound hammer and strike lightly with a choked-up grip. The use of a heavy hammer here prevents excess bounce, which can be very troublesome.

When you have marked all your lines, wet the cutting edge of your chisel with some lubricating oil or rub it with a candle so that some wax sticks to it. Lay the piece on the cutting plate, which you have placed in the middle of the anvil face, and start your cut, but do not cut through. Strike only hard

enough to nearly cut through along all your marks. Now place a portion of the shaded area in the vise and bend it back and forth until it breaks off. Do this with each shaded portion until you have gone all around (Fig. 6-16). Watch out for finger-cutting edges.

All the edges must be filed. Replace the work in the vise with one edge about 3/4 inch above the jaws and with the edge to be filed parallel to the top of the vise. Using the bastard-cut file, draw-file the edges until they are fairly smooth. Keep one 12-inch or 14-inch file just for this type of fine work. Draw-filing is like planing in that individual knives within the file do the cutting during the entire stroke (Fig. 6-17). With your work properly in the vise as above, take the tang end of the file in your right hand and the other end in your left. Place the file on the edge nearest you. Have it square across the work piece, level with the floor to start (Fig. 6-18).

With moderate down-pressure from both hands, push the file along the edge. Stop the stroke while about one-half the file's width is still on the work. Don't go off the far end because this tends to round the corners. Lift all downward pressure, pull the file back to the beginning point, and repeat your stroke. The file will try to go endo; don't let it. When the edge of the work is smooth, tip the file to right or left and take several cuts with light downward pressure on the push stroke. This will smooth any remaining sharp edges.

If you hold the tang of the file in your left hand instead of your right, the pull stroke is the one that cuts. Everything else is the same. Smooth all the edges of the blade blank before the next process.

Working the Blade of the Shovel

This section is all cold work. No heat is used. This process is a departure from what you have been doing, but follow each step carefully, and all should turn out fine. You will be introduced to the use of a *swage block*, a heavy chunk of cast iron about 3 1/2 inches thick and from 14 to 16 inches square. It has holes of varied shapes and sizes cast into it and has a variety of notches, grooves, and circle parts cast all around the edges. The swage block

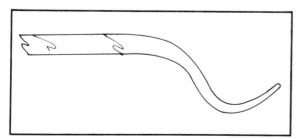

Fig. 6-14. The blade end of the shovel handle has been bent to its approximate final shape. It is ready to receive the blade.

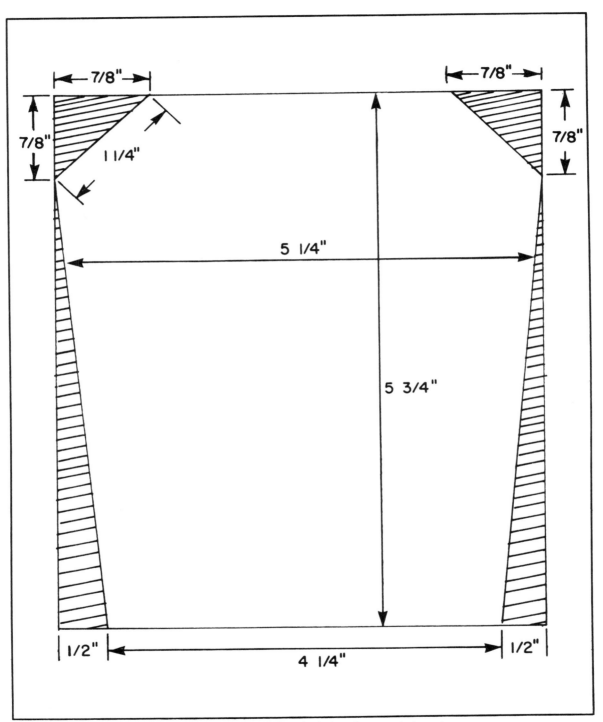

Fig. 6-15. Lay out your shovel blade as shown here. The shaded portions are to be cut away.

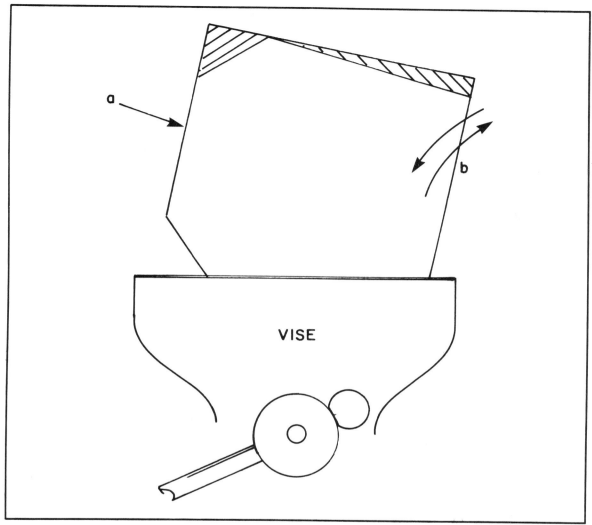

Fig. 6-16. Hold the portion to be cut away in the vise and rock the blank back and forth to complete the cut. The top of the blade is marked "a;" "b" is at the bottom.

would be useful for the next step in making your shovel, but it is not necessary. Directions for making a wooden substitute for a swage block follow the directions for making the shovel.

You will do well to practice on a piece of scrap the same thickness as the blade stock before you tackle your carefully prepared blade blank. You should protect your ears with plugs or earmuffs. Wear a heavy leather glove on your holding hand. The shock waves set up in this sort of work can

actually blister and bruise unprotected fingers. In all cases hold the work very firmly against the anvil or swage block.

On the blade blank you have just prepared, lay out a horseshoe-shaped line according to the measurements in Fig. 6-19. Use a 1-pound ball peen hammer or the 1 1/2 pounder if you have it. Peen a 3/8-inch strip all around, centering on the mark. Peen very thoroughly and hit rather hard (Fig. 6-19). Do all of this on the smooth face of your an-

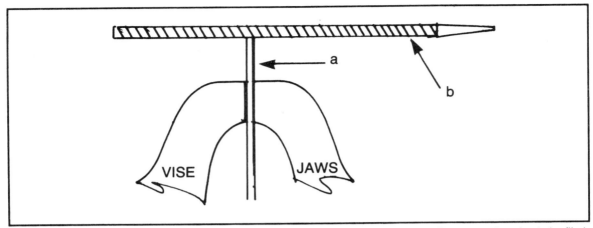

Fig. 6-17. The work, shown at "a," is held in the vise. The file, shown at "b," should be flat across the edge to be filed.

vil. Note that the edges outside the peening are turning up and the center is "bellying up."

Move the work to the swage block and use a round trough with about a 2 1/2-inch radius or your largest round trough. If you do not have a swage block or anvil swages, use the firewood method, explained at the end of this segment. Study Fig. 6-20. Line "Y" is the strike line for the peen. Don't try to work in the bottom of the trough along line "CL." Line "Y" passes through at about 3/4 inch below the top edge of the trough and is the aiming point for every blow. You move the work around under the hammer. Don't strike the hammer off the "Y" line.

Start in the middle of either shoulder of the blade (Fig. 6-21). Pass the peened area under the hammer to the other shoulder (Fig. 6-22). Continue to the lip along the side area and then return to the starting point and peen the other side out to the lip. Work back and forth until the work lays well into the radius. You may peen between the edges of the metal and the mark line, but do not get into the belly or bottom area yet. Do not peen the edge of the metal. Leave 1/8 inch to 3/16 inch of metal untouched all around.

Move the work to a trough with a smaller radius and repeat the process. In this type of work, you are stretching the metal between the bottom and the edges, particularly in the back half under the shoulders, and you are pushing it out to form

a partial bowl in the shoulder areas (Fig. 6-23).

Lay the work on the anvil. With the face of the hammer, flatten the bottom. As you progress with the shaping, the work will need to be flattened

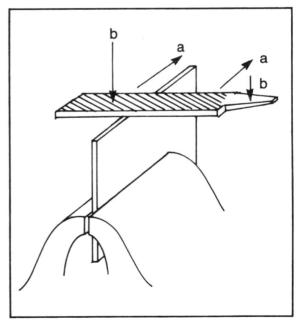

Fig. 6-18. When you are draw filing to finish up an edge, keep downward pressure equal at points "b" and "b." Keep the push pressure equal at "a" and "a." If you pull the file toward you to cut, turn it end for end. Keep the pressure equal. The term for this is draw filing whether you cut on the push or the pull.

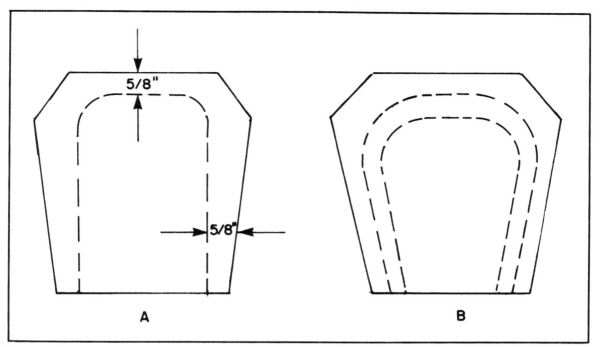

Fig. 6-19. Start peening on the dotted line shown in ''A.'' As you peen, try to stay within the dotted lines shown at ''B.''

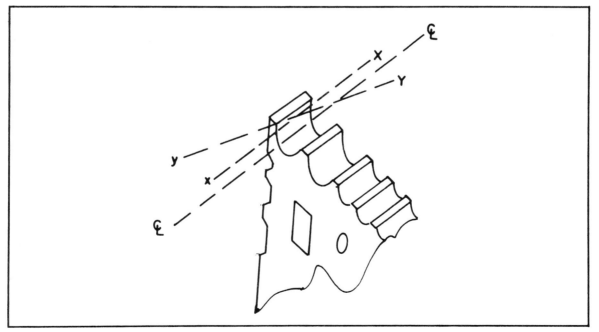

Fig. 6-20. Troughs in the swage block. Line ''CL'' represents a center line through the bottom of the trough. You will work in the area between lines ''x'' and ''y.''

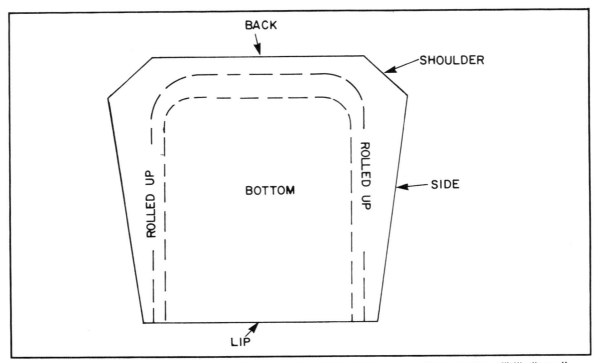

Fig. 6-21. As you begin to peen, the edges and the shoulder will start to turn up and the bottom will "belly-up."

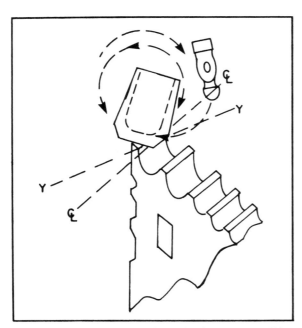

Fig. 6-22. Turn the work as shown by the arrows, striking at line "y."

several times. If the work twists, grab the lip in the vise and twist the blade back true again (Fig. 6-24). Use a gloved hand only.

Continue shaping, using smaller and smaller troughs on your swage block, until only the sides are being worked. The sides require about a 3/8-inch radius. The edges may be bumped to help true up the work. Regardless of the size of the trough being used, the "Y"-line principle (Fig. 6-20) applies.

Riveting

Riveting is a process of fastening two parts together without welding them or using screws or nuts and bolts. A rivet looks much like a bolt with a round or flat head, but it has no threads (Fig. 6-25). Many types of rivets are available. Sometimes they are hard to find because they are not used much in to-day's industry. Ask for them in hardware stores, sheet metal shops, or from iron and steel suppliers.

To effect the fastening, the two parts are put

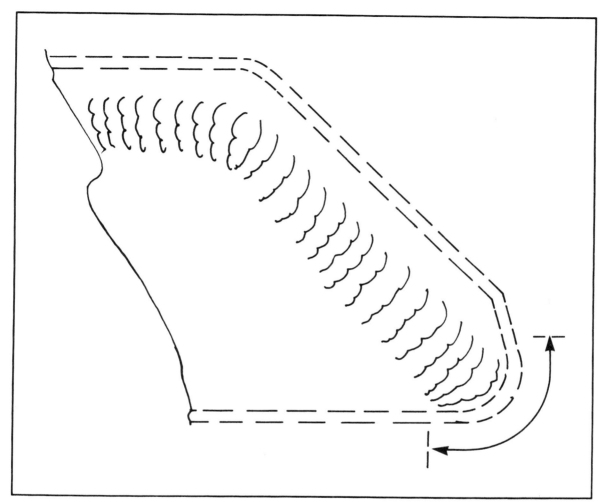

Fig. 6-23. The shoulder rolls up to form a bowllike shape. Arrows show the limit of the peened area.

together, and a rivet is passed through a hole common to both parts. The head of the rivet is backed up or *bucked* with a heavy object. The parts are held together tightly, and the end of the rivet is battered over. This forms a second head. When properly done, riveting is an excellent way to fasten parts together. The next time you are near a steel bridge notice all the rivet heads.

Riveting may be done hot or cold. In hot riveting a *bucker* places a red-hot rivet in the hole, and a rivet set, usually driven by air, is placed on the other end of the rivet. The bucker holds a heavy *bucking bar* against the head to keep the *setter* or

riveter from pushing the rivet out. The setter pulls the trigger on the rivet set and the rivet is headed (Fig. 6-26). This is all done as fast as possible to hold the heat in the rivet. As the rivet cools it shrinks, drawing the two parts together securely. When a hot rivet is properly headed, it is very tight. The job is permanent and will not vibrate loose.

Cold riveting is done in much the same manner, but it is easier to handle and allows more time for the work. Hot riveting is not practical for most of the work done in a small blacksmith shop. You will use cold riveting only.

In hand hammer work, rivets from 1/8-inch

73

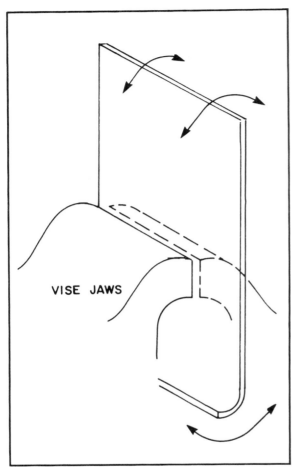

Fig. 6-24. Twist the work back into alignment by holding the bottom of the blade in the vise and twisting by hand.

parts and stick out about one to one and one-half times the diameter of the hole (Fig. 6-27).

Place the work so that the head of the rivet is directly down on the anvil or on a heavy flat-ended bar sticking up out of the hardy hole or the vise.

Use the ball of your 1-pound ball peen hammer and start striking the end of the rivet on its outer edge (Fig. 6-28). Do not hit the center. In this way you are peening down the sides of the rivet all around to form a second head. While you are doing this, keep the parts pressed tightly together.

When the head is partly formed and the end is mushroomed down, but before it is set down tightly, hit the center of the rivet two or three firm blows with the face of the hammer (Fig. 6-29). This fills the hole full of rivet stock (Fig. 6-30). Then ham-

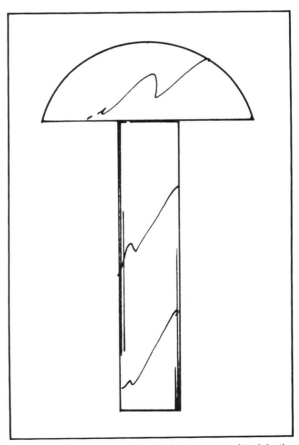

Fig. 6-25. Common roundhead rivets are used to join the shovel blade to the handle.

through 3/8-inch diameter are practical. You can use rivets of 7/16-inch diameter and larger, but you will find them difficult to handle. I recommend bolts and nuts for these larger sizes.

When a rivet is installed and properly tightened up in the work, we say that the rivet is *set*. Installing rivets is called *setting rivets*. When a rivet is used as a pin, as in a set of tongs, it is called a *pivot set* or *hinge set*. The rivet is not set up tight, thus allowing a flexible joint. Now you are ready to try a practice piece.

Drill holes in the parts to be riveted and line them up.

Cut off a rivet so that it will pass through both

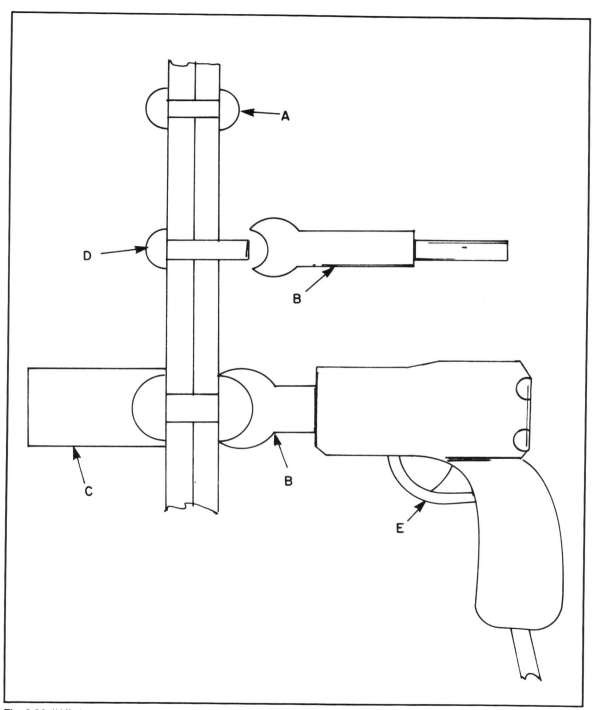

Fig. 6-26. "A" shows a completed rivet joining. "B" is the rivet set. "C" shows a bucking bar. "D" shows the rivet before it is set. "E" shows a power riveting gun as it sets a rivet against the bucking bar.

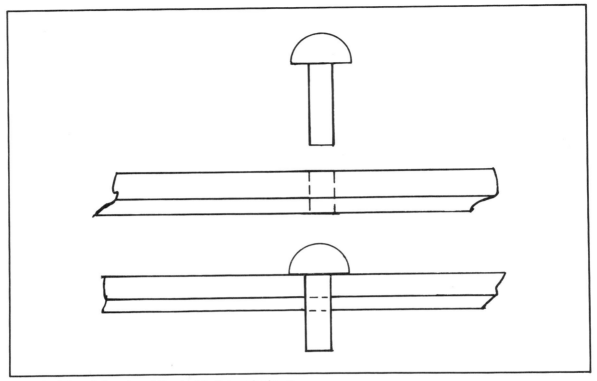

Fig. 6-27. The relative size of the rivet to the work pieces.

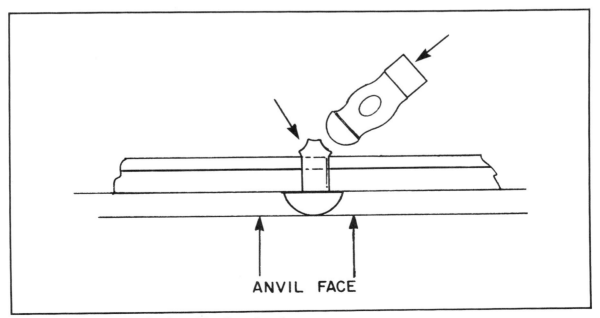

ANVIL FACE

Fig. 6-28. Start setting the rivet by striking the outer edges.

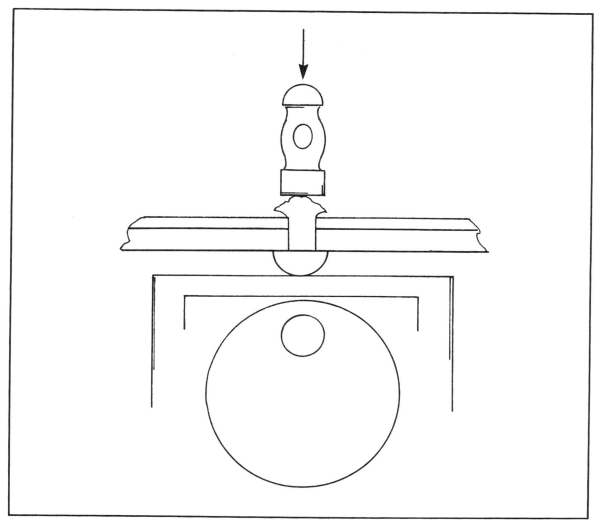

Fig. 6-29. This blow fills the hole with the shank of the rivet.

mer again around the mushroom to make an even, round finish. It will be very tight.

Riveting the Shovel Blade to the Handle

Go to the kitchen and find a large spoon that has a pleasing line. Keep this pleasing line in mind when you are assembling your hearth shovel. Appearance is important in the design of the shovel.

You will rivet the handle to the inside of the blade. The round head of the rivet will also be inside.

Drill a number 11 hole on the center line 1/4 inch from the end of the tongue on the handle. A regular 1/4-inch electric drill will serve well for both holes needed in this riveting job. Nest the tongue down into the blade. Fit as needed, align it well, and mark the tongue with a punch. Drill the blade through the hole in the tongue using a number 11 drill (Fig. 6-31). You may use a 3/16-inch drill in place of the number 11 drill in this exercise.

Cut your 3/16-inch rivet to about 5/16 inch long. It should stick through the tongue and the blade

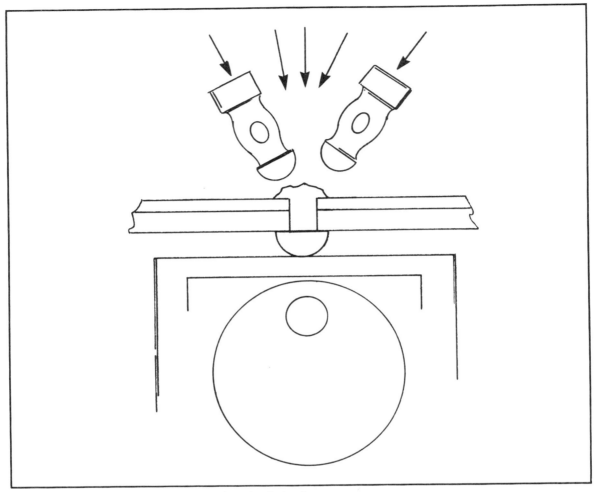

Fig. 6-30. Final blows of the hammer complete the rivet set.

with 3/16 inch (the diameter of the rivet) extending. Set it in place and peen it over, but not too tight yet. Align the handle and the blade, and then tighten up the rivet enough to hold them in line (Fig. 6-32).

On the inside, mark the center line of the tongue with a punch mark about 5/8 inch up the tongue from the other rivet. After making sure that all is in alignment, drill another number 11 hole through the tongue and the blade. Place another 3/16-inch or 3/8-inch (or longer as noted above) rivet in the hole and peen it. Tighten up both rivets so that the blade and the tongue seem to be in one

piece. The peened part of the rivets should be rounded out, not flattened.

Do any minor alignment that is needed, keeping the lines of the kitchen spoon in mind, brush all the work with a hand wire brush and oil it up. Your hearth shovel is complete (Fig. 6-33).

The Woodblock Method
for Forming Your Shovel Blade

If you do not have a swage block or anvil swages, you can make an acceptable substitute. Find a piece of hardwood about 12 inches by 12 inches square. It can be square or round and between 12 inches

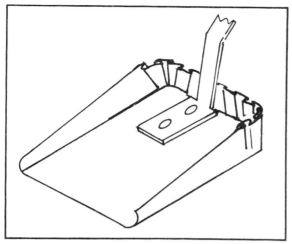

Fig. 6-31. The shovel handle and blade are ready for the first rivet.

and 18 inches long. A woodstove or fireplace log will do. The wood must be dry and solid. Eucalyptus, madrone, oak, maple, ash, and mesquite are all suitable. Cut off both ends square so that the piece will sit firmly on its end and the working face will be level.

Use a hot iron to burn small depressions on the end grain of the wood. This will give you a basin or cup into which you will hammer your metal for final shaping. Your original shaping is done on the anvil; then it is finished on the woodblock. The depression for the hearth shovel needs to be 3/8 inch to 1/2 inch deep and about the diameter of a 50-cent piece. It should be shaped like a bowl.

To do this, heat a 1/2-inch round bar and round off the end a bit to dull the sharp edges. Don't bend it. On the wood stump, mark the spot where you

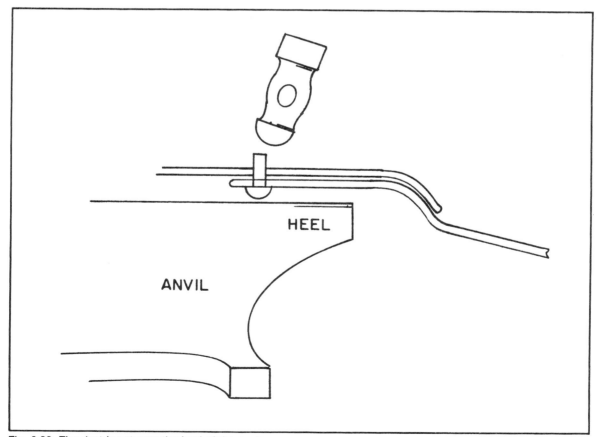

HEEL

ANVIL

Fig. 6-32. The rivet is set over the heel of the anvil.

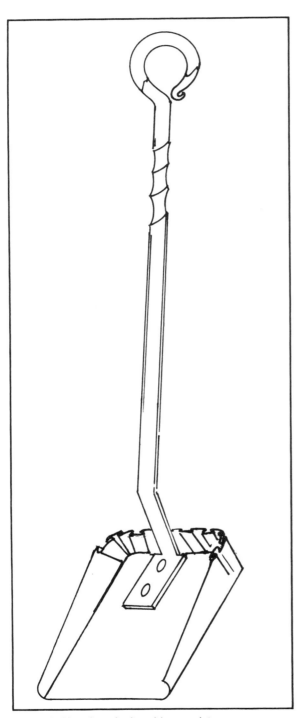

Fig. 6-33. Your hearth shovel is complete.

want your forming cup. Heat the end of the bar to an orange heat. Place the hot end in the center of the spot. Hold the bar at about a 15- or 20-degree angle to the face of the block. Keeping the point on the spot, work the bar around in a circle much like the minute hand of a clock. Don't move too slowly, or you might make a poorly shaped cup. You may need to make two or three revolutions. Do this work when the bar is at orange heat—hot! As soon as the orange color drops into the red tones, reheat the bar (Fig. 6-34).

Next burn a groove in the stump in a line that crosses the annual rings at an angle to any diameter line as shown in Fig. 6-34. This groove should be about 6 inches long, 1/2 inch wide, and about 1/4 inch deep. The groove will be used to shape the rolled sides of the blade.

Avoid cooking the wood. This will happen if the bar is too cold. You want to actually remove the wood by burning it instantly almost as if you were cutting it with a gouge. Burning this way leaves the wood very hard, but not weakened. You may use a gouge to carve out the cup instead of burning it out. If you choose this method, do your flash burn anyway to harden the cup. Be careful; there will be lots of smoke and flame.

To use the woodblock cup to shape the metal, first stretch the metal on the anvil under the ball peen hammer (Fig. 6-23). Then shape the stretch in the cup. Repeat the process as needed (Fig. 6-35). In doing this you keep the part to be formed moving under the hammer. Keep the hammer striking over the center of the cup. Do not try to force the metal down into the cup. Instead coax it into the cup. If it will not go without hard blows, it isn't ready. Just start the metal moving a little more in the desired direction on the face of the anvil. As you peen the iron, you will notice the movement of the iron around the peened area and see the edges of the iron or sheet metal move out of alignment. These movements are your guides.

The only difference between using an iron swage and a woodblock is that the wood cup cannot tolerate the pressures the iron swage can. Using the iron swage, you stretch and shape at the same time under each hammer blow. In using the

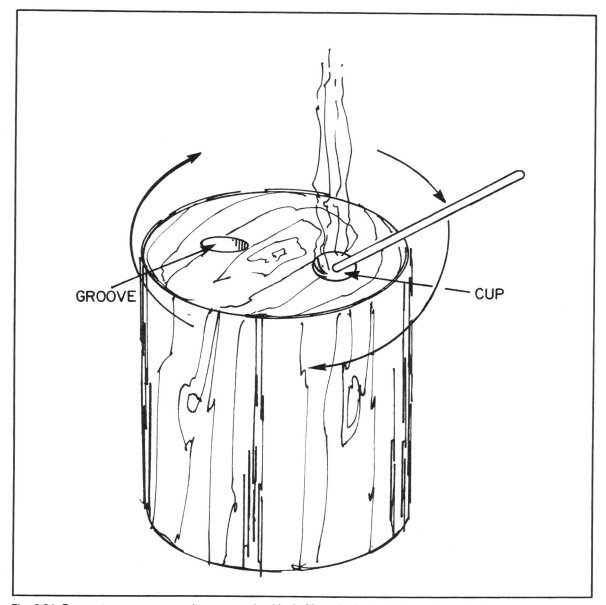

Fig. 6-34. Burn out cups or grooves in your wooden block. Move the heated bar as shown by the arrows.

woodblock cup, you shape up only what you have stretched on the anvil. Working on the woodblock is slower. However, in many cases you can obtain a finer finish. Many smiths prefer a woodblock for very fine work. Let me warn you that although the wood is hard, it can be destroyed in a hurry. Even

a 1-pound ball peen hammer striking a piece of 16-gauge metal can ruin your block if you overdo it. As you practice this method, you will find that your forming cups will last for many jobs. Never try to form hot metal on your woodblock. You will destroy the block.

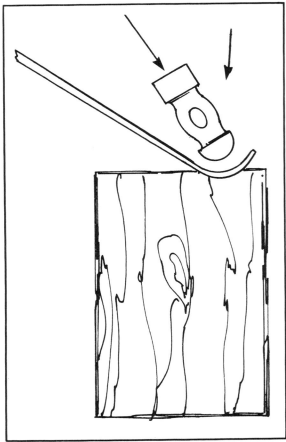

Fig. 6-35. When you shape the peened area in the wood-block, strike straight into the radius of the peened area. This will allow firm pressure against the surface of the cup.

A LANCE POKER

The lance poker is very useful in cleaning up your fire and removing large clinkers in one piece. When you make this tool you will be working flat stock edgeways, which will present some problems not encountered in working square or round stock. This project includes shaping a cutting edge with your hammer. Some of the work may seem simple, but be careful and take each step in its turn. As always, record what is happening in dimension changes as you go along. In a project like this, you want to move the same amount of metal on each side of the flat bar during any one heat. Don't try to move too much metal at one heat. I will explain this as you

go along. Doing too much too fast can cause damage that cannot be repaired.

Have your heat right when you are working flat bar stock edgeways. It must be hot enough so that when you work it into a point the center portion of the flat bar stock will tend to extrude. As this happens the corners will, in effect, follow in toward the center, then outward toward the point you are forming. Study Fig. 6-36 carefully. Use a piece of scrap to see at just what heat this movement occurs and, in general, experiment with edge forging.

You will need a light yellow-orange heat. It will be hotter than the temperatures you have been using up to now. The iron will form scale rather quickly when you take it out of the fire.

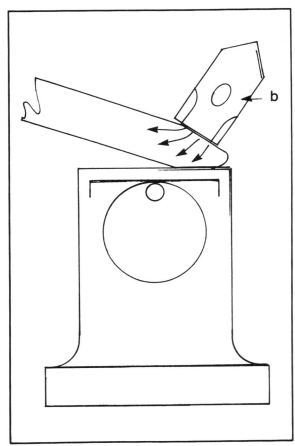

Fig. 6-36. Notice the direction of the hammer blow shown by the arrow at "b" as you begin to taper flat stock edgeways.

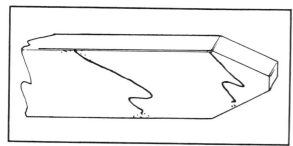

Fig. 6-37. The started edge-forging of the flat stock should look like this. Notice that there is no swelling, bulging, or upsetting.

Stock Required

1/4-inch by 3/4-inch by 18-inch flat stock, M.S.

Procedure

First you will draw out the blade of the poker. Draw out the bar to a 1/4-inch by 1/4-inch point in about

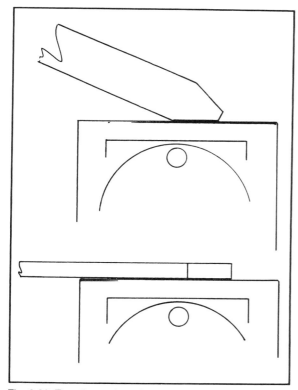

Fig. 6-38. Turn the work so that you alternate between edge hammering and flat-side hammering.

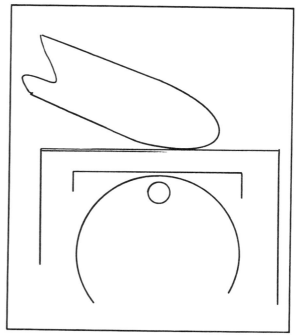

Fig. 6-39. Round the shoulders slightly.

2 inches (Fig. 6-37). While you are doing this, maintain the 1/4-inch thickness of the stock. As the stock *upsets*, becomes thicker, from beating on its edge, hammer it back to a 1/4-inch thickness. In this type of forging you go back and forth from edge hammering to flat-side hammering so that no portion of the work gets too far ahead of the other (Fig. 6-38). Do some measuring while you work the lance. You will find it very helpful to have these measurements in your records later.

Round the shoulders slightly where the taper of the point meets the whole size of the stock (Fig. 6-39).

Before you go back into the fire for your next heat, lay the edge of the tapered part on the face of the anvil at the back radius. It should not hang over. Tip it up a bit. Now lay the hammer face on the edge of the taper. Tip the hammer face so that it has the same angle to the iron as the anvil does. When seen at anvil-face level, the angle of the hammer and the angle of the anvil should describe the sides of a knife blade (Fig. 6-40).

Heat to a light yellow-orange and start work-

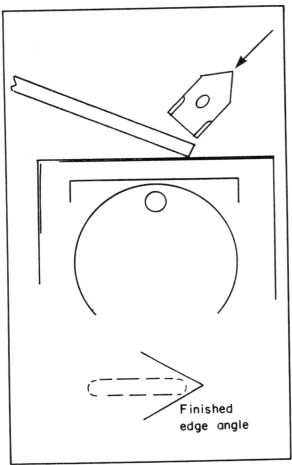

Fig. 6-40. Hammer face and the anvil face are at the proper angle for forming the knifelike edge.

waist 2 1/2 inches long and 1/2 inch wide. Center at 7 1/2 inches from the point as shown in Fig. 6-43.

Lay the edge of the waist over the back of the horn and forge it to shape, working all from one edge. Keep the waist 1/4 inch thick. It will grow quite a bit. Record the growth. When the waist has the desired center dimension, work it over to the center line, using the face of the anvil (Fig. 6-44).

Return to the edge of the lance; continue working it back toward the waist until it is starting into the waist about an inch or less. Don't make the blade more than 1 1/2 inches wide at the widest point. As you approach the waist, let the blade get duller. This will keep it narrower until the blade blends into the stock and the edges disappear (Fig. 6-45).

Study the figures. Push yourself to make a perfect tool that will resemble the drawing as closely as you can make it; be as neat as you can. There may be no way to correct an error here. You may hit the edges of your blade to help shape it, but don't overdo this. Don't try to work the blade after it reaches a low red heat. Reheat as many times as you need to. Remember you are learning this trade, so don't be surprised if you have a failure and have to do something over.

No one will scold you if you make mistakes.

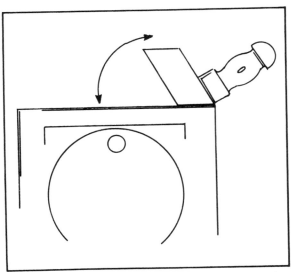

Fig. 6-41. Keep turning the work from side to side so that the blade will not curve beyond recovery.

ing into the metal to obtain the edge you visualized (Fig. 6-41). Work first on one edge, then on the other, back and forth. Do this by turning the stock over and over. You will notice that as you forge the blade on one side, the center line of the metal moves over and bends the bar. This movement occurs because the metal on the edge is being elongated as well as widened, and it moves the center line along with it (Fig. 6-42). Continue to work both sides together, bringing the edges down to about 1/32 inch. Do not make the edges sharp. Work back from the point into the curve and stop there.

Start at the handle end of the curve, which is now about 3 inches from the point, and lay out a

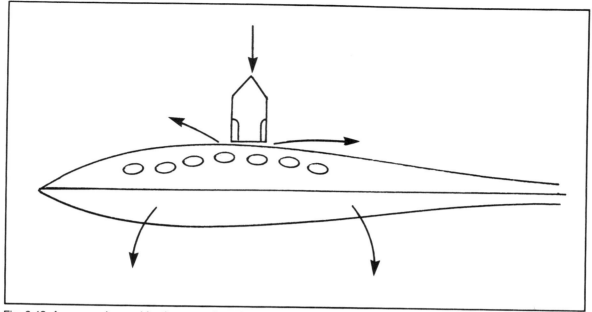

Fig. 6-42. As you work one side, the center line of the blade will bend as shown by the arrows. The small circles indicate where the hammer blows have fallen.

Let the blade cool in the air until all the heat color is gone; then quench to room temperature.

You will form the eye on the handle end of the poker. First draw out a *rat-tail*. This is really a taper, but it has shoulders all around it. It does, not start at stock dimension as does the eye taper. The rat-tail should be 4 inches long with a 1/16-inch round point and a 1/4-inch by 3/8-inch base. Lay about 1 1/4 inches of the handle over the anvil at

the smallest radius on the anvil (about 1/16 inch or so). Use the cross peen of your hammer to strike. Refer to Fig. 6-46 to see how this job is done (Fig. 6-47). This makes a groove in one edge and a flat spot in the other edge. Turn it over and gently work a groove in the flat spot. This allows you to start the taper without having the hammer strike the anvil. Avoid letting the stock behind the groove rest on the anvil and avoid hitting it. Draw this rat-tail

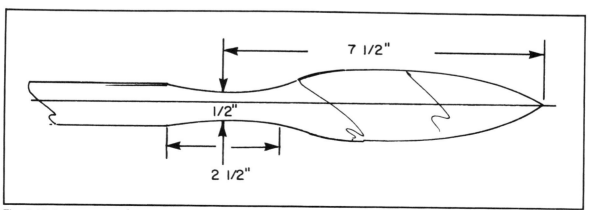

Fig. 6-43. Lay out the waist behind the blade as shown here.

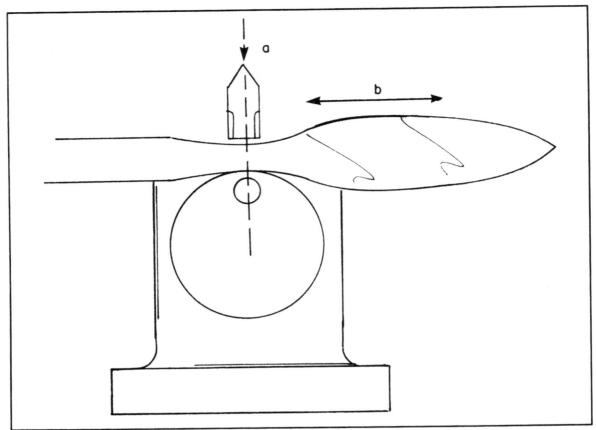

Fig. 6-44. True up the blade in the waist area. Work directly down over the top of the horn, close to the base as shown at "a." The arrows at "b" show the direction of growth that will occur in both the waist and the blade.

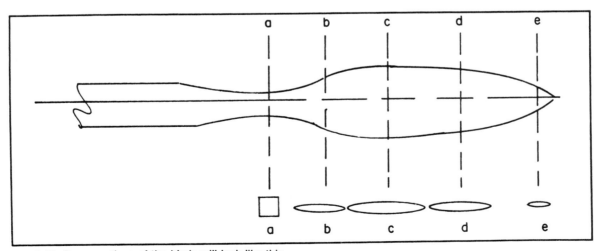

Fig. 6-45. Cross sections of the blade will look like this.

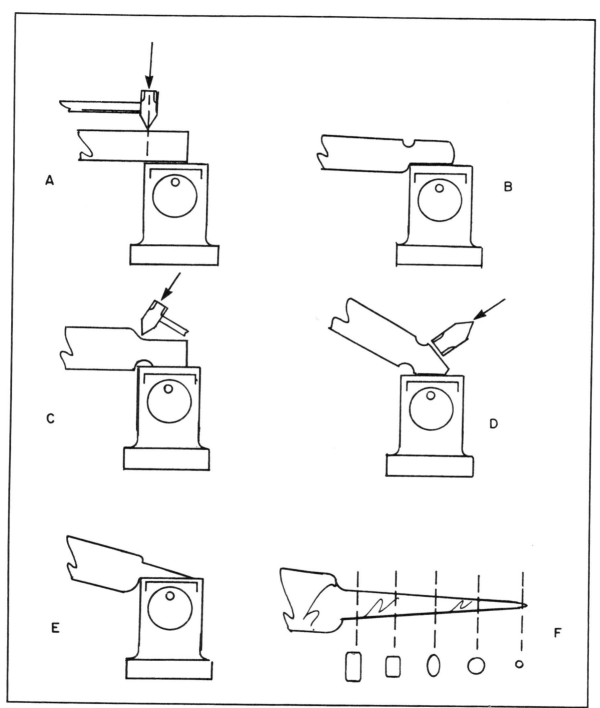

Fig. 6-46. The steps for making a rat-tail taper. The arrows show the force line of the hammer. "F" shows cross sections of the rat-tail.

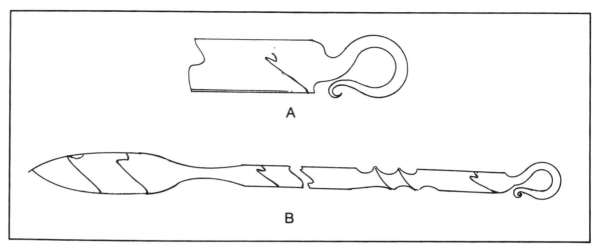

Fig. 6-47. "A" shows the completed handle end of the lance poker. "B" shows how the handle will line up with the blade in the completed poker.

taper out to the same length as the taper on the other two hearth pieces.

Forge a little eye in the end of the rat-tail; then form your big eye. Tuck the little eye into the shoulder area of the handle so it matches the other pieces of the set (Fig. 6-47).

Lay off the area for the twist the same way you worked the first poker. You want the two pokers to match. Heat the work and twist one full turn. Finish the turn so the wide faces of the set are facing in the same plane. Twist slowly, but complete the twist in one heat. About eight seconds is the maximum twisting time.

Wire brush your poker, true it up as needed, and oil it.

You have now forged a complete set of hearth tools. Use the tools as you work at your forge. Some problems occur every time a forging fire is used for an hour or more, and your tools are designed to handle these problems. I will explain how to use them as you go along.

Chapter 7

Upsetting

IN THIS CHAPTER YOU WILL LEARN HOW TO upset bar stock. This is a technique you will use many times in your future work. You will also learn something about planning the sequence of work so that you keep work processes in the right order.

A PRACTICE PIECE

Upsetting is the process of building up the thickness of the end or a portion of the bar somewhere between the ends. This is called *upsetting the end* or *upsetting the shank*. Upsetting is simple, but it requires practice and an understanding of what is happening to the metal being upset.

When you upset a bar you increase the diameter of a portion of it by using some of the stock in the length. You are pushing a portion of the bar back into itself. As a result that portion begins to swell relative to the amount of length consumed.

Stock Required

Square or round stock, 1/2 inch by 10 inches, M.S.

Procedure

Prepare both ends of the bar, be it round or square stock, by rounding up the ends. This way the energy delivered into the bar by the hammer travels through the center (Fig. 7-1).

Heat the iron to a yellow-orange, heating only the area to be upset. Heat control is probably the most important part of upsetting. Note that the movement of metal within a heated area is nearly unpredictable in both the lateral and the axial directions. Proper handling as described in these steps will control this movement.

Hold the bar truly vertical on the anvil face. Push down with your hand as shown in Fig. 7-1. Avoid any torsion or kinking pressure as it will cause the metal to buckle (Fig. 7-2). If the bar end, top or bottom, is not rounded, the off-center contact point pushes the bar into a buckle.

Strike the top of the bar with your cross peen hammer. If the motion of the hammer is not true, the bar will buckle in the upset opposite to the hammer direction (Fig. 7-2). Your hand becomes the

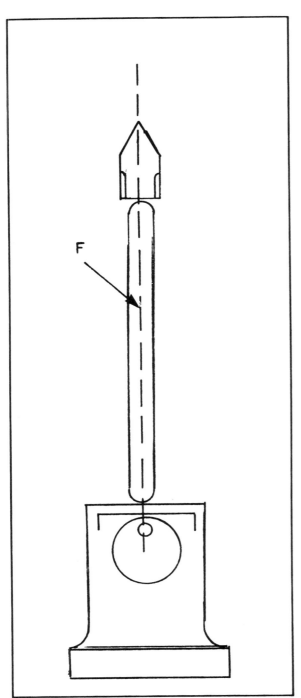

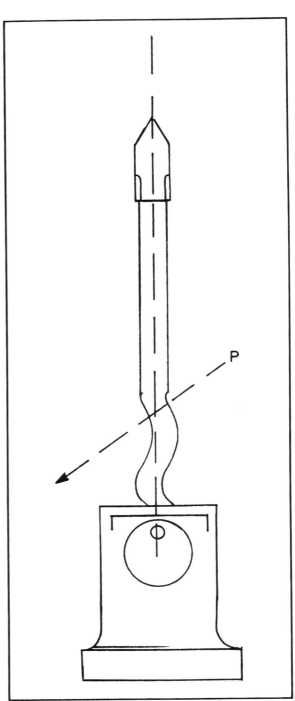

Fig. 7-1. This bar is properly prepared for upsetting. The force line is perpendicular to the anvil face. The force line "F" must be through the center of the hammer and the bar.

Fig. 7-2. If there is any side pressure on the bar, it will bend. Dotted line "P" represents side pressure from the holding hand. Poorly shaped ends will cause bending.

pivot point, and, unless the hammer blow is true, a buckle will occur even if every other precaution is taken.

You may overcome some of the problems of upsetting by using the step of the anvil or a swage. The swage acts as a socket for the metal to swell into. This keeps the iron from jumping around. In all cases revolve the bar a quarter turn after each blow. This helps to keep the upset in line (Fig. 7-3).

All the foregoing conditions and requirements hold true when you are upsetting a portion between the ends of a bar, but the job is more difficult. If a kink or a buckle appears, take it out on the anvil before the next heat. Stop your upsetting blows at a red heat. If the buckle closes itself, or the metal gets a crease or a crimp, start over because the metal will break at the closure. The closed-up buckle is a tight crimp or, in blacksmith terms, a *cold shut*, whether it is on the end or in the middle of the bar.

In upsetting it is particularly important that you observe the result of every move you make. Ana-

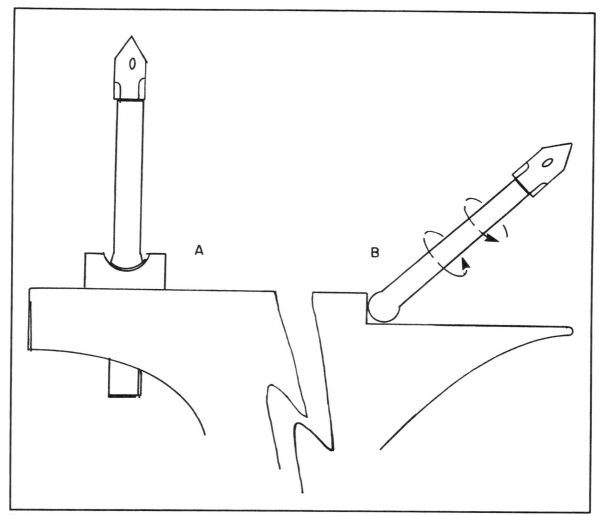

Fig. 7-3. A hardy bottom swage as shown at "A," or the step of the anvil, shown at "B," is quite helpful in upsetting. In all cases keep the line of force going straight through the bar. Keep turning the bar.

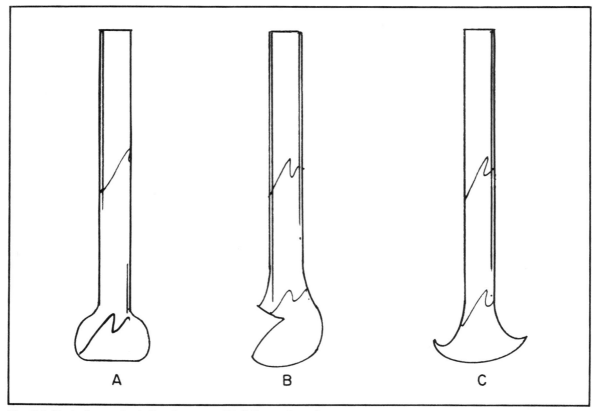

Fig. 7-4. Try to form a knob like the one at "A." If you shape it as you go, all will be fine. "B" has developed a kink and "C" has developed a mushroom face. You probably won't be able to correct these.

lyze the results so that you can develop the good ones and avoid the bad ones. Measure the bar before and after the upsetting. This is the only way to learn what to expect regarding changes in bar length. As the upset bulk increases, the bar length decreases.

A TOOL HANGER

The tool hanger (or plant hanger) is a small item. Making it will require you to think about planning your sequence of events. In this exercise it is possible to *lock yourself out* by doing any process in the wrong order. That is, if certain steps are done out of order, the balance of them cannot be done at all.

The hanger is forged from a piece of stock that is longer than necessary to show how to postpone the use of tongs or pliers as long as possible. It uses stock that is oversized for the item in order to show how stock can be reduced to suit your purpose.

The work will be performed on one end of the stock while the other end is used as a handle. All work will be at a yellow-orange heat. Stop working at a red heat.

Stock Required

Round stock, 3/8 inch by 14 inches, M.S.

Procedure

Upset one end of the stock to about 1 1/2 times the diameter of the bar for about 3/4 inch (Fig. 7-4).

Dress the upset end over the back radius of the anvil to obtain the desired shape as shown in Fig. 7-5.

Lay the bar across the anvil so that the upset

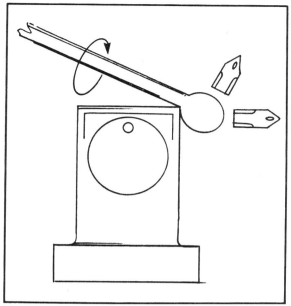

Fig. 7-5. Shape up the upset end over the back edge of the anvil.

just clears the back radius; draw the round shank down to 1/4-inch square for about 1 1/2 inches (Fig. 7-6). Carry the square as close to the upset or knob as you can.

Lay only the knob on the anvil face. Have it right up to the front radius and flatten it to 3/32 inch thick. As you flatten, shape it to create a neat rounded or oval shape (Fig. 7-7). This will make a sloping shoulder at the point where the squared shank and the flattened knob meet. The flattened part is called a *pad*.

Start at the end of the squared portion and continue to draw out a square taper to about 1/8-inch square in the 4 1/2 inches (Fig. 7-8). As much as is practical, avoid heating any of the previously completed work. To do this push that portion beyond the center of the fire.

Lay the bar across the anvil face so that the beginning of the shoulder of the pad is exactly at the beginning of the back radius. Have the shoulder facing down (Fig. 7-9). Use a wiping blow and bend

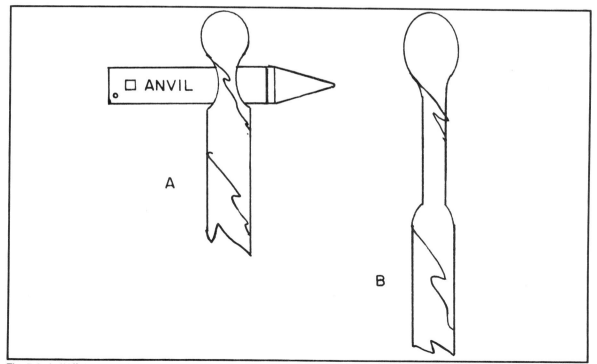

Fig. 7-6. At "A" the upset is beyond the back edge. The stock is ready to be drawn down to 1/4 inch square as shown at "B."

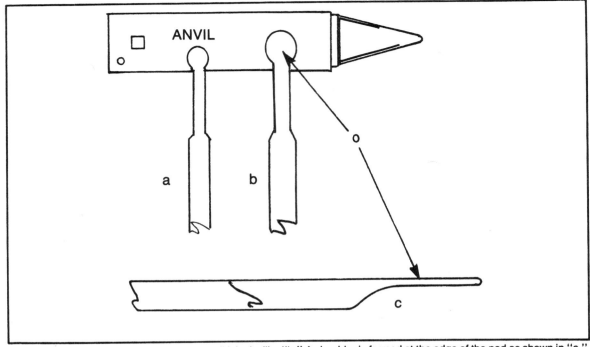

Fig. 7-7. Flatten the upset knob, "a," only until it looks like "b." A shoulder is formed at the edge of the pad as shown in "c."

the pad down over the radius to a 90-degree bend. Use about a 3/16-inch anvil edge radius for this work (Fig. 7-9).

Turn the bar over so the pad points up and extends 1 inch beyond the back side of the anvil. Make another 90-degree bend at this point using the same back radius. This will be opposite to the first one (Fig. 7-10). Line up the pad and the squared portions by bending and twisting while you hold the work in the vise.

Cut the taper off the handle at the thinnest part of the taper. From now on use your vise-grip or locking pliers to hold the work (Fig. 7-11).

Heat the entire portion from the bend to the cut-off and complete a square taper down to a 1/16-inch square point. Then roll a very small eye as you did for the hearth set handles in Chapter 6. The eye points the same way as the nearest bend (Fig. 7-12).

Carefully heat the small eye and about 2 inches of the taper. Quickly quench only the eye to a black. This quench helps to preserve the delicate small

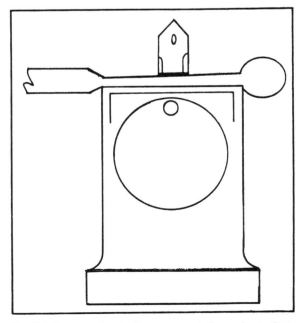

Fig. 7-8. Draw out the stock some more to form a long, slow, square taper.

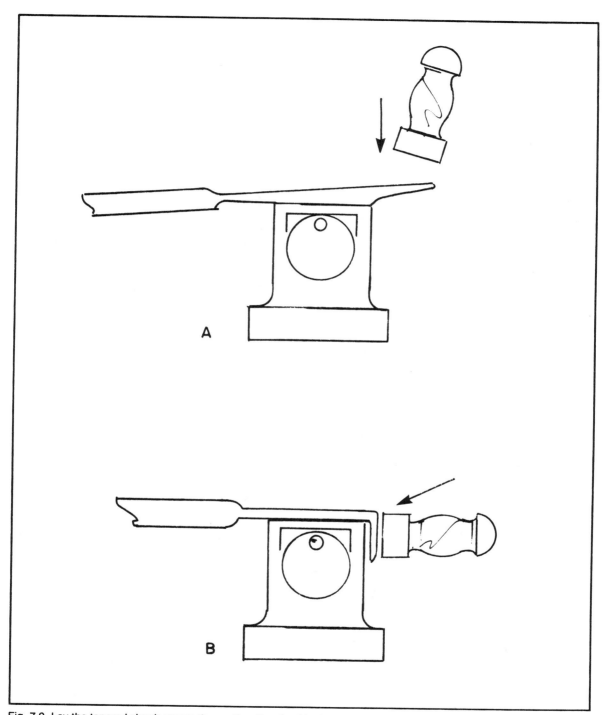

Fig. 7-9. Lay the tapered shank across the anvil so the shoulder is right on the edge of the anvil as shown at "A." Bend the pad down as shown at "B."

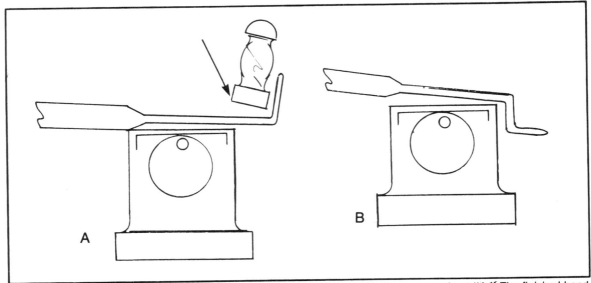

Fig. 7-10. Make the second bend in the shank. Notice the force line and the hammer angle at "A." The finished bend should look like "B."

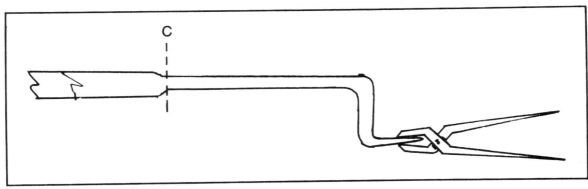

Fig. 7-11. Cut the work away from the 3/8-inch bar.

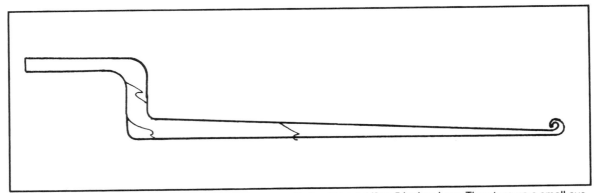

Fig. 7-12. Draw out the square portion to 1/16 inch square. It should be 4 1/2 to 5 inches long. Then turn up a small eye.

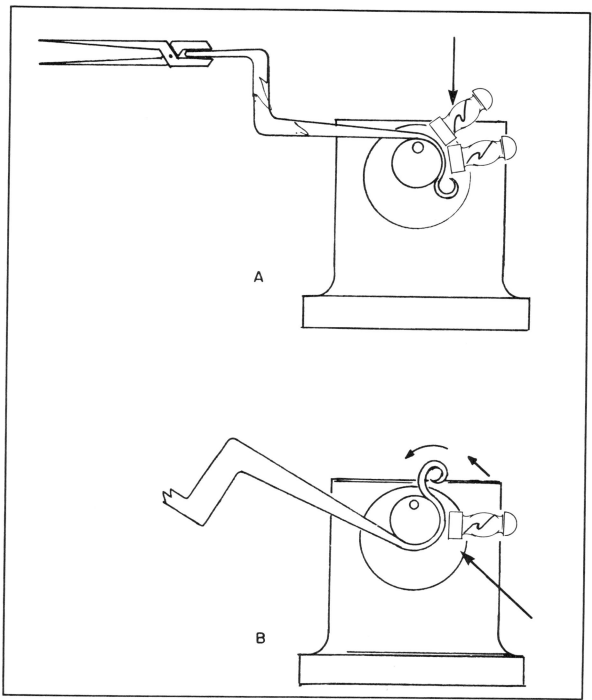

Fig. 7-13. Start to turn a hook over the horn as at "A." Turn the work over again and roll the hook up around the beak using light wiping blows as indicated by the arrows at "B."

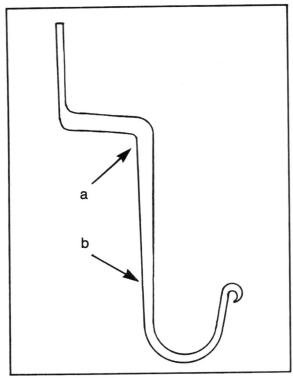

Fig. 7-14. The hook should now look like this. Heat for the twist between lines "a" and "b."

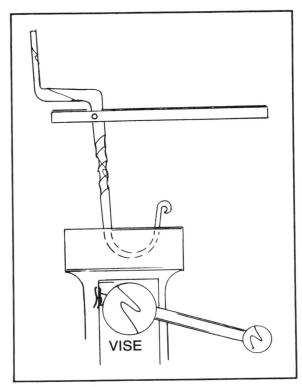

Fig. 7-15. Make one full turn in the twist.

eye while you are working close to it. Then hold the eye in the up position out over the beak of the anvil and bend it down in a roll (Fig. 7-13). In this same heat, if you can, hook the roll up under the horn beak and complete the rolling as you feed the work into upward wiping blows (Fig. 7-13). Make a roll that a nickel would fit into, about 7/8 inch across (Fig. 7-14).

Heat to an orange-red between the roll, which has become the completed hook portion, and the first bend (Fig. 7-14). Place the hook in the vise and grab the square shank right up under the first bend (Fig. 7-15). Make one full turn, clockwise as you look down on it.

If you have made a mistake and it appears that the hook is headed the wrong way, go a half turn or more as needed to correct the situation.

Wire brush the unit and oil it. Now drill a 3/16-inch hole in the center of the pad. Remove the drilling burr, and your hook is ready to hang.

Chapter 8

Hot-Punching and Drifting

HOT-PUNCHING A HOLE HAS MANY ADVAN-
tages over drilling a hole. It also has some
drawbacks. For example, if the work has a rather
intricate configuration, a hot-punched hole close to
the intricate work can distort the work beyond repair unless great care is taken and the timing is
right. When you are hot-punching, most of the
metal in the way of the hole is pushed into the side
wall. This increases some of the dimensions around
the hole (Fig. 8-1). Only a very thin flake of metal,
the size of the hot-punch point, will be removed
(Fig. 8-2). When a hole is drilled, the entire mass
of the metal in the way of the hole is removed. It
is possible and rather simple to hot-punch a 1/2-inch
hole through a 1/2-inch bar. On the other hand, if
a 1/2-inch hole is drilled through a 1/2-inch bar, the
bar will be cut in two. Remember this rule: every
time a bar—square or round—is hot-punched, the
length of the bar will increase.

A HOT-PUNCH

You will make a hand-held hot-punch for average
work. Forge at a light orange heat. Do not continue
to forge after the metal reaches a low red heat. Use
your 2 1/2-pound hammer.

Stock Required

5/8-inch-by-8-inch round stock, M.S.

Procedure

Draw out a round taper 1 1/2 inches long to a
5/32-inch point. Bump the point back to keep it flat
as you proceed. Keep all sections of the work as
round as possible. Keep the point concentric with
the stock.

When your point is nearly finished, use a
1-pound hammer and heat the point to a red-orange.
Lay the point on the anvil and refine to finish size
in this heat (Fig. 8-3). Use rapid, light blows while
rolling the point so that the hammer never hits the
same place twice. Don't strike the end in the final
finish. If it cups a little, file it flat after the work
cools and before hardening.

Let the punch cool to about 300 degrees. Then

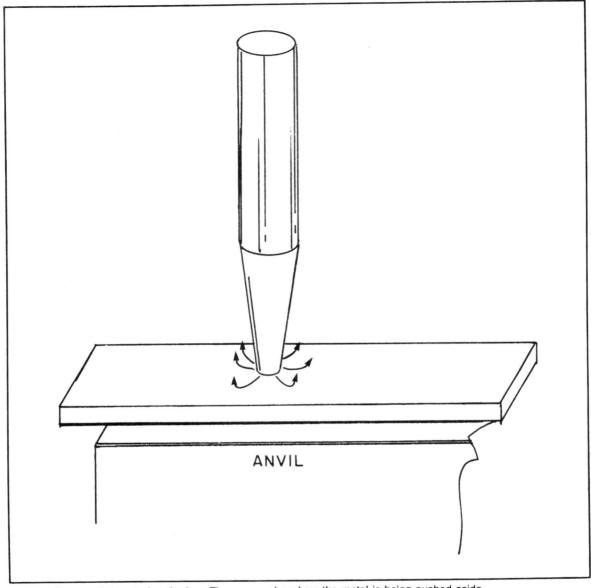

Fig. 8-1. The punch is entering the bar. The arrows show how the metal is being pushed aside.

heat to full red, no orange showing, and be sure the entire shaped portion is the same color. Remove it from the fire and jam it into a pile of the dry coke at the edge of the forge. The coke should be ground up for this treatment, so the metal gets good contact throughout the heat. Don't wet out the flame and smoke that will appear. After 3 or 4 minutes, move the punch to a new spot in the coke pile and let it cool to room temperature. Wet out the old location if necessary, but don't wet the new location. In this process you are soaking some of the carbon out of the coke and into the iron. In a small way this causes case-hardening of the mild steel.

Reheat the point slowly to a low red for most

of its length. Then quench. Thrust the point straight down into the water, but don't let the punch touch the bottom or sides of the quench bucket. Wet the entire punch and keep it moving around until it is cold. Don't temper. This punch makes a good stand-in until you make one of tool steel. It will also help you decide what size punches you might need, and it is an ideal punch to lend. In very little time, you can make a punch of any size to use once or twice.

USING THE PUNCH

In this exercise you will learn how to use the mild steel punch you just made.

Stock Required

Any M.S. scrap, 3/4 inch wide, 1/4 inch thick, and long enough to handle.

Supplies

A pint can of water and a pint can with animal fat. Pork, lamb, beef, or bacon fat, or a mixture of fats is fine. I call it kitchen fat. It need not be melted. A couple of inches in your can is enough.

Procedure

With a center-punch, punch mark the exact spot where the center of the hole is to be. Mark it deep, or the mark will be hard to find when the work is heated.

Clean the anvil and place the hot-punch and hammer where they will be easy to pick up.

Heat the stock at the mark to a light orange forging heat. Lay the work on the anvil. Place the hot-punch vertically, directly on the punch mark, and strike with a 1 1/2-pound hammer or a 2 1/2-pound hammer. Strike rather hard. This must

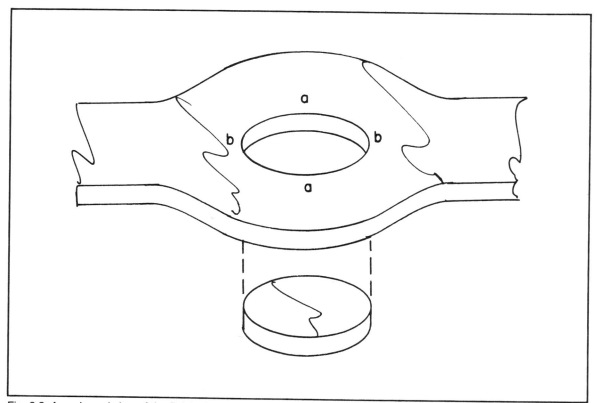

Fig. 8-2. An enlarged view of the finished hole shows the wafer that was pushed out by the punch: "a" indicates metal movement to the side of the bar, "b" indicates lengthwise movement, which makes the bar longer.

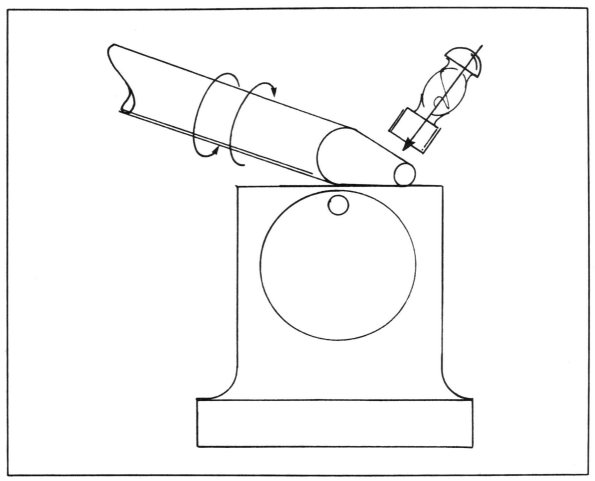

Fig. 8-3. Roll the nose of the punch under the hammer as indicated by the arrows.

be done quickly. If you let the hot-punch rest on the hot work, you will soften its point. After the first strike, dip about 1/2 inch of the punch point into the fat. Put it back quickly in the dimple you just made and hit it hard twice. Then redip the point in the fat. The punch point will heat up very rapidly and lose its hardness if you do not keep cooling it in the fat. Keep up this strike and dip until the dimple becomes a hole as deep as the metal is thick. This might take two heats the first few times you hot-punch. Turn the metal over and see if a rosette has formed directly in the way of the hole. If it has, center the hot-punch on the rosette and hit hard. There should still be good color in the work. If not,

go back and reheat to forging heat. Lay the work on the face of the anvil, rosette up, and drive out the center of the rosette. Cool your punch in water. Check the hole. It should be through, and a thin wafer left on the anvil.

Flatten the stock around the hole to stock thickness. It will be "pooched-up" a little. Move the hole in the bar over the pritchel hole, and with the hot-punch, dress the hole to size. Work from both sides, cooling the punch in the fat, then in the water, then into the hole. Rotate the punch as you work so that out-of-roundness will not be a problem.

Always punch the hole through the stock from both sides on the face of the anvil before you go to the pritchel hole or to a *bolster* for sizing and true-ing. A bolster is a piece of steel that contains various sized holes.

It may be necessary to dress the punch point from time to time as it tends to swell in use and stick in the hole. Dress the punch by working the point down cold, just as you did on the last heat in its construction.

If the hole is deep, sometimes the fat will pop or explode in the hole. This popping tends to drive the punch out of the hole and lessen punch sticking. The fat does not burn off the punch very quickly, so it continues to act as a lubricant. All punching and cutting tools, hot or cold, should be lubricated to reduce wear and tear, to carry away the heat, and to speed up the work.

A DRIFT

The drift is used to shape or enlarge the hole after it has been hot-punched (Fig. 8-4). A drift may be made for general-purpose, round-hole work or for square, hexagonal, oblong, three-cornered work, or whatever is needed, with one major exception. A drift cannot have grooves in it that will require the metal to move toward the center of a hole. There may be some argument on this point, but for practical purposes the rule stands. Figure 8-5 shows the types of shapes that cannot be made with a drift.

The drift does not use a mating piece to do its work, such as a two-piece die would have. All that the drift needs is a hole in a bolster or an anvil into which it can go without jamming as it is driven through the work. The drift has a round nose for a point. Never use your drift for any kind of punching. The drift for round or shaped holes is a long, even taper with a cross section the shape of the desired finish hole. The body of most drifts is only a little more than twice the diameter of the smallest end. For example, a 1/2-inch drift will work holes from 1/4-inch diameter to 1/2-inch diameter. A 1-inch drift will usually work a hole from 1/2 inch to 1 inch. However, because a drift is tapered, unless it is driven through onto the shank, a finishing drift will be required.

The amount of taper will depend on the length of taper on the drift. If the drift is well made, the

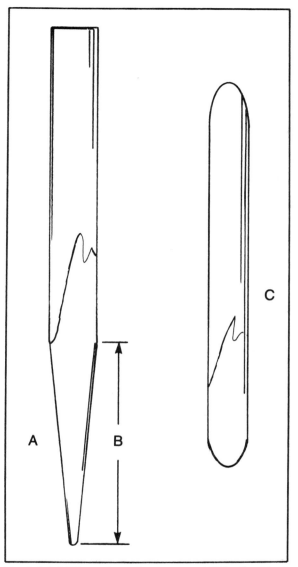

Fig. 8-4. A drift has a long, slow taper as at "B" with a blunt nose as at "A." This tool must be finished smooth and true. "C" shows the slug drift.

taper in the hole will not be a problem, and drifting clear through may not be necessary. Three tapered drifts will cover most work encountered. You will need one that is 3/16 inch to 3/8 inch by 9 inches long with a 4 inch taper, one that is 1/4 inch to 1/2 inch by 9 inches long with 4 1/2 inches to 5 inches of taper, and one that is 1/2 inch to 1 inch by 12

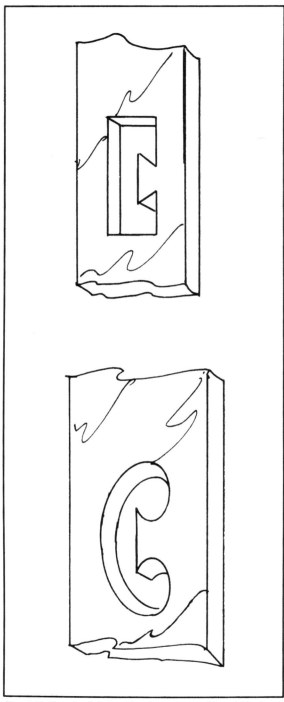

Fig. 8-5. Punched holes like these cannot be drifted out. Some form of die will be required.

inches long with 6 to 7 inches of taper.

Before you begin this exercise, go to Chapter 11 and read the section on using used automotive springs, finding the critical point, and on oil quenching. Pay particular attention to the cautions on oil quenching.

Stock Required

One salvage automobile spring. These come in a variety of diameters, giving you a wide selection.

Your best tools will be made from new steel suitable for your purpose. However, many of the new tool steels, although they make superior tools, do not lend themselves to working on an open forge.

Try to get coil front springs from large U.S.-made cars manufactured before 1975 because, in most cases, the metal will forge better for your purpose. Straighten the spring by heating it and bending it in the vise. Steel from auto springs will be ruined if it is overheated. Work at an orange heat and stop working at a full red heat. Do not quench. Let it air cool. Scar it as little as possible.

Never work spring steel cold or in the black heats because it will work internally and shatter under strain or when you heat treat it. Use a clean fire and keep the work well covered to avoid oxidation. When your steel is oxidizing, it is also losing carbon.

Cut off a length sufficient for your drift, about 8 inches long.

Procedure

Draw out the point or taper as in any other type of round or square taper work. When shaping by the hammer is completed, heat the entire area being worked to a low forging heat. Push the work through the fire a little at a time until the entire worked area has reached a low forging heat. Then lay it in a warm place near the fire and let it cool out completely. This is called *normalizing* and is a very important step in all tool making. The cooling time may be several hours, or overnight, depending on the size of the tool.

Read Chapter 11 for information on heat treating and find the critical point. Bring the entire tapered portion to a dull red heat and test with the magnet. Make sure the color of the work is the same throughout; then quench in light oil as explained in Chapter 11. Go straight down until the entire tool is in oil. Keep it moving in a figure eight. Do not let it touch the bottom of the container. Check it from time to time, and when the tapered portion of the tool is still smoking, but the oil is not flowing off it much, place the tapered portion back into the fire. Do not use the air blast on the fire. Keep the work moving. Bring it to a heat that burns off most, but not all of the oil. If all the oil burns off, the piece has become too hot. Keep the heat even. When the correct heat has been reached, put the tool aside in a cool place with no wind on it and let it cool to room temperature.

Your tool is now ready to use. Don't blame yourself too much if the tool breaks the first time you use it. It was a used spring and might have been fractured internally. These internal fractures do not always show up in forging, but might during or after the hardening and tempering process.

You might find that some salvage metal does not respond to oil hardening. One good way to avoid trouble in heat treating is to make test pieces first. An automobile coil spring is very long when it is straightened out, so sacrifice a little of it. This test is valuable because there is no practical way to know what the carbon and alloy content is. These properties vary with the automobile and the date of manufacture.

USING THE DRIFT

In this exercise you will learn to use the drift and how to make a finish drift.

After the hole is punched, heat the work to a good forging temperature and place it over the pritchel or hardy hole as needed. With a stick put a little kitchen fat on the portion of the drift that will touch the sides of the hole. Start the drift straight down into the hole and drive it in about 1/2 inch. Strike the work on a cold part to set up a vibration as you pull the drift out. If this does not work the first time, put the point of the drift on the anvil face and bump the work off.

Flip the work over and repeat. Keep a little kitchen fat on the drift as you repeat the process until the desired hole size is reached. All the while watch that you do not overheat the drift. Quench it in water from time to time. Have a sample piece of stock at hand to test the hole size as you go along. An oversized hole is very difficult to correct.

When a drift is to be driven clear through the work, you do not want the hammered end to be flared out that it jams in the hole. To avoid this, forge or grind the last inch or so of the drift to reduce its diameter. This will cause the drift to drop on through as the reduced diameter reaches the hole. This shaped drift is a *finish drift*.

You can easily drift holes out to a given dimension with straight side walls by using *slug drifts*. Make these out of short pieces of stock. They need not be more than 4 to 6 inches long and of the desired finish size of the hole. Forge or grind a short taper on each end of the slug about the same angle as the taper of your long drift; 1 inch of taper is usually enough (Fig. 8-4).

To use one of these slugs, drift the hole out to nearly finish size, then lubricate the slug with kitchen fat, enter it into the hole, and drive it clear through. Turn the work piece over and hammer the stock flat where it may have become thickened; drive the slug back through again. Repeat this as needed to finish the hole. With care you can punch and drift holes accurately to any size you desire. Make up long starter drifts and follow-up slug drifts as you need them. Keep them on your tool rack.

Never try to drift out a hole after the red color is gone from the work. A hole can be corrected a small amount after the metal has been at room temperature for 15 minutes or more.

Chapter 9

Two Methods for Making Blacksmith Tongs

MY STUDENTS AND MY YOUNG FRIENDS WHO have their own shops find that the making of tongs somehow rings a romantic bell. Perhaps this is warranted. Tongs are a very necessary tool in blacksmithing. The workmanship in a pair of tongs made by hand, hammer, and anvil alone certainly reveals the ability and pride of the maker. It also reveals how practical his thinking is. Some smiths think big, heavy, long-handled tongs are just right. Well, if you have three arms and three hands, two of each to handle the tongs and one for the work they hold, go ahead. I want light, well-made, easy-to-handle tongs that do the job they are supposed to do and are pleasing to look at.

The work involved in making the tongs in the first exercise will include every process you have studied so far and will add some new processes. You will wind up with tools of very good quality, size and balance, traditionally designed and made.

In the second exercise you will make quickie, flat-stock tongs. These will do the same job as tongs of traditional design, but they will look different and are constructed differently. Methods of construc-

tion are not interchangeable from style to style. Each is complete in itself. Learn from them both.

In the first exercise you will be making a pair of traditional tongs using the traditional method. As noted before, there is a great deal of romance and folklore about blacksmith tongs. The multitude of tongs of infinite variety gives rise to this lore. You rarely find a modern, practicing blacksmith who can tell you what all the different antique tongs were used for. Every tong was made to fit a particular need. Many times that particular need never arose again in the shop.

A pair of blacksmith tongs makes it possible for the smith to handle hot metal, in and out of the fire and at the anvil. A good pair of tongs must allow the smith or his helper to handle the hot work with the least possible fatigue. It must hold the work securely so that the work won't fly out of its grip. This happens even with the best tongs and can be very frustrating.

Any antique looks great nailed up on the shop wall, but the tongs you work with and that serve you best probably won't be antiques. Instead they will be ones made in modern shops or bought from modern suppliers.

To judge a pair of tongs for yourself, look for the following features: they must be lightweight. The *reins*, or handles, must be somewhat springy. The handles for a one-hand hold should be 14 to 18 inches long, measured from the pivot pin or hinge pin. They should be from 3/8 inch to 7/16 inch in diameter in the gripping area. The jaws should not be over 2 1/2 inches long, except for special needs. The right length is usually about 1 1/2 inches to 2 inches. The jaws will have to fit the piece of metal to be worked in a manner that does not require excessive gripping pressure by your hand. Such pressure is fatiguing, and hand fatigue is as much a reason for the tongs' not holding as is a wrong shape to the jaws. The illustrations in Fig. 9-1 show most of the commonly used types of tongs. There is an endless variety of special purpose tongs.

When you make a pair of tongs, remember that each half is exactly like the other. You must realize that they are not mirror images or rights and lefts. To demonstrate this to your own satisfaction, draw a pair of tongs on a piece of paper. Now draw two left halves (or right halves), making them as much alike as you can. Punch a small hole in each of the halves where the pivot pin would go. Carefully cut out the tongs with scissors and lay the two identical pieces on the table side by side. Now take one piece only and turn it over. Lay it down on top of the other so that the punched holes line up and so that it crosses the other. Most students find some mystery in making tongs because they visualize the two halves as being different. You can now see that the halves are the same, and you should have no difficulty.

The tongs most commonly used in small shops are straight-jaw tongs, bolt tongs, and ring tongs (Fig. 9-1). After you have made these three types of tongs, you will be able to make special purpose tongs for yourself.

Any pair of tongs that is to be held in one hand need not be made of stock any heavier than 5/8-inch round stock or 1/2-inch square stock. Lightweight, strong tongs can be made from 1/2-inch round stock. The average length of tongs for the small shop should be 16 to 20 inches.

TRADITIONAL SQUARE-LIPPED BOLT TONGS

The first pair of tongs you will make is designed to handle 3/8-inch to 1/2-inch round or square stock (Fig. 9-1). The pair should be about 18 inches long overall. As always, it is a good idea to do a practice piece on any part of the project that is new to you. For practice use any piece of suitable scrap.

Stock Required

1/2-inch- × -15-inch square stock, M.S.

Procedure

You will form the lip first, then the reins. After that you will shape the jaws and finally assemble the tongs.

Forming the Lip

Draw out a 3 1/4-inch flat taper to form the lip. Forge this to dimension as shown in Fig. 9-2. Be accurate. Just before your taper is completed, place a small center punch mark at 3 1/2 inches from the lip. Don't reduce the stock size beyond this punch mark.

Rotate the stock one-quarter turn to the left (Fig. 9-3). Swing the handle end to the left to about a 30-degree angle to the anvil edge. Extend the lip out over the back radius, using a small radius, 1/8 inch or so, so that the punch mark is directly over the radius and is visible (Fig. 9-3). Keep the iron down flat on the anvil face. Keeping this position, hit hard with *half a hammer over* to form a shoulder. Figure 9-3 shows hitting in this way. Let the iron spread all it will, don't forge it down to less than one-half the stock thickness: in this case 1/4 inch. If you finish at less than 1/4 inch, the tongs will be weak. When you are working another time with metal that is thicker or thinner than that used for this project, remember that the pivot area must be no less than one half the thickness of that metal. This is measured in a line parallel to the pivot axis.

Be accurate. Continue the thinning and spread-

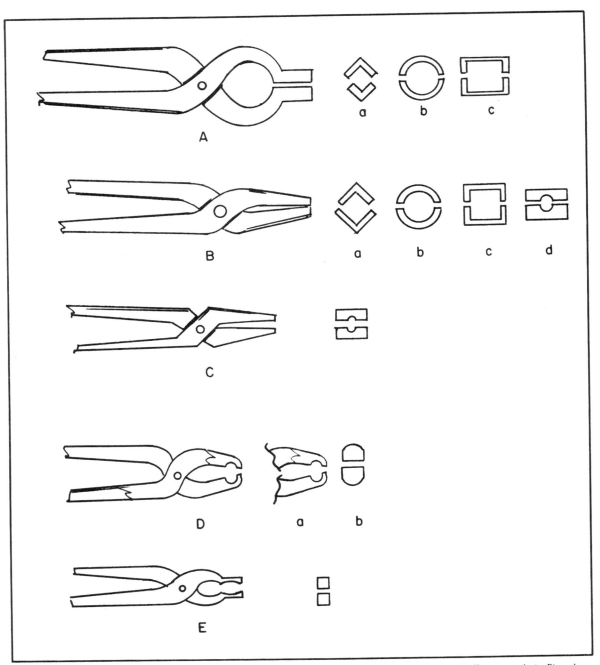

Fig. 9-1. "A" shows bolt or bow tongs with various bites: "a" will grip square or round stock, "b" was made to fit a given round stock, "c" for a particular flat stock. "B" shows straight-jaw or regular tongs and various bite shapes. "a," "b," and "c" are used in the same ways as "a," "b," and "c" in "A." "d" is made for flat stock or sheet metal. "C" shows straight tongs with a single-purpose bite. Notice the slight grooving in the center of the bite. This increases the holding power of the bite. "D" shows ring tongs. A sideview is shown at "a," the end view at "b." "E" shows pick-up tongs. This is a delicate tong. The points of the bite are about 1/16 inch to 1/18 inch wide.

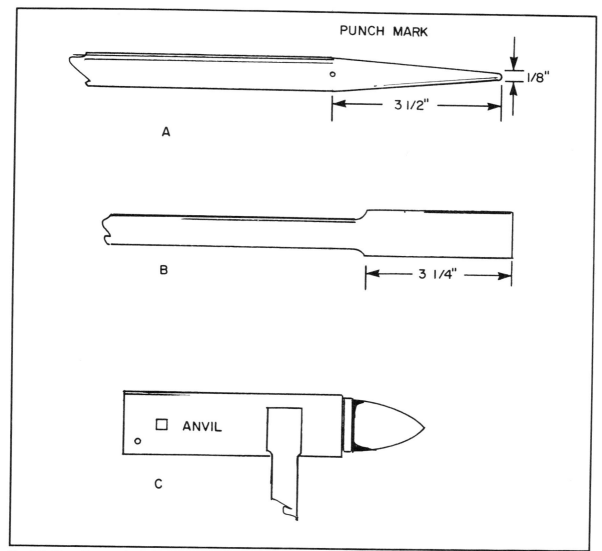

Fig. 9-2. Place the punch mark as shown at "A." Notice that this is on the edge of the jaw rather than the flat of it. "B" shows a flat view of the jaw. Draw out a flat taper to form the jaw and the lip as shown at "C."

ing until you are about 2 inches from the shoulder. Then taper back up until you reach stock size (Fig. 9-4).

Forming the Rein

In this process you are going to use your anvil horn. It will act as a fuller, which moves metal in one direction in the process of forming an indentation (Fig. 9-5).

Draw out the rein to 3/8-inch round by starting 3/4 inch from the place where the pivot area has returned to 1/2-inch square stock. You are not going to reduce size much, only 1/16 inch to the side, so take it easy (Fig. 9-5).

Draw out the rein to 3/8-inch square, 3 1/2 inches from the starting point following the instructions above. This is a long, slow taper. Do this work near the base of the horn of the anvil, about 2 1/2

109

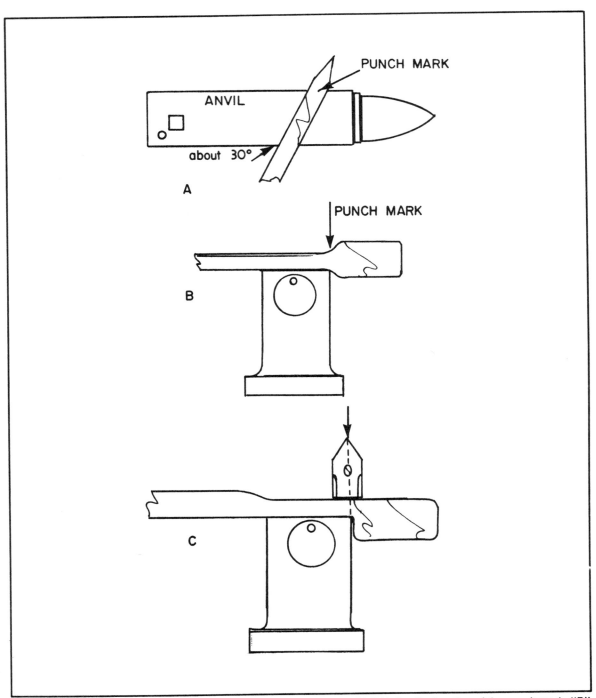

Fig. 9-3. Place the jaw on the back edge of the anvil edge as shown at "A." Notice the location of the punch mark. "B" shows another view of the punch mark location. At "C" you have moved the jaw over to form a step. Notice the location of the hammer and the punch mark. This move is called hitting with half a hammer over.

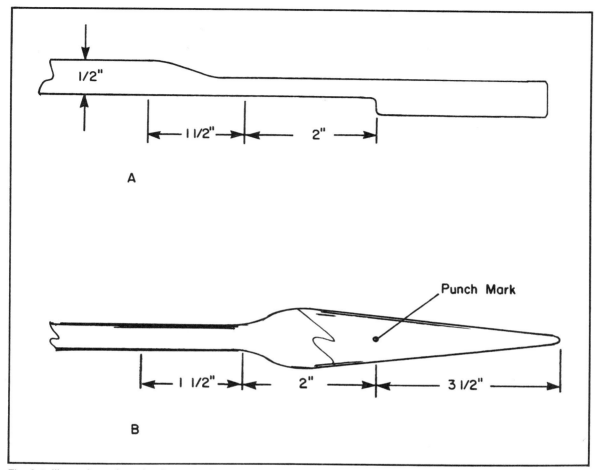

Fig. 9-4. Illustrations show the drawn-out hinge area. Note that the rein is on the wrong side in view "A." Don't correct it now. "B" is a view at 90 degrees to "A," seen from what will be the outside face of the hinge.

inches from the table. This area will not mark up the anvil side of your work so much. Smooth it out as you go. If you get undersized, you will not be able to correct your error, and the rein will be weak.

Now convert the 3/8-inch square to a 3/8-inch round in the next 3 inches or so. You will first be squaring and then rounding as you go. Keep up this rounding until you have converted the balance of the 1/2-inch square stock into 3/8-inch round stock. This will make the rein a little long, but don't trim it yet. Remember to work the iron hot. Always have it showing color. As you work, use portions of the anvil as required. When I work on a piece like this, I work over the small or outer portion of the horn

for fast drawing, over the base of the horn for slow drawing and initial smoothing, and on the anvil face for final smoothing and straightening (Fig. 9-5).

Use a piece of scrap 1/2-inch square stock for your practice run. Work it between the ends as if it were the rein. Work to the dimensions called for in the rein. This process is a little more difficult than regular tapering. Avoid going undersize because there is no way to correct back to full size.

When you have completed drawing the rein, lay it aside. Don't quench it. Let it cool slowly.

Now make a second rein piece exactly like the first one. This is the other half of your tongs. Remember your paper cutouts.

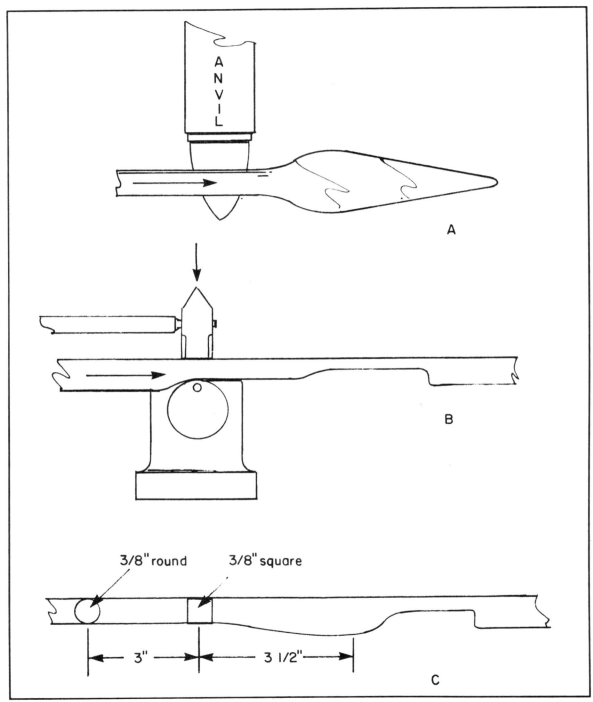

3/8" round

3/8" square

3"

3 1/2"

A

B

C

Fig. 9-5. At "A" you are starting the long, slow taper. "B" shows a side view of drawing out the rein. The arrow indicates feed across the horn. "C" is a general side view showing the 3/8-inch square turning into a 3/8-inch round.

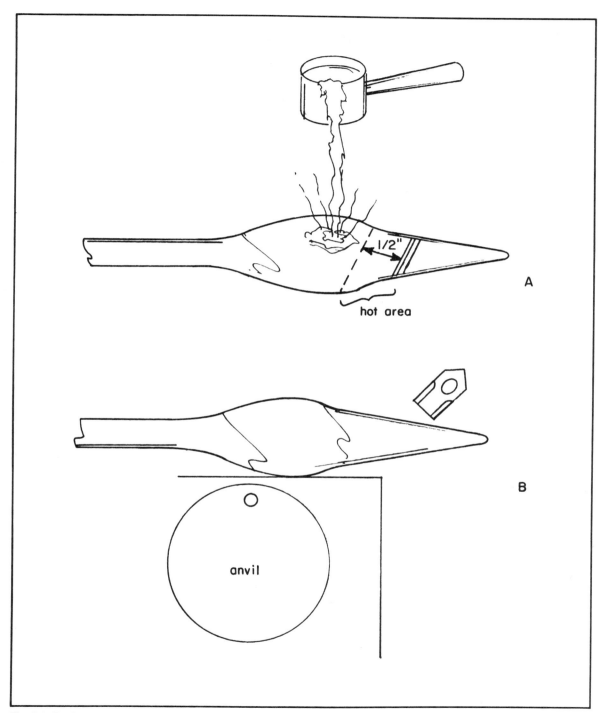

Fig. 9-6. Begin to shape the jaws. Locally cool the pivot portion of the jaws at "A." Start the bend, using the wiping blow as at "B."

Shaping the Jaws

When you have completed the two pieces, you are ready for final shaping of the jaws. The jaws are the entire portion of the tong from the pivot pin to the end opposite the rein or handle end. There will be some minor adjustments after the tongs are assembled.

Heat the area where the step of the jaw meets the pivot area. The bend is going to be right in the step. Carefully study the steps in Figs. 9-6 and 9-7. Locally cool the pivot portion to about 1/2 inch from the step (Fig. 9-6). See Chapter 16 for information on how to do local cooling.

Place the pivot portion on the face of the anvil, straight across it, letting the jaw hang out over the back radius as shown in Fig. 9-6. The rivet area is on edge, not flat on the anvil. The step faces to the right. The portion of the step in contact with the anvil should exactly contact the large back radius as shown in Fig. 9-6.

Bend the jaw down over the radius to about 40 degrees from horizontal (Fig. 9-7). Do not change

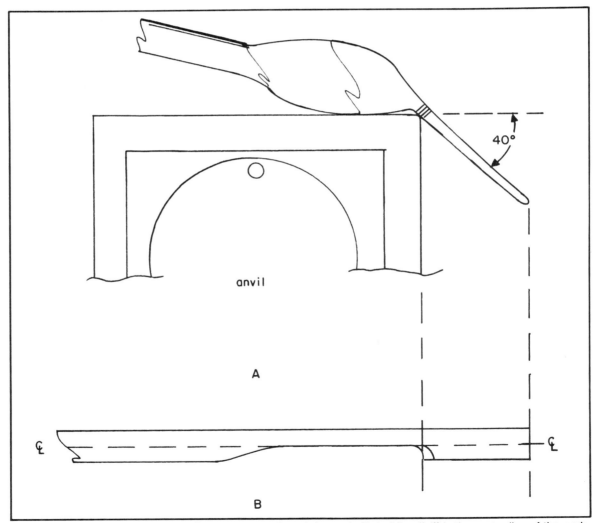

Fig. 9-7. "A" shows the bent jaw. "B" shows a side view of the work. Dotted line "cl" is the center line of the work.

114

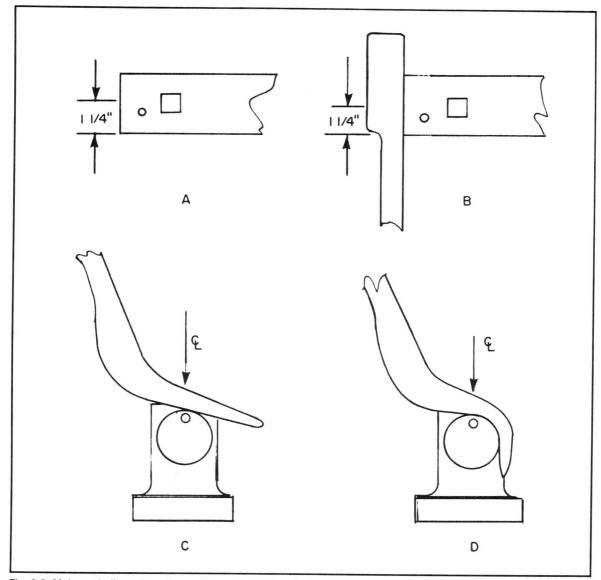

Fig. 9-8. Make a chalk mark on the anvil as at "A." Transfer the chalk onto the jaw as shown at "B." Place the chalk line directly over the center of the horn as at "C." Start a part of a circle as shown at "D."

any forged dimension. This move is strictly bending. Now check to see that the step, the side face of the pivot area, and the jaw center line are still lined up as in Fig. 9-7. Allow the step to cool to dark red, but don't let it chill completely.

Figure 9-8 is a series of pictures showing how the jaw is shaped. Mark a chalk line on the heel of the anvil as shown in Fig. 9-8. Heat the entire jaw to an orange heat. Quickly cool the entire hinge area and the edge of the step to no color (Fig. 9-8). Hold the jaw with the step to your left along the heel of the anvil and lay off a chalk mark 1 1/4 inches from the step as shown in Fig. 9-8.

Lay the jaw across the beak of the horn so that

the chalk mark is directly over the horn center line (Fig. 9-8).

Bend the jaw down about 80 degrees (Fig. 9-8). Make a smooth turn in the bend. You are creating part of a circle.

Reheat the jaw to an orange heat from the "D" bend to the end and cool the "D" bend somewhat so you won't spoil it in the next bend. In this same heat turn the work over so the step is toward your right.

Make a chalk mark 3/4 inch from the end of

the jaw. Place the jaw, at the mark, up against the 1/16-inch front radius of the anvil and bend the end, which will become the lip, down onto the anvil face. Study Fig. 9-9 carefully, and you will have no trouble completing the jaw and hinge portion of the work.

Repeat these steps to shape the second half of the tongs. Try to match the two halves perfectly. When you have completed the two halves, turn one over and lay the steps together with a little clearance. Imagine the location of the pivot pin hole.

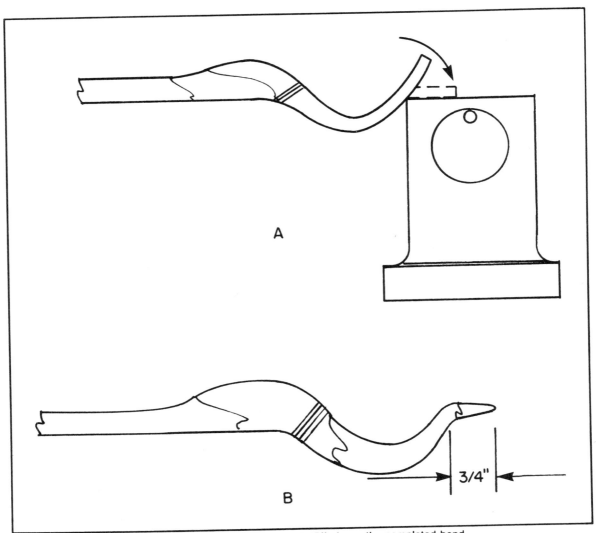

Fig. 9-9. Line up of the work on the anvil is shown at "A." "B" shows the completed bend.

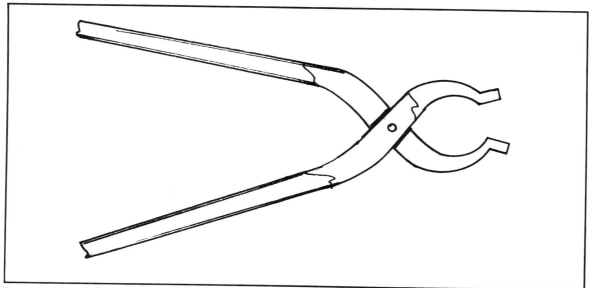

Fig. 9-10. Line up the two halves of the tongs to locate the hinge pin.

Assembly

You are now ready to start the assembly and completion of the tongs, that is fitting the two halves together and shaping them to their final form. You will find that most people refer to the completed joint of a pair of pliers or tongs as a hinge because the movement of the two parts is very limited. In this lesson on tongs, I will refer to the joint as a hinge and to the bolt or rivet that joins them as the hinge pin.

Match up the two pieces for their best positioning to locate the hinge pin (Fig. 9-10). When you have found the point for the pin, mark it with a center-punch. This point should be about 5/8 inch from the shoulder or step.

The holes for the pin should be hot-punched, not drilled, because this makes a stronger hinge. To hot-punch, heat the work to orange heat. Lay the part on the anvil face with the shoulder down and the jaw extending beyond the back side. Punch the hole from the outside first. Go through until you form a rosette on the anvil side. This will bend your work a little, but this is all right (Fig. 9-11). When you turn the piece over to punch out the rosette, you will straighten it again. Punch the hole to just under 5/16 inch; then drift it out to a true 5/16 inch.

Make the drift for this out of a scrap of 5/16-inch round stock with one end tapered a little for easy entry (Fig. 9-12).

Dress out any disfigurement caused by the punching and drifting. Pass the drift through a time or two if necessary, but don't oversize the hole. Drive the drift completely through. Most of this work can be done over the pritchel hole. Don't let the drift rest in the hole. As the work cools, the hole will shrink around the drift, and you may not be able to get it out without spoiling your work.

Lay this punched piece over the unpunched piece and arrange for the best position for the second hole. Disregard the reins at this point. Consider the hinge area and the jaw alignment only. Mark through the first hole to locate the second one.

Now look over the new location. If it is not centered from side to side on the pivot area, shift it until it is. You want the same amount of metal on each side of the pin in every case. If there is a slight misalignment, it may be adjusted later.

Make a deep center-punch mark in the center of the pin location. Heat the piece to orange heat and hot-punch directly over the mark. This time you will be starting the hole from the shoulder side.

Find a 5/16-inch bolt with enough shank below

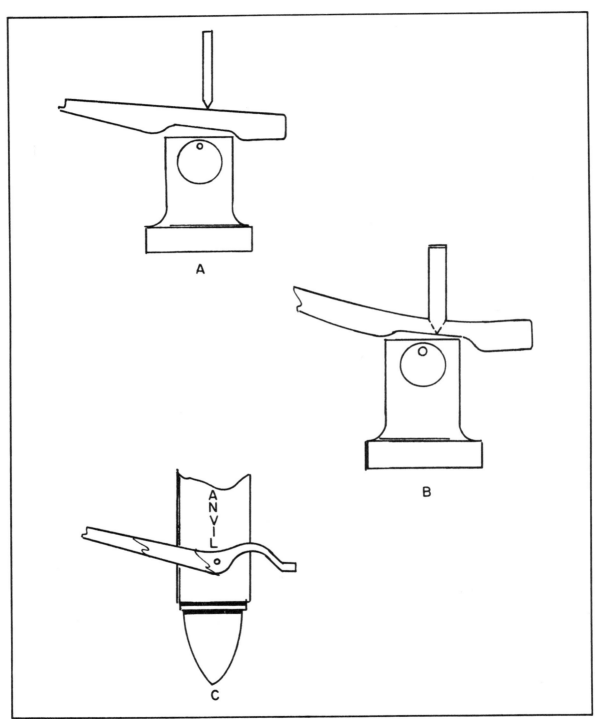

Fig. 9-11. Start the pin hole as at "A." The work may bend at this point, as shown at "B."

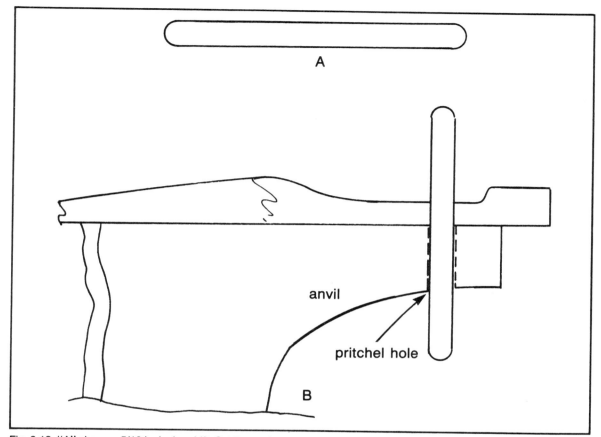

Fig. 9-12. "A" shows a 5/16-inch slug drift. Set the work over the pritchel hole so the drift can go through as shown at "B."

A

anvil

pritchel hole

B

the threads to keep the threads out of the hole. Assemble the tongs tightly and true up the line-up of the hinge and the jaws, disregarding the reins. Any side-to-side trueing up can be done cold by holding the assembly in the vise at the base of the jaws. The reins will straddle the vise screw. Use washers if necessary to ensure a tight bolt.

If the pivot area is rough and keeps the jaw from working easily, grab each half in the vise. Take it by the edge so that you can file out the rough spots and flatten the mating surfaces of the hinge for easy movement (Fig. 9-13). Remember that the hinge will move very little in actual use.

Form the "V" in the lips. If you have a swage block, use the 90-degree "V." If you have a 90-degree bottom swage that is large enough, you may use it (Fig. 9-14).

Heat the lip and about 1/2 inch of the bow of the jaw to an orange heat. Have the top swage handy to the swage "V." The top swage can be made out of an 8-inch or 10-inch piece of 1/2-inch or 5/8-inch square stock (Fig. 9-14).

Lay the lip flat on the "V" with the rein in line with the groove of the "V." Press the bow against the end of the "V" (Fig. 9-14). Lay the rein against your chest or belly. (Be sure you have on an apron.) Lay the top swage on top of the lip in line with the groove of the "V" and press it down hard with your holding hand. Make sure that everything is lined up.

Strike fairly hard on the top swage. Study Fig. 9-14 carefully. Force the lip down tightly into the bottom of the "V" of the swage being sure that the "V" line in the lip extends onto the bow a bit (Fig.

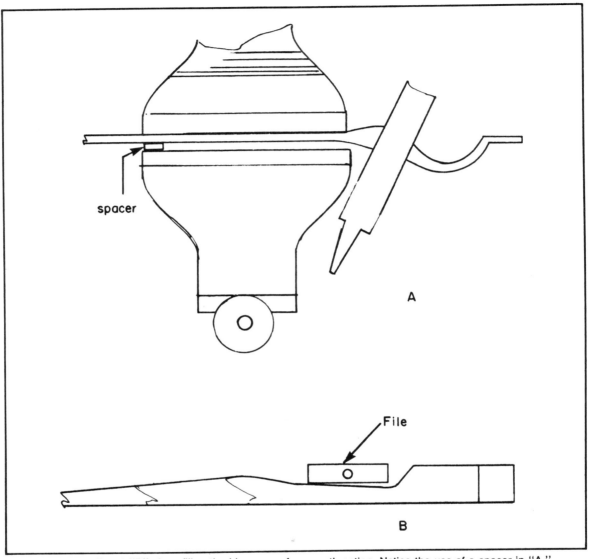

spacer

A

File

B

Fig. 9-13. Both "A" and "B" show filing the hinge area for smooth action. Notice the use of a spacer in "A."

9-14). Try not to change the angle of the lip to the bow or the arc of the bow (Fig. 9-14). Now repeat this with the second half. Do not quench.

After the halves have cooled, assemble them and realign the hinge and jaws as needed.

Now test the jaws. Close them together and see if they will hold a piece of 3/8-inch round stock. If the bite is too big, file the lips of the bits until they hold the 3/8-inch round firmly (Fig. 9-15).

You are ready to adjust the reins. Study Fig. 9-16 before you start this next move. Close the tongs on a piece of 3/8-inch square stock and tighten the bolt. Lay the tongs flat over the fire so the reins will be heated for about 3 inches and right up to the bolt. Sprinkle a small amount of water on the bolt so it won't overheat. Keep it black. When the reins are heated to a low orange, grab the closed jaws in the vise. Bring the reins together in line with

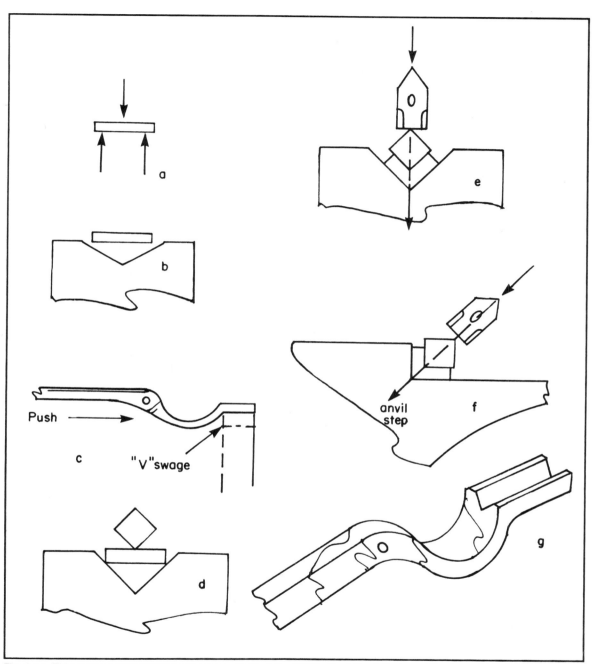

Fig. 9-14. This series of illustrations shows how to form the "V" in the bite of the jaw of the tong. At "a" the jaw is flat. At "b" the jaw has been placed into the swage, and at "c" it is pushed against the swage. "d" is an end view of the jaw bite, the top swage, and the square bar stock in place. The force line of the hammer blow is shown at "e." At "f" you see how the step of the anvil may be used for a bottom swage. The sequence of actions will be the same as if you had used a swage. The final jaw and lip should look like illustration "g." In forming the "V" always follow the sequence exactly.

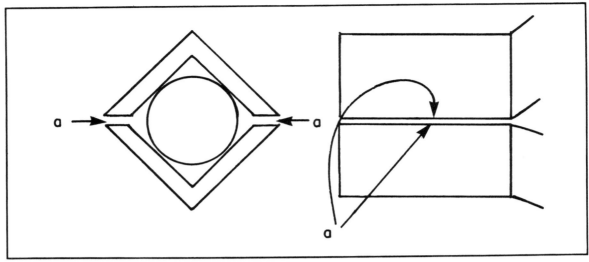

Fig. 9-15. Fit the bite size around a piece of 3/8-inch round stock.

the jaws until they are about 2 1/2 inches apart at a point about 14 inches from the bolt. Keep the bend in the heated area and the balance of the reins straight (Fig. 1-16). When everything is aligned and spaced, remove the tongs from the vise and let them cool. Wire brush them thoroughly and install the final hinge pin.

This hinge pin may be either a bolt or a rivet. I like bolts because they are easy to adjust and because they are made of better steel than the rivets. If you use a bolt, get a good one. Try your welding supply store or any industrial retail-wholesale supply house. Ask for a black, number 5, HEX (hexagonal) head bolt with NC (national coarse) thread and a shank that fills the length of the holes well but that doesn't stick out and keep the nut from tightening. You don't need a washer here (Fig. 9-17).

Bolt the two halves together and add a drop of oil in the joint. Finger tighten the new bolt and nut. Saw off all but one full thread. File out the saw marks and peen the thread down just a little so that the nut won't back off. Don't make a rivet of the bolt. Use a wrench to tighten it up a little more until there is just a little drag in the action. Peen the thread down a little more if needed. This helps to keep the nut from backing off when the tongs are worked.

If you use a rivet as a hinge pin, you may buy it or make it. Refer to Chapter 6 to review riveting. Complete all the same steps using a bolt. Complete the tongs except for cutting off the bolt threads. Instead remove the bolt and save it to use when you make your next pair of tongs. Replace the bolt with the rivet. Brad the rivet over until it reaches the preferred tension. Oil it up, and you're done.

You may hear a suggestion to put the whole works in a fire and "heat'em up and work'em in the quench tub." This is a bad practice that will result in frequent pin failure, because of loosening, or in outright pin breakage. I suggest you don't do this. Make a good working joint in the first instance.

Your tongs are now ready to use. Do not ruin them by overheating them in the fire as you use them. Most of the tongs you make will be this size, weight, and length. A 5/16-inch bolt will serve very well for them all.

QUICKIE FLAT-STOCK TONGS

You will now make a pair of lightweight ring tongs for 1/4-inch and 5/16-inch round stock. Ring tongs are like other tongs, but they are designed to hold small pieces of stock crossways in the jaws. They are most useful in making rings, links, and chains. These tongs may be bolted or riveted in the hinges.

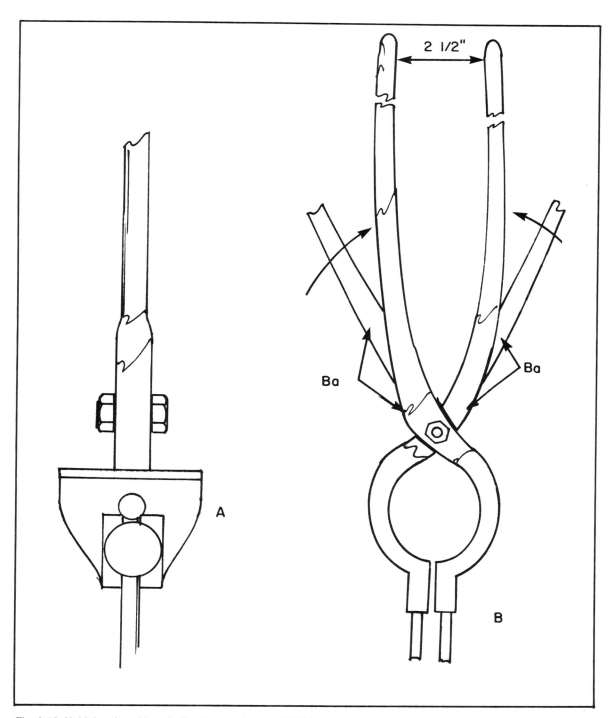

Fig. 9-16. Hold the closed jaws in the vise as shown at "A." Move the reins together as shown at "B." "Ba" shows the area of the bend.

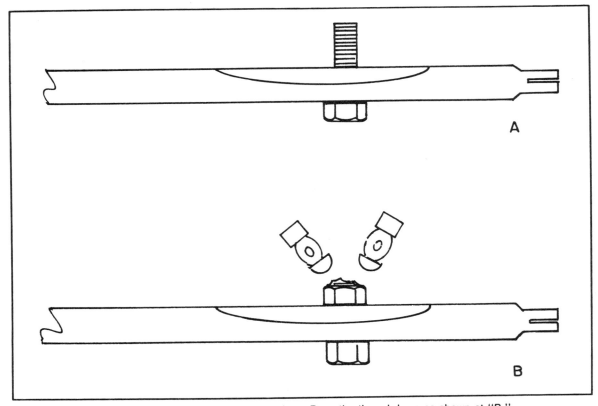

Fig. 9-17. "A" shows the final hinge pin, the bolt, in place. Peen the thread down as shown at "B."

Here again, rivets look more attractive, but bolts are easier to assemble.

The following method eliminates unnecessary work in making a pair of tongs for average work, but also works well for special purpose tongs in most cases. It requires little fuel because few heats are required. Tongs made in this fashion are equal in working and holding ability to any other design I know. Their appearance, strength, and lasting qualities are equal to all other designs. These tongs are made from stock that is twice as wide as it is thick.

Stock Required

Two pieces of 1/4-inch by 1/2-inch flat stock, 14 inches long, M.S.

One 1/4-inch bolt and nut or one 1/4-inch roundhead rivet.

Two 1/4-inch SAE flat washers.

Procedure

Work the following at a light orange heat.

Making the Jaws and Lips

Heat one end of a piece of stock and lay it edgeways on the back anvil face. Taper from 1/2 inch to 5/16 inch in 1 1/2 inches of length. Do not thin to stock size; let it spread. Bump the end and square it up nicely (Fig. 9-18). This will become the jaw and lip.

Hang the point 1 1/2 inches over the back small radius (1/8 inch) and bend it down edgeways 45 degrees as shown in Fig. 9-18. Use wiping blows. Don't reduce the dimension of the stock.

Rotate the stock to the other edge, a 180-degree rotation, and extend it out over the same back ra-

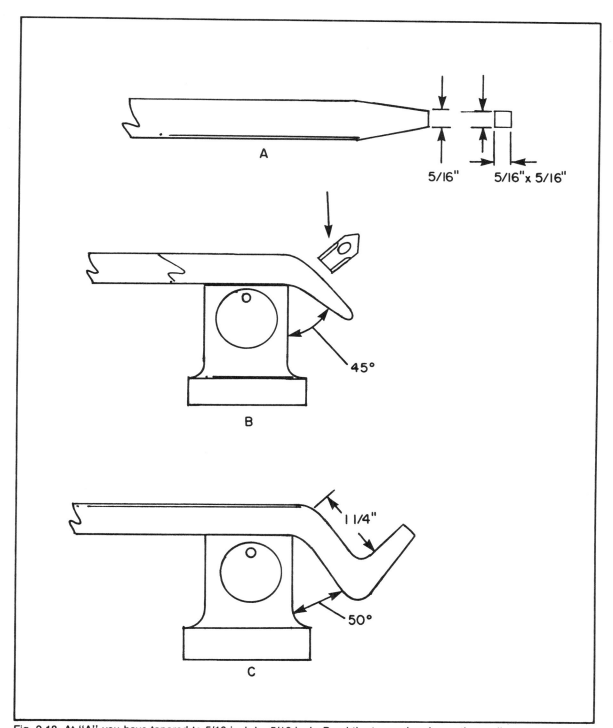

A

5/16"

5/16" x 5/16"

45°

B

1 1/4"

50°

C

Fig. 9-18. At "A" you have tapered to 5/16 inch by 5/16 inch. Bend the tapered end over the anvil as shown at "B."

dius 1 1/4 inches farther. Using the same wiping blows, bend it down 40 degrees. Be careful not to alter your first bend or reduce dimension. Do not quench (Fig. 9-18).

Bend the second piece of flat stock exactly as you did the first. Again, do not quench. It will help you to duplicate the first piece if you lay these angles out in chalk on the face of your anvil. The bends should be accurate.

Assembly

Lay the two pieces together in scissors fashion. Arrange them so that the offsets are centered over each other. Bring the lips together. This must leave space at the bottom of the jaws (Fig. 9-19). Center-punch the exact center of the hinge cross point; hot-punch and drift for a 1 1/4-inch hinge pin in both halves.

Bolt the two halves together, adjusting them so that the lips touch at their ends, and set the bolt up a little snug. Check for free movement. If the metal in between the bends became distorted, flatten the hinge area until the movement is correct. Now rebolt and tighten. Place the jaws in the fire. Don't go in too far. You want to heat the entire jaw area evenly to a high red heat, but keep the bolt cool (Fig. 9-20). Use the dribble can for this. Make

sure that the vise jaw guards are in place. (See Chapter 16 for a discussion of vise jaw guards.)

Holding the reins up, place the jaw in the vise pointing straight down, with the lips together and the bolt plumb over the vise screw (Fig. 9-21). Locate the bolt so there is 1/2-inch clearance, no more, between it and the top of the vise jaw guards. Now slam the vise hard shut. Use an adjustable end wrench if necessary to grab the bolt and hinge. Twist as needed until the bolt is straight across the vise jaws and the hinge dividing line is exactly in line with the jaws (Fig. 9-21). Work quickly because the bolt is getting hot and might stretch. The jaws are now aligned. Quench the jaw and hinge area until it is cool enough to handle.

Shaping and Reins

There should be about 1 1/2 inches between the ends of the reins. If not, unbolt them and cold bend each half over the end of the horn, just behind the hinge bend. Don't disfigure the hinge area. Adjust each rein the amount needed to result in a 1 1/2-inch space between the ends. Now remove the bolt for the next step.

Starting about 7 1/2 inches from the rein end, heat and forge out a long taper toward the end of the rein. Finish with a 5/16-inch square end. As you

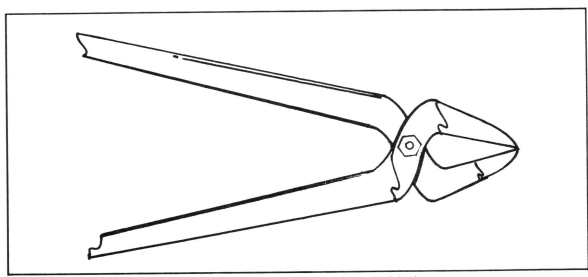

Fig. 9-19. Locate the hinge pin hole so there will be a space at the bottom of the jaws.

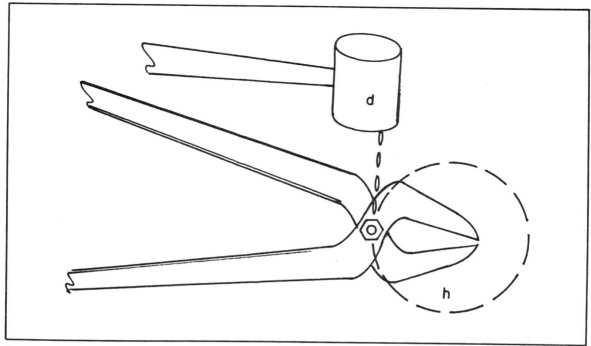

Fig. 9-20. Cool the hinge pin with water from the dribble can.

taper, let the rein swell sideways as it wants to (Fig. 9-22). This process is called *softening* the corners or edges. Make both reins the same.

Reassemble the tongs. Set the cold tongs, reins down, one on each side of the vise screw until the bolt is 1 1/2 inches above the jaw guards. Close the reins together so that they just clear the vise screw and the tongs are vertical. Tighten the bolt (Fig. 9-23).

Remove the tongs from the vise, maintaining the spacing of the reins. If the bolt has loosened, tighten it. Keep the reins in the same position and heat them 1 1/2 inches from the bolt. Heat both reins equally to a light red. Center the heat 1 1/2 inches from the bolt. Keep the bolt cool with the dribble can. When the reins are heated, grab them with the vise jaw just as they were prepared in the last step. Hold them about 2 1/2 inches below the bolt. Slam the jaws shut (Fig. 9-24). Grab the hinge area just under the bolt and twist the hinge into alignment as you did with the jaw alignment.

Remove the tongs from the vise and let them

cool to no heat color. Then quench them until they are cool enough to handle. Remove the bolt.

Finishing the Jaws

Your tongs may be a little wide at the end of the reins, but don't adjust any more yet. Assemble the tongs and file a mark crossways on the contact face of the jaw 1/4 inch from the end of the shorter jaw (Fig. 9-25). Close up the jaws and file off the long jaw to match the short one. Then file a "V" about 1/16 inch deep on the file mark to match the shallow "V" on the other jaw. Be sure the "V" ways are square across the jaws (Fig. 9-25).

Have a piece of 1/4-inch round stock 3 or 4 inches long at hand on the anvil. A long 1/4-inch bolt will do. Grip the bolt or round stock in the "V's" to make sure it won't slip out. Put it aside. Have the hinge bolt snug, but not tight. Heat just the tips of the jaws to an orange heat. Keep the hinge bolt cool. Take the round stock in the "V's" of the jaw, lining it straight across the jaw. While squeezing on the reins lightly, being careful not to

127

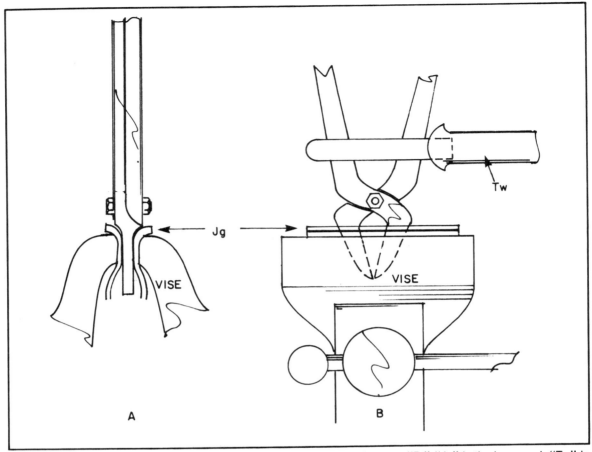

A   B

Fig. 9-21. Locate the hot jaws in the vise as at "A." Align the jaws as shown at "B." "Jg" is the jaw guard. "Tw" is the twisting wrench.

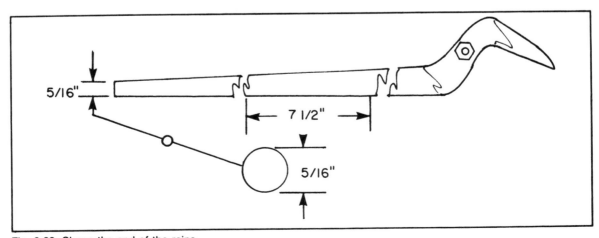

Fig. 9-22. Shape the end of the reins.

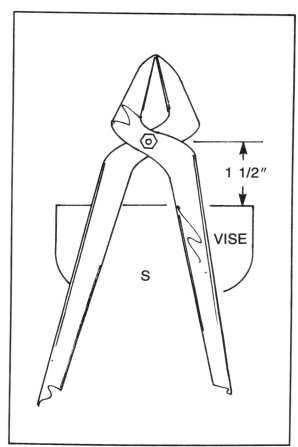

Fig. 9-23. Adjust the reins.

before. You may use a rivet. If you do, put a washer against each half under the heads of the rivet. Adjust the reins up close to the hinge by cold bending them until 1 inch remains between the ends when the jaws are empty and closed together.

This pair of tongs will handle 3/16-inch, 1/4-inch, and 5/16-inch round stock and 1/4-inch square stock.

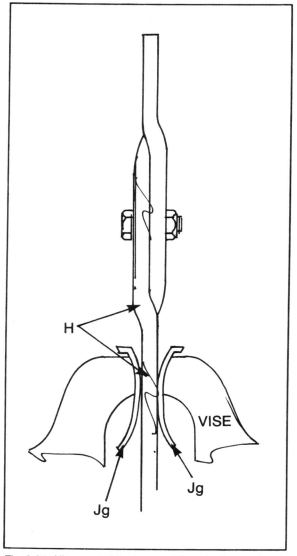

Fig. 9-24. Alignment of the jaws and the reins is completed. Notice the use of jaw guards.

bend the jaw ends, lay the bottom jaw squarely down on the anvil. Hit the top jaw directly over the round stock. Don't hit too hard (Fig. 9-26).

Hang on to the round stock and turn the tongs over and hit the same way again. Repeat as needed to form a round valley in each jaw. These do not need to be exactly the same depth. You may heat up one jaw more than the other if it is not moving as fast as the other. Keep working until the jaws have about 1/16 inch of space between them at the very tip while you still hold the round stock. Don't let the jaw tips come together. The valleys will have rounded shoulders. Don't change this (Fig. 9-26).

Finishing

Replace the bolt with a new one and finish off as

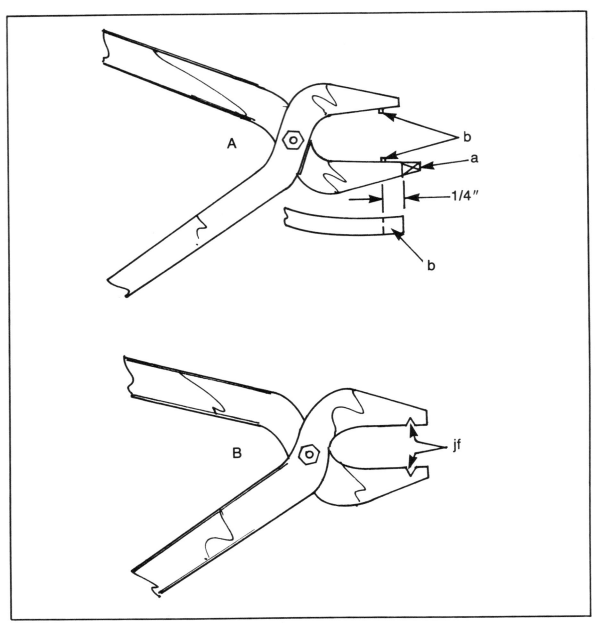

Fig. 9-25. File a mark at ''b'' in illustration ''A'' and file off the portion at ''a'' so that the jaws match. File a ''V'' shaped notch at ''jf'' in illustration ''B.''

Oil the joint and wire brush the tongs. Cut off excess reins to make the tongs 18 inches or less overall. Wipe them down with some oil to prevent rust (Fig. 9-27).

MEDIUM WEIGHT QUICKIE TONGS

In this exercise you will make a medium weight, flat-stock, hollow-bit tong for holding 5/8-inch round, 1/2-inch round, and 1/2-inch square stock.

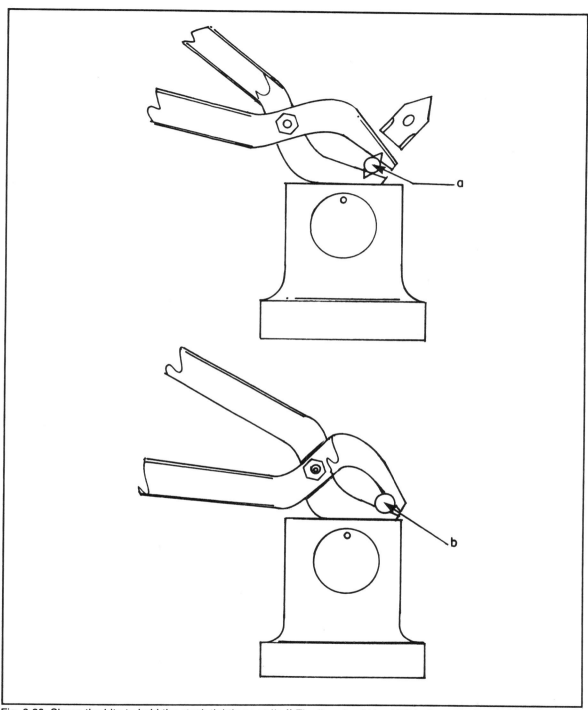

Fig. 9-26. Shape the bite to hold the stock tightly as at "a." The lips should be 1/16 inch apart when holding the stock as shown at "b."

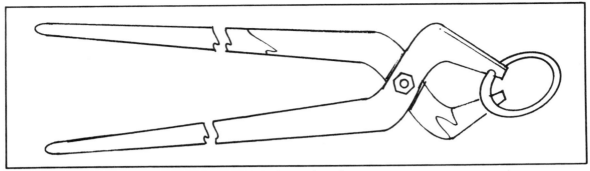
Fig. 9-27. The finished tong is holding a ring of 1/4-inch round stock.

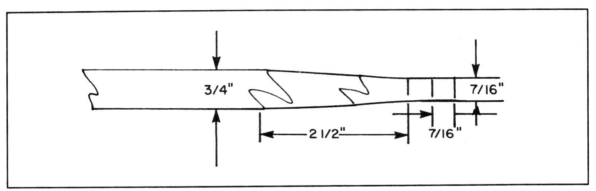
Fig. 9-28. Draw out the jaws to these measurements.

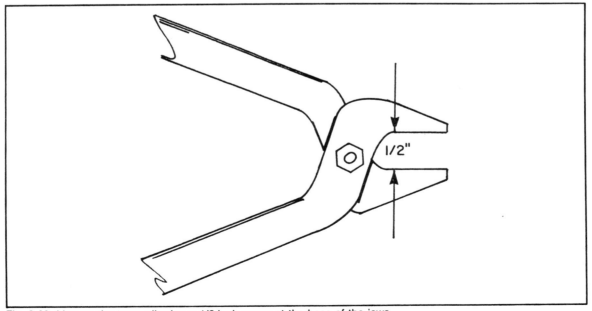
Fig. 9-29. Line up the tong, allowing a 1/2-inch space at the base of the jaws.

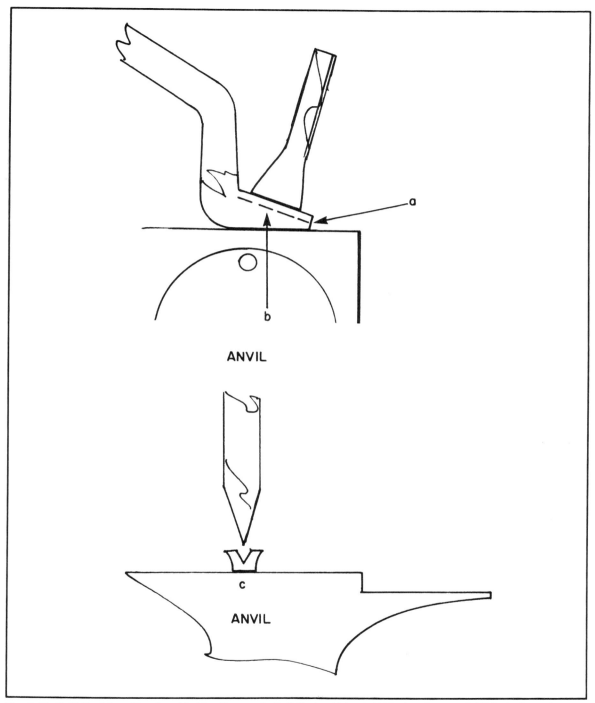

ANVIL

ANVIL

Fig. 9-30. Split the bite with a hand-held splitter at "a." "b" should be 1 1/4 inches long and 1/4 inch deep. A cross section of the jaw and the splitter should look like "c."

These tongs will hold as well as the traditional tongs, but they will not have the bow type jaws. They will be straight. With a few exceptions the method follows that of the lightweight quickie tongs.

Stock Required

Two pieces of bar stock 3/8 inch by 3/4 inch by 14 inch, M.S.

One 5/16-inch bolt and nut or one 5/16-inch round-head rivet.

One piece of 1/2-inch square stock with a good smooth end, for testing the bite.

Procedure

Work at yellow orange heat.

Draw out a 2 1/2-inch taper edgeways on the stock to a 7/16-inch square end (Fig. 9-28). Extend the taper 2 1/2 inches over the back small anvil radius and bend it down sideways 45 degrees. As you did in making the light tongs, revolve the stock 180 degrees and extend it 1 1/2 inches farther over the

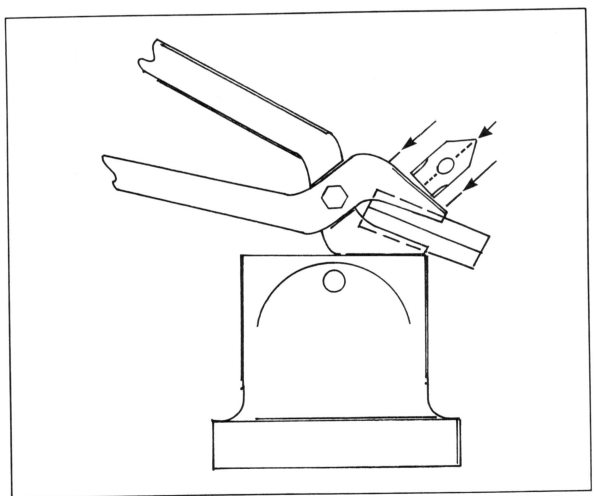

Fig. 9-31. Grab the square stock in the bite. Start working the jaws down over the stock, turning the work from bit edge to bit edge as you go. The 1/2-inch square-stock plug should be fitted into the bite. Don't let the lips come together. Let them spread out.

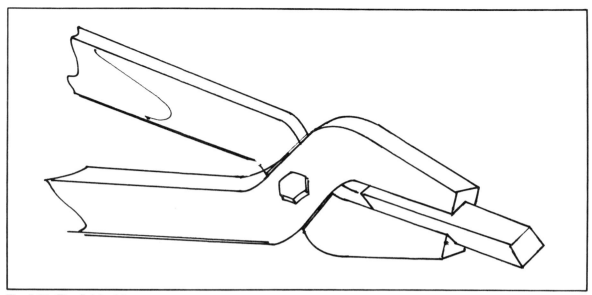

Fig. 9-32. The finished tongs.

same radius and bend it back 50 degrees (Fig. 9-18).

Repeat the locating process for the hinge pin as you did in the light tongs. Punch and drift a 5/16-inch pin hole. Now make the second half. Using the bolt method, line up the entire tong, allowing 1/2-inch space at the base of the jaws (Fig. 9-29). Start 3 1/2 inches from the pin and draw out a taper for the rein. This should go from full stock size to 3/8-inch square in 6 inches.

The balance of the rein should be forged out to 3/8-inch round, first squaring and then rounding it. Don't set the spacing of the reins until the bits are cut. The tongs should be fully aligned before the bits are cut and grooved. This is done in the same way as for the quickie ring tongs.

Dismantle the tongs. Heat the bit for 1 1/4 inches to a light orange. Figures 9-30, 9-31, and 9-32 show the finishing steps. Place the bit firmly on its back on the anvil face with the "bite" side up. Use a hand-held splitter to split the bit on the center line (Fig. 9-30). (This splitter is discussed in Chapter 11.) Split the bit about 1/4 inch deep for about 1 1/4 inches. Repeat on the second half.

Assemble the tongs with a bolt. They should be snug. Heat the two bits to the same heat. Quickly place the short piece of 1/2-inch square stock in the jaws as far as the split goes. Squeeze the reins and lay the bits edgeways on the anvil face (Fig. 9-31). Hit fairly hard, then turn the whole assembly over 180 degrees and strike again. Repeat until you have a nicely fitting pair of bits holding the square stock. Remove the square stock and quench it. It will have picked up a lot of heat by now.

Reheat the bits, grab the square stock, tighten the bolt and line up the bits as needed (Fig. 9-32). Replace the bolt with a new one or use a rivet as you did in the light tongs. If you rivet this, washers will not be needed.

Now that you have learned the methods, let your imagination go. Draw pictures of the tongs you want and make them either from bar stock or from flat stock. You will find that 1/2-inch round stock makes very attractive lightweight tongs. Try it. You should be able to duplicate a pair of tongs just from seeing a picture of them.

Chapter 10

Rules for Working to Dimension

THROUGHOUT THIS BOOK YOU HAVE BEEN learning to work to desired dimensions, in addition to learning how to forge an object to form a given shape. When you are attempting to determine how to arrive at certain dimensions, you can use a variety of rules and formulas that will give the same results. The following rules have been chosen because I think they are the simplest and the best for general purposes. They are used regularly in my shop. Study the rules carefully because you will be applying them in the following lessons. The records you have been making of measurement changes will help you to establish variations to the rules to fit your particular way of working.

First I will give you the rule for determining the length of stock to cut in order to forge a piece with a butt weld. The rule for a scarf weld or a lapped weld will follow. These welds would be used in making rings and in joining two separate measured pieces. (You will learn how to make rings in Chapter 15.) After the rules for rings you will take up the rule for determining the length of stock to cut for "U" bolts, "Z" bars, and other specific shapes.

The measurements are done by the same rule whether you will be bending the stock the flat way or the edge way.

RINGS AND LINKS

The rules for determining how much stock length you will need for various rings and links are shown below.

The Butt Joint Ring

Stock length = the inside diameter of the ring + the thickness of the metal × Pi. The value of Pi is 3.14159265. For your purposes, use the value 3.14.

For a flat bend or roll, the thickness of the metal is measured in the plane of the bend or roll in the radial or flat view (Fig. 10-1).

To calculate the stock when making a ring of any stock, all measurements are in the plane of the diameter only.

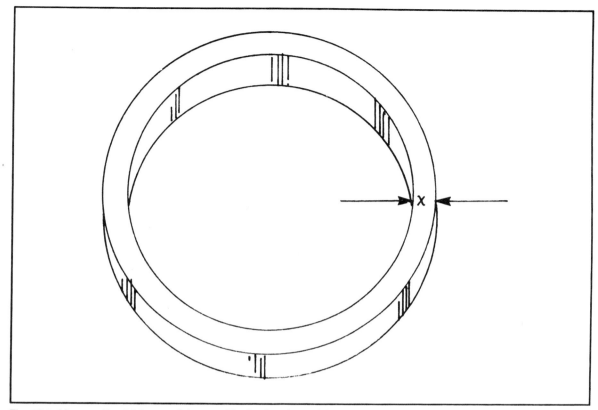

Fig. 10-1. Measure the thickness of the metal in the flat plane of the roll or bend or circle as shown at "x." To calculate stock needed, always measure the inside diameter regardless of the shape or size of the stock.

Always use only the inside diameter in calculating.

For example; let us suppose that you are required to make a 6-inch ring of 1/2-inch square stock. You would figure it as follows:

Inside diameter of the ring	6 inches
Thickness of the metal	1/2 inch
Total	6 1/2 inches

6 1/2 inches × Pi (3.14) = 20 3/8 inches = the stock length needed for a butt joint ring (Fig. 10-2).

The Scarf Welded Ring

Stock length = the inside diameter of the ring + (2 × the stock thickness) × Pi.

As an example suppose you need to make a scarf welded ring with a 6-inch inside diameter from 1/2-inch square stock.

Inside diameter of the ring	6 inches
2 × 1/2 inch (the stock thickness)	1 inch
Total	7 inches

7 inches × Pi = 21.98 inches = the stock length needed for a scarf welded ring (Fig. 10-3).

If the stock used in the above examples had been 1/8-inch by 1/2-inch flat stock bent edgeways (instead of 1/2-inch square stock), the measurements would be the same. The formula allows for upsetting after the stock is cut. Upsetting is used

137

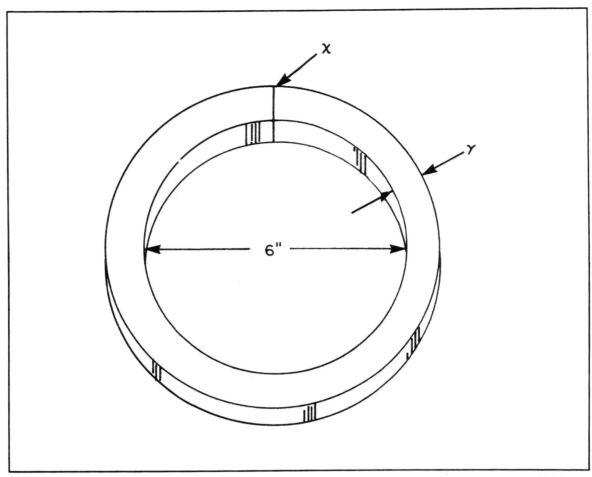

Fig. 10-2. Measure the side diameter of the ring (6 inches) and the thickness of the stock in the same plane. Thickness is measured at "y." The location of the butt joint is shown at "x."

in some types of welds. When you are making fire welded rings, upset any stock that is less than 3/8 inch thick.

The Link

To determine the stock length needed when you are making a link, add twice the length of one side, that is, the straight part, to the completed formula for a ring (Fig. 10-4).

To find the length of the side of a link, subtract the small diameter from the large diameter. The result is the length of either side. Study Fig. 10-4 to understand the rule.

"U" BOLTS AND "Z" BENDS

These rules will vary according to the type and shape of the bends.

The Radius Bend "U" Bolt

To find the stock length required for a radius bend "U" bolt, add twice the thickness of the metal to the overall inside total length.

For example, assume that you are required to make a radius bend "U" bolt 2 inches wide by 6 inches long, made from 1/2-inch stock.

2 × 1/2 inch (the stock
thickness)   1 inch

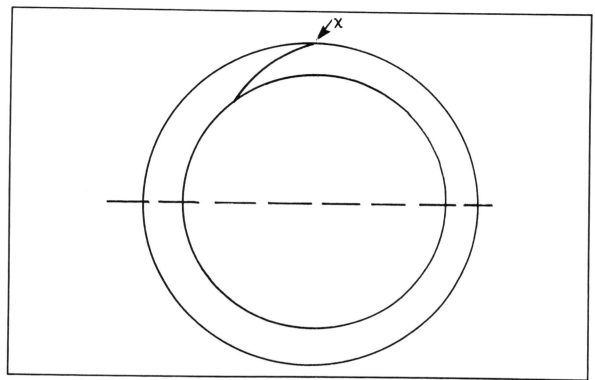

Fig. 10-3. The weld in a scarf welded ring is shown at "x."

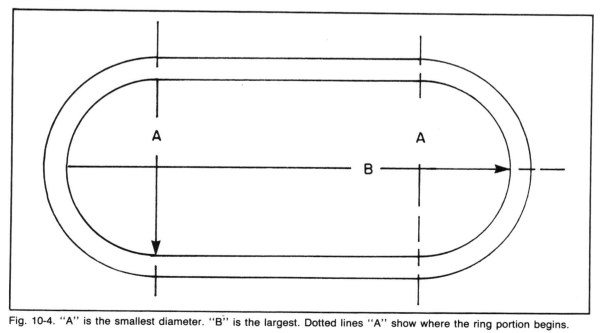

Fig. 10-4. "A" is the smallest diameter. "B" is the largest. Dotted lines "A" show where the ring portion begins.

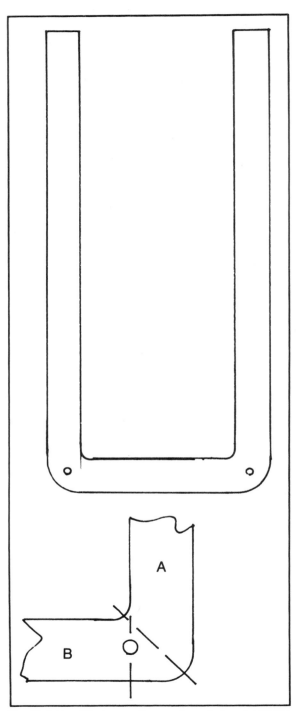

Fig. 10-5. Bend the legs so the punch mark stays inside the leg, "A." It should remain on the center line of the base, "B."

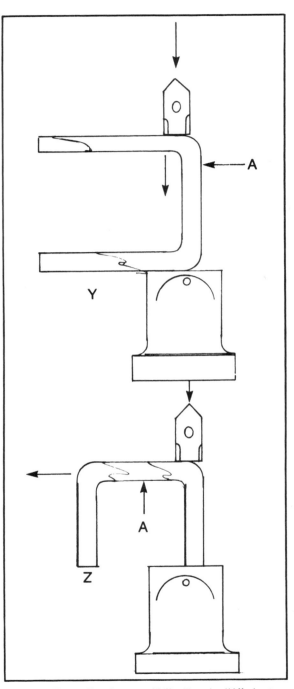

Fig. 10-6. The strike shown at "Y" will make "A" shorter. Strike as in "Z" to make "A" longer. Make these strikes light. For minor corrections the iron can be at a red heat or cold.

140

Inside length of one side	6 inches
Inside width of the bolt	2 inches

1 inch + 6 inches + 2 inches + 6 inches = 15 inches = stock length required (Fig. 10-5).

Forging the Radius Bend "U" Bolt

To forge the "U" bolt, mark the stock at the desired inside width.

Working at an orange heat, bend the stock so that the inside radius of the bend is equal to 1/2 the thickness of the stock. (Remember that a radius is 1/2 a diameter.) The outside of the bend will follow the dictates of the inside. When you are making this bend, keep your marks in the middle of the bend. When the "U" bolt is finished, the marks will line up with the inside of the legs (Fig. 10-5).

This type of bending should be done over the horn or over a good radius on the anvil edge. Keep your marks on the side of the work so that they can be seen and so that they will not start a crack. If the bends need to be moved, stand the bolt on one leg on the anvil and bump the base of the "U" bolt near the bend or lay one leg on the anvil face and bump the opposite leg near the bend (Fig. 10-6).

For final trueing up use a swage or the step of the anvil. To thread the "U" bolt, bend a leg to clear the die stock; then true it up when the threads are completed (Fig. 10-7).

The "Z" Bend or Crank

To find the stock length for a "Z" bend or for a crank, use the rule for "U" bolts. To forge this bend, simply bend one leg opposite to the other. If one leg is to be longer than the other, offset the marks accordingly (Fig. 10-8).

A Round Bottomed "U" Bolt

To make a round bottomed "U" bolt, use the rule

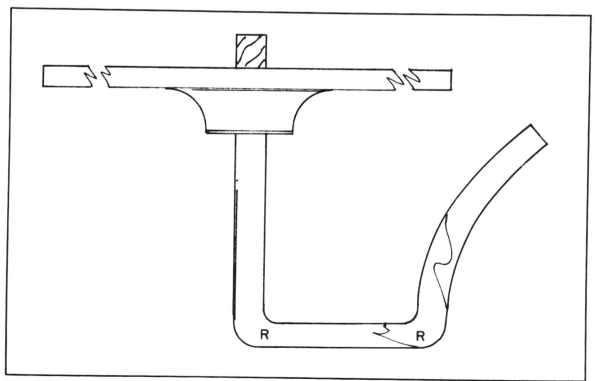

Fig. 10-7. When threading a "U" bolt, bend one leg out of the way. Don't bend in the radius bend "R."

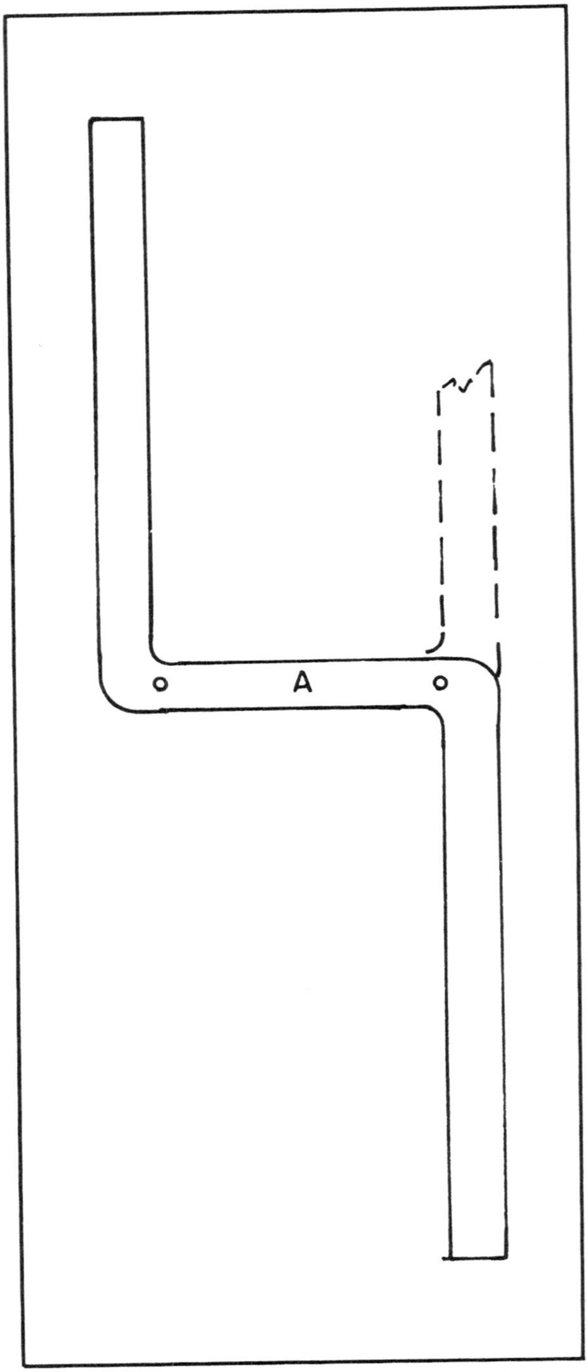

Fig. 10-8. The "Z" bend is done exactly like a radius bend "U" bolt except that the legs are opposed. Correct the length of "A" as you would the base of a "U" bolt.

for a ring of a radius equal to the bottom of the "U" bolt, and add together the length of both legs and 1/2 the ring.

As an example, let us say that you are required to make a 6-inch "U" bolt with a 1-inch radius in its base from 1/2-inch round stock (Fig. 10-9). This is called a round bottomed "U" bolt. Note that a 1-inch radius equals a 2-inch diameter. First you will need to find the length of stock needed for the bottom round:

Inside diameter or space between the legs	2 inches
Metal thickness	1/2 inch
Total	2 1/2 inches

2 1/2 inches × Pi = 7.81 inches ÷ 2 = 3.93 inches = length of stock needed for the bottom turn.

Next you will determine the length needed for the legs:

Length of the finished bolt	6 inches
Minus 1/2 the diameter of the base	1 inch
Length of each leg	5 inches

2 × 5 inches (or 10 inches) + 3.93 inches (length of bottom turn) = 13.93 inches = length of stock required.

As a practical matter you will require 14 inches of 1/2-inch round stock because for blacksmith work the difference between 13.93 inches and 14 inches is negligible.

The round bottomed "U" bolt is forged around the horn. The horn of your anvil is close to round at any given cross section. When you want a certain measurement as in this "U" bolt, use a pair of calipers and hold it straight down over the horn to find the 2-inch diameter. Then shape the "U" bolt over that portion of the horn (Fig. 10-13). In effect you are using the horn as a cone. Use either spring or slide calipers.

"U" Bolts with Inside Square Corners

Stock length for "U" bolts with inside square

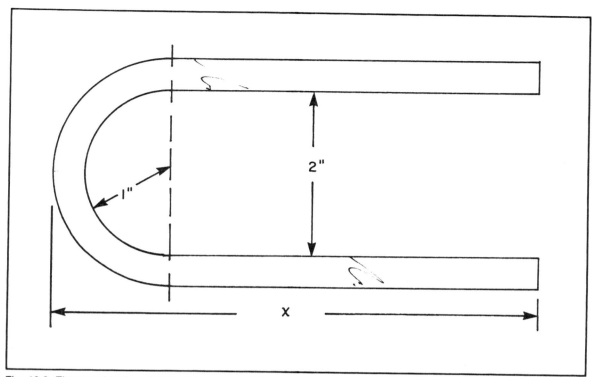

Fig. 10-9. The round bottom "U" bolt is measured like a radius bend "U" bolt, from the end of the legs, "X," to the inside bottom of the "U."

corners is determined by the same rule as for the radius bend "U" bolt.

Forging "U" Bolts
with Inside Square Corners

When you make this type of bend, it is important that you work at a yellow-orange heat. Do not work in the deep reds. Be very careful not to scar the work inside the bends because it may break before you finish it. In forging this bend, the inside and the outside must be worked alternately a bit at a time. The sides must be kept at stock dimension as you go along. They will tend to bulge in the bend because of the upset type of forging used in making the bend. Keep your marks on the side of the bend so that you can see them as you work (Fig. 10-5). If the mark is kept lined up with the inside of the leg, the inside dimension will be correct.

Place the heated metal over the back radius so that the leg is past the anvil face and the mark is

lined up with the back of the anvil body. Bend to about 45 degrees, no more.

Figure 10-10 describes the first forging blows. Note that they are wiping blows and that the hammer for 1/2-inch stock should be about 1 1/2 pounds. The reason for using this lighter hammer is that as you bend you are, in a sense, also upsetting the metal within the bend. You want to keep the shock of the hammer within the bending area only. Also you are taking advantage of the resistance of the weight of the cold part of the metal to act as an extension of the anvil right up into the bend. Most of the work on the outside of the bend will be up in the air above the anvil with only the end of the leg on the anvil (Fig. 10-11).

Continue to work the metal back into itself so there will be some to fill out the outside corner. From time to time it will be necessary to do a little shaping on the inside of the bend. Do this over the edge of the anvil near the heel. When you do this,

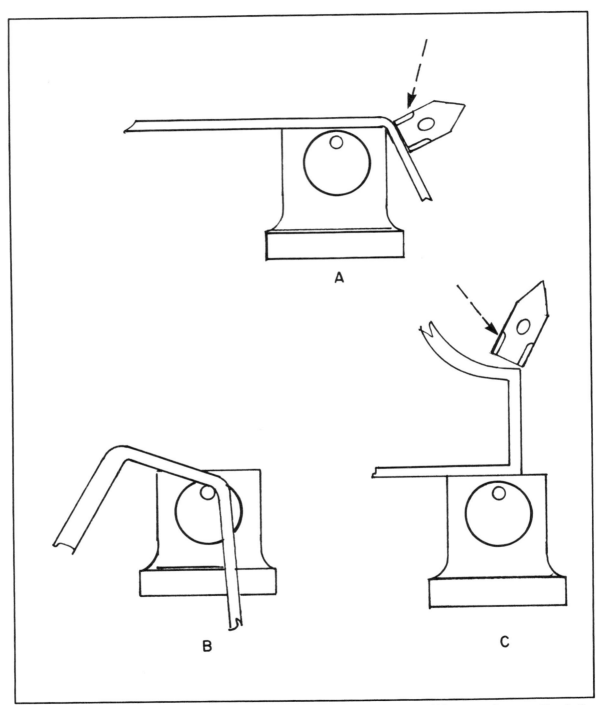

Fig. 10-10. "U" bolts with inside square corners must be worked quite hot. Avoid hard blows to reduce upsetting in the corners. Follow the sequence "A," "B," and "C." Arrows indicate force lines.

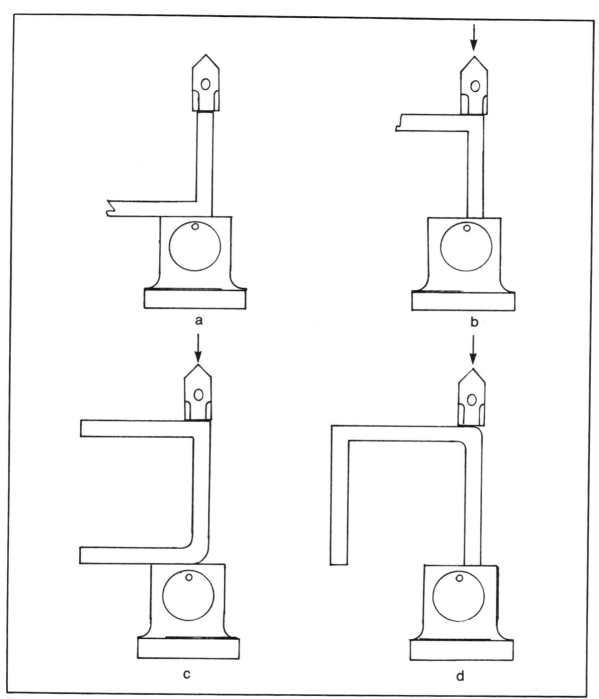

Fig. 10-11. After the primary bends, most of the work will be up in the air with only the leg or corner on the anvil. Make a few blows with the leg up, then a few with the base up. Bring both legs and corners along together. Heat only one corner at a time.

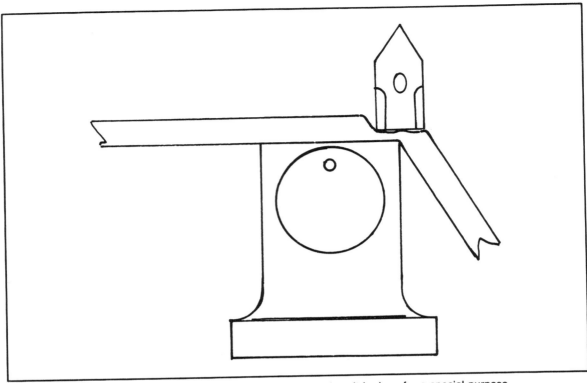

Fig. 10-12. A half a hammer over stroke is almost always bad unless it is done for a special purpose.

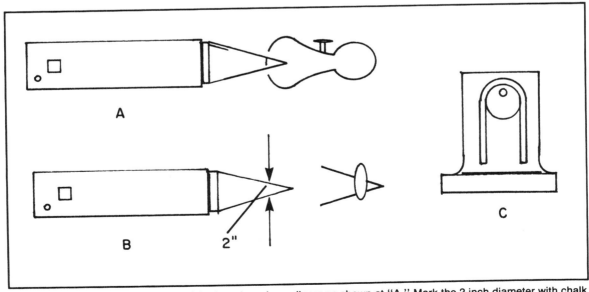

A

B

2"

C

Fig. 10-13. Find the 2-inch diameter of the horn by using calipers as shown at "A." Mark the 2-inch diameter with chalk down on the side and a little under the horn as at "B." Work out the true round bottom of the "U" bolt over the 2-inch portion of the horn as at "C."

be sure that you don't do any "half a hammer over" strokes, of your work will be ruined (Fig. 10-12).

To make the second bend, work over the beak of the anvil (Fig. 10-10). Close up the bend as you go along, working all sides. This progressive action will give you the best results (Fig. 10-11). This type of bend is not easy to do, but it is well worth mastering because it has many uses besides the bends in "U" bolts (Fig. 10-13).

Making the bends is a slow process, and you lose metal to scale because of the high heat required and the number of heats you need. By now, however, you should be getting more work done in each heat. Work toward improving this ratio.

The foregoing work helps you to better understand why and how a bend or a ring or similar shape uses more metal than would be indicated by mathematical calculation alone.

Chapter 11

Heat Treating

BEFORE YOU BEGIN MAKING HAND TOOLS, you need to understand the processes of hardening and tempering. These processes are known as heat treating.

Heat treating the completed tool is necessary because in the heat treating you control the hardness, toughness, brittleness, softness, or any combination of these qualities in the finished product. And when you finish making a tool, no matter what steel is used, heat treating is needed to relieve internal stresses and strains set up within the metal during the forging. If you do not heat treat your finished tool, there is a very good chance the tool will fail. The only steel that will not be affected much by heat treating is mild steel.

WATER HARDENING
TEST FOR SALVAGE STEEL

In the next chapter you will be making hand-held tools from salvage steels. In order to save yourself time and frustration, you must determine what temperatures are needed to forge, harden, and temper

salvage steels. This chapter will explain how to test all salvage metal, but you must be patient and observant and make notes so that you have records.

Stock Required

One automotive front coil spring that appears to be in good condition. (The stock in a coil spring is usually called the "wire" or "spring wire," regardless of its size or the size of the spring.) The diameter of the coil in our example is 4 1/2 inches from center to center. The coil wire is 27/32 inch more or less, round in section, and has seven full turns. Straightened out, the spring will give you about 8 feet, 3 inches of steel.

This measurement is the result of the formula: diameter of the coil, center to center, × Pi × the number of turns = length of the metal when it is straightened out. Following this formula, we see that 4 1/2 inches × 3.14 = 14.137 inches. 14.137 inches × 7 turns = 98.358 inches. 98.358 inches ÷ 12 inches = 8.20 feet.

In this study you will assume that the spring

wire is made of water hardening steel.

A bucket with at least 2 gallons of water in it for quenching. The water must be between 70 degrees Fahrenheit and 85 degrees Fahrenheit. Temperature of this quench water is important.

A used mill file.

A magnet. Any magnet will be fine as long as it is strong enough to pick up a 1/2-inch-×-1 1/2-inch bolt.

Procedure

Heat one end of the coil to a reddish orange heat. Don't get it any hotter than is necessary to bend the wire.

Slip a piece of pipe over an inch or so of the hot end and jam the coil, hot end down, between two bars stuck in the hardy hole. Uncoil the spring. Repeat this process until you have uncoiled the spring or the amount of stock needed for the current work (Fig. 11-1).

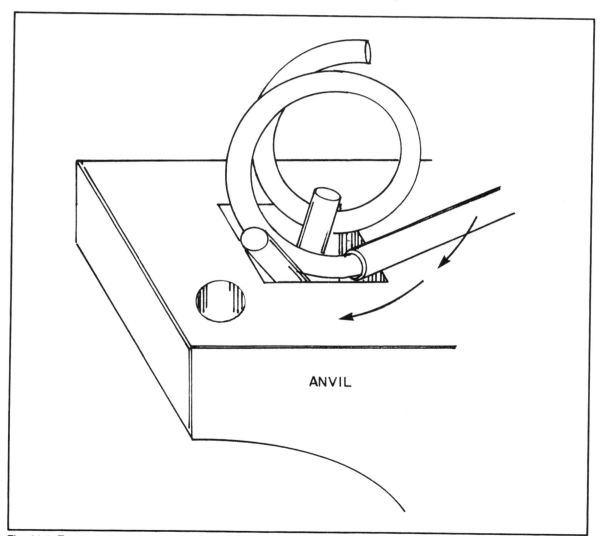

ANVIL

Fig. 11-1. To open up an automobile coil spring, stick two rods in the hardy hole on the anvil. Use your bending fork or a piece of pipe to straighten the hot coil.

When the spring wire has cooled naturally to room temperature it can be cut with a hacksaw. Cut off about 10 inches and set the rest aside. Do not quench any stock until so instructed.

Heat about 1 inch of the 10-inch piece to an orange heat. Bring the heat up slowly. Use your dribble can to keep the other end cool enough to handle with your bare hand.

Draw out the end to 1/4-inch square, about 3 inches long. In the first two or three blows it should be forming a nose on the end. If it isn't, hit harder. This type of steel is tough. If the end is cupping or looking wrinkled, the metal is not hot enough. Stop forging when the metal reaches a dull red. At this temperature it may become tough to forge, or it may suddenly take on a different feel under your hammer. Watch for a change of feel and sound. This will happen long before the color has gone. When it happens, stop forging. If you continue, there is a good chance of shattering or cracking the metal internally. You won't be able to see it, but it will appear if you harden and temper a finished tool.

Forge the 1/4-inch square tongue to an even shape the same thickness throughout. When the tongue is finished, put it in the fire and bring it up to a dull red. Set it aside to cool and normalize. Do not cut off this test end (Fig. 11-2).

When the test end is cool enough to handle, file a shallow notch about every 1/2 inch, starting from the end (Fig. 11-2). Place it in the fire and bring the end, including all of the first 1/2-inch section and some of the second section, to a low forging heat. Arrange the piece in the fire so that the balance of the test piece is progressively cooler as it approaches the parent stock. At the junction with the parent stock, the test piece should be black. Study the figure and make a good mental note of your color pattern.

Quickly quench the piece endways in the

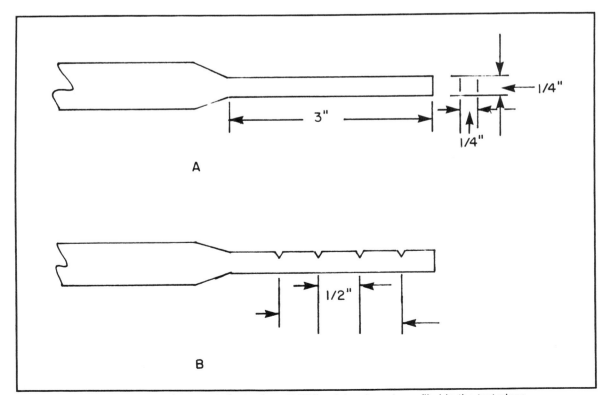

Fig. 11-2. "A" shows the test piece ready for testing. At "B" notches have been filed in the test piece.

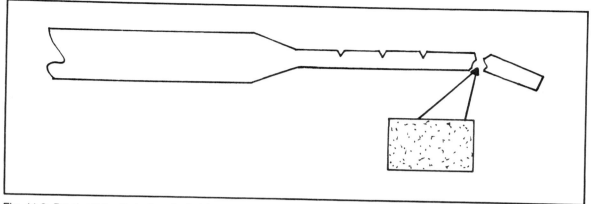

Fig. 11-3. Break off the first piece by holding the notch over the back edge of the anvil and striking with a bar of iron. Observe the grain structure. It will be grainy and ragged. As you proceed to break off more pieces the grain structure will change.

quench bucket you have prepared. Keep making a figure-eight motion in the quench while you continue to hold the test piece vertically. Do not take it out of the water until you are sure that the 1/4-inch square portion is at water temperature. Give it a full minute so the parent stock will be cool as well.

Continue to make your notes. Hold the test end close to the anvil edge for support. Attempt to file it. Does the file really "zing" across it with no effort and without cutting it? If so, it is very hard. Break off the first 1/2-inch section of the test end, using a bar of iron for a hammer (Fig. 11-3). The end piece may be so hard that it will mark the face of your improvised hammer. Study the appearance of the grain in the break. If the grain is coarse and the break is not clean (that is, it is off at an angle or some shattering has occurred), the metal is brittle and weak. It will not stand impact or flexing.

Test file the remainder of the stock as before, then break off another 1/2-inch piece. File the exposed break, remembering the feel of the file across the grain structure. Repeat this break testing without reheating until you have reached the place in the bar where it will no longer break off, but will just bend. If you have recorded this test as you proceeded, you should have a clear graphic sketch and notes of each test that will show the heat range of the various test breaks and that will include color and file tests.

Among your test breaks there will be a grain structure that has a very fine, even, almost silky look. It will be too hard to file. The break will be clean with no chips out of the side. It will just look like a fine sample. The heat that produced this fine sample is your desired hardening heat. It will probably be in the deep reds. You might be surprised at how low the best hardening heat is.

The next section of the sample should be soft enough to file somewhat and perhaps will bend without breaking. This indicates the piece was not hot enough to harden.

Remember, the more light you have in your shop and the brighter the fire in your forge, the deeper or darker the hardening temperature will appear.

The next test establishes the critical point, which must also be known when you heat treat metal. Turn the test piece end for end. Take your magnet and hold it lightly between your fingers. Hold the cold test piece in your other hand in a horizontal position with the heavy end pointing at the magnet. Keep it about 2 inches from the magnet (Fig. 11-4).

Pass the magnet up and down in front of the blunt end of the test piece. Do not let it touch. While you are moving the magnet past the test piece, notice the feel of the pull as the magnet approaches and leaves the bar. Notice the increase and decrease of pull. When you lose the feeling of magnetic pull,

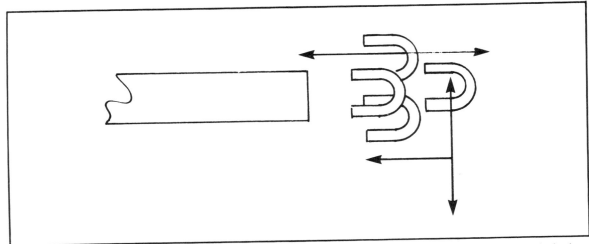

Fig. 11-4. As the bar is heated, keep passing the magnet back and forth and side to side. Never let it touch the bar.

note the feeling of the moment when you are no longer aware of magnetic pull. When this test is done with hot metal, it will show you the critical point in the heat range that you must reach as a hardening heat.

You must not exceed this heat by more than 75 or 100 degrees Fahrenheit. This will be the hardening heat, the heat at which the work is quenched.

You will find the critical point in your test piece. Pay close attention to your work because this point comes and goes in a very narrow heat range.

Put the heavy end of the test piece in the fire and start heating it slowly. Every few minutes as the heat is increasing, try the magnet test just as you did with the cold metal. Don't let the magnet touch the test piece at any time. Keep heating the piece slowly and watch for color. At the first sign of color, you know that you are approaching the critical point. Continue magnet testing as you continue to increase the heat. Somewhere in the very low deep red color, the magnetic pull will disappear.

Move the magnet to within 3/8 inch of the test piece. There should still be no magnetic pull. Keep the magnet passing by the test piece as you approach the 3/8-inch clearance point. Never allow the test piece and the magnet to approach each other on a common line (Fig. 11-4). If you do, the test piece will pick up some magnetism within the part

of its mass that is below the critical temperature, and the proper sense of magnetic pull or the lack of it will be lost. Your test would then be worthless. For the same reason never let the magnet touch the steel during these tests. A magnet test taken on the side of the bar is also worthless.

Make complete notes on all this because each different alloy and each different carbon steel will have a different critical temperature. As you make the magnet test, keep observing the heat color.

When the test piece reaches its critical point, the temperature at which the metal loses magnetic attraction, put the piece back in the fire. Count to 10 quickly. This allows for replacing the heat lost in the last test. Pull the test piece and quench it. Keep making figure-eight movements in the water.

Feel the shock of the cooling that the steel feels and keep an eye on it. As the sound changes pitch (it rises), as the bubbles stop rising, and the tremble goes out of the steel, take it out of the quench. If it is frying or sizzling hot, quickly requench just a little. The objective here is to bring it down as soon as possible to a temperature between 200 and 300 degrees Fahrenheit in the water quench. When it is cool enough to touch, but too hot to hold, quench no more. Now give it the file test. It should be too hard to file (Fig. 11-5).

After you have completed these tests, you have the information necessary to temper the balance of this coil spring to the desired hardness or toughness or both.

These processes are useful for testing any steel you might have, whether it is automotive, old tool steel bars and the like, or other salvage material. I find the magnetic test is faster and is about as accurate as the break test. I use it more frequently. If the tool you are about to make is important, use both test methods on a sample of the steel you plan to use.

I have had very good success using auto salvage dated 1973 and earlier. Some of the steels used since 1973 and a few of those manufactured earlier are high-alloy steels that cannot be heat treated successfully by the simple methods available to the average blacksmith. "Heat treating" and "hardening and tempering" mean the same thing within the context of this book.

OIL HARDENING
TEST FOR SALVAGE STEEL

For any steels that the average blacksmith will use, oil hardening is very much like water hardening. Here again you will be using automotive salvage steels, junkyard scrap, and old-style carbon steels. New carbon steels above 100 points carbon and many alloy and exotic steels are beyond the scope of this book. For heat treating on those steels, consult the supplier or the manufacturer.

Stock Required

One 10-inch piece of automotive coil spring or similar salvage steel.

40 or more gallons of oil. There are several commercial oils that may be used for your heat treating. I find 20W motor oil, nondetergent, is quite satisfactory. I use the low-cost oil that is sold in large food markets or discount stores. It comes in 2-gallon cans and is clearly identified. Do not use multiviscosity oil such as 10-30 or 10-40. Do not use used oil because the impurities that may be in it will affect your work in unpredictable ways.

One 40-pound grease bucket. A 40-pound grease bucket makes a great quench bucket for most of your work. Four gallons of oil will fill it to about

3 inches from the top. Save the lid to cover the oil when it is not in use. Keep this quenching oil clean and free of water.

Procedure

Caution! Smoke and flame usually occur in this process! If the piece is rather large, say 1 1/2 pounds or more, flames may reach 3 feet or higher

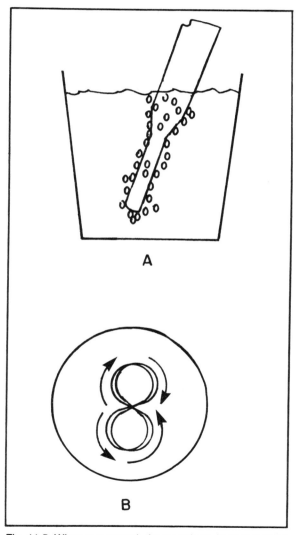

Fig. 11-5. When you quench the test piece, keep it moving to wash the vapor blanket away as at "A." Use a figure-eight motion as shown at "B." Do not allow the piece to touch any part of the quench container.

when you put the metal in the oil quench! Wear a heavy glove on your holding hand! Place your oil quench where it will not burn down your shop! Oil quenching is not child's play. It can be a real hazard to your well-being. Sometimes the hot oil splatters! *Never* under any circumstances use water on an oil fire!

Make up a test sample as you did for water hardening.

Bring the test sample to the same heat range that you reached in water hardening.

Hold the test sample with tongs to quench in the oil.

Check to make sure you fully understand the cautions given above. Quench in the oil, plunging the heated sample into the center of the mass of oil and moving it in a figure eight. Do not let the work touch the bottom or sides of the bucket. The sample will cool much more slowly in oil than in water, and the action of the liquid will be much less violent. The 1/4-inch piece will cool to a smoking heat in about 1 minute. Water quench, on the other hand, would take only about 15 seconds.

Pull out the test piece and check it visually. If it is frying hot, put it back for more quenching. Pull it out when the oil on it would be too cold to fry a hamburger, about 175 degrees Fahrenheit. Let it finish cooling in the air. Wipe it off as soon as you can. It must have no free oil on it for the break test.

Break and inspect the sample as you did in the water quench test. You will find the metal much different, piece for piece and color for color. If it is an oil hardening steel, it will harden up in the oil in the same fashion that the water hardening sample did. If it is not an oil hardening steel, it probably won't harden up. However, it may get so tough that it won't break and will require a hard pressure or blow to bend it.

In most cases oil hardening is not needed for the steels used in this book.

AN AIR HARDENING TEST

Sometimes you will find that salvage steel will air harden. To test for this, make up a test piece as you did in the water or the oil test, but to cool it

simply wave it rapidly in cool air or move it around in front of a strong fan or air jet. In most cases it will not become hard enough to serve your purpose. However, if it does, you will not need to temper it after it is hardened.

HARDENING NEW STEELS

In my shop I use new steel for all customer work and usually reserve salvage steels for my own tools and personal uses.

I have found that it is not practical for the average small shop to purchase the exotic tool steels available today. In order to get satisfactory results from them much more accurate temperature controls and quenching methods are needed than are usually available to the small blacksmith shop. However, I have found the following new steels quite adaptable to small shop service. They are all basically carbon steels.

Columbia's Unannealed AISI, Type W1 Steel

Columbia unannealed AISI, type W1 steel is recommended for knives, hammers, cold-cutters and chisels, swages and anvil tools, and similar items where forging is used to shape the tool. This steel has the highest carbon content needed around any blacksmith shop. "W1" means water hardening, 100-point carbon steel, no alloy included. It is designed as a water hardening steel. Typical analysis is carbon, 0.95-1.10 percent; manganese, 0.20-0.30 percent, silicon, 0.20-0.30 percent. Forge it at a full high heat, dark orange to light orange. Maximum heat should be between 1,500 degrees and 2,000 degrees Fahrenheit. Keep your fire exceptionally clean to avoid incorporating dirt at these high heats.

Anneal at 1,450 degrees Fahrenheit (the critical point) in dry wood ash or mica granules.

When you purchase new metal, get complete information on forging, annealing, hardening, and tempering from the supplier. Be sure you understand the dope sheet on high-carbon steels of this type. These steels are too expensive for guess work. They are tough and of very high quality, but they will not stand for much casual handling while being processed into tools. There is a broad size selection in W1 steels. Tools from W1 steel can be made to be extremely hard and tough.

AISI C 1070/90 Steel

Another steel very good for your purposes is AISI C 1070/90 tool steel. It is less expensive and more easily processed than AISI type W1. Ask your supplier about this one. 1050 or 1060 plow steel is also very good.

When you are inquiring about tool steels of any kind, be sure you inform the supplier that the steel will be hand forged and heated in an open coal and coke fire, blacksmith style. Many of the tool steels do not forge well by hand.

If you have a piece of new tool steel and do not have any information on it, test it as if it were scrap. If the test piece shatters in the water quench, try an oil quench. This is the only method available to the blacksmith shop. Other methods require a metallurgist's laboratory. Your attention to detail and changing conditions in the sample will determine the value of your test. One last reminder: keep records and mark all stock you have tested so you can identify it later.

TEMPERING

Tempering is the process of modifying the hardness of steel to a serviceable hardness and toughness. In all blacksmithing usage the hardness is reduced, brittleness is reduced, and toughness is increased. Resistance to impact is increased.

The secret in tempering steel is to be complete. Allow the steel to go through its entire cooling process after each heat before you reheat.

After hardening is completed, you should ordinarily start tempering immediately. The tempering heat should be applied slowly to get the proper heat throughout the part to be tempered. As the heat begins to rise above about 300 degrees Fahrenheit, hardness begins to decrease, brittleness decreases, and toughness increases.

Tempering for Hot-Cutting Tools

The object in tempering a tool that is to be used for hot cutting is to eliminate brittleness and to maintain a hard, tough core so that the cutting edge will not deform easily. The actual cutting edge will lose hardness in its first two or three cuts. It only needs to be softened (tempered) enough to prevent cracking or chipping resulting from the sudden shock of entering hot metal and the shock of the hammer after the first two or three blows. The hot-cutting edge depends entirely on its backing to maintain its edge and general shape.

Tempering for Cold-Cutting Tools

For cold-cutting edges the demand on the tool is a little different, so you will harden and temper to allow for this. The internal steel behind the cutting edge must be both hard and tough so that the cutting edge will have good support behind it. If the support is weak, the cutting edge will bend under the cutting load and crack or break. The cutting edge itself must be quite hard so that it can maintain sharpness for a reasonable time. This hardness must be deep enough to allow you to sharpen the tool several times by grinding it.

With this understanding of the requirements of the tools, study Fig. 11-5 and observe the method of heating and quenching to temper for these requirements.

TEMPERING TO A DESIRED HARDNESS

The process of forge tempering depends on color to determine the point at which you have reached the desired heat range (Fig. 11-6). You cannot see these colors unless you clean the tool of all old scale and oxide. Use a brick, sandpaper, or a piece of a grinding wheel. Any abrasive you can hold in your hand will do if the grit is between 80 and 100. It must be free of any oil or wax.

If you are working with oil-hardened tools, the oil residue can be a problem. Be sure to clean off all the oil before beginning the tempering process.

Test your tool with a slightly dull mill file. The tool should be so hard that the file slides across it without cutting the metal. Use a slow stroke and considerable pressure. If the file won't cut it, the tool is hard enough to require tempering. If the file

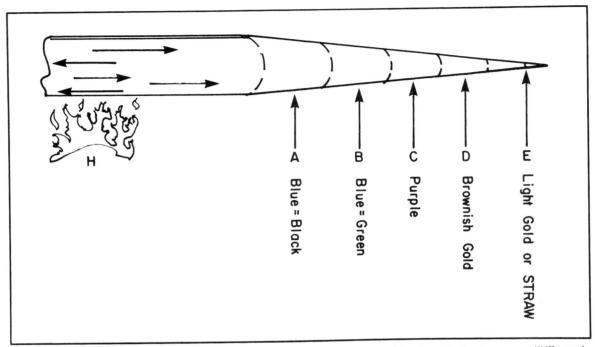

Fig. 11-6. The heat source must be behind the area being heat treated or tested. Heat from the heat source at "H" travels toward the point "E." Section "A" will become blue-black at 650 degrees Fahrenheit. Section "E" will be a light gold or straw color at about 400 degrees Fahrenheit and will be almost brittle. Colors indicate temperature only.

can be made to cut the freshly hardened tool, there is no need to temper the tool. However, it may not hold up in service.

Procedure

Scrub off all the old scale and oxide on one side of the cutting edge. Scrub back about 2 inches from the cutting edge or point. Make it bright so that it reflects light well. Use the brick or stone or sandpaper for this. Don't wipe the dust off with your hand or anything else that has oil or wax on it.

Lay the tool across the fire so the cutting edge is beyond it. Adjust the tool so good light reflects off it from a window or a door. Let the tool heat up slowly behind the cutting edge. Do not use the air blast because you will heat the tool too quickly. Soon the color will begin to change in the part of the steel that has been polished or scrubbed bright. The first color will be light yellow or a brassy color, also called a light straw color. Your steel is now at approximately 460 degrees Fahrenheit. The color

will travel toward the cutting edge. As it does, the color following it will darken until it is a deep golden brown, also called a dark straw color or a brown straw color. This occurs at about 500 degrees Fahrenheit. As the heat continues to rise and drift toward the edge, the tool will become light purple at about 530 degrees Fahrenheit, a pale blue at 610 degrees Fahrenheit, and then a blue tinged with green at 630 degrees Fahrenheit (Fig. 11-6).

The higher the tempering heat, the softer the steel becomes. As you can see, the metal behind the cutting edge is losing hardness sooner than the cutting edge because it is getting hot sooner than the cutting edge.

When the color indicates that you have reached the desired heat at the cutting edge, quickly quench the entire tool in water or oil, whichever is appropriate. Keep the temperature of the quench between 70 and 85 degrees Fahrenheit. Keep moving the tool in the quench until all heat is gone. This includes internal heat.

When you are quenching tools of any kind during any phase of hardening or tempering, keep the tool moving. Never let it touch the side or the bottom of the container.

Sometimes for blacksmith purposes, oil hardening or oil-hardened steel will tolerate a 75- or 80-degree Fahrenheit water quench for the tempering process. You should experiment with different heat treating processes.

A Tempering Guide

Here is a guide that shows suggested heats for tempering various types of tools.

Temperature	Color	Purpose
430° F.	Pale yellow, very light straw	Steel engraving tools, hammer faces, paper cutter, bone-carving tools
460-500° F.	Brown yellow, dark straw	Rock drills, pocket knives, pen knives, stone-cutting tools, chasing tools, and hardies
530° F.	Light purple	Woodworking tools and hardies
550° F.	Dark purple	Earth augers, cold-cuts and chisels, hot-cuts and splitters, axes, and fullers
570° F.	Dark blue	Springs and woodcutting tools
610° F.	Pale blue	
630° F.	Greenish blue	

Most steel will remain tough and durable, that is, it will be hard to bend and break, when it is tempered at 570 degrees Fahrenheit. However, it will not hold an edge well. At blue green, or 630 degrees Fahrenheit, the steel is no longer hard enough for most practical uses. This is certainly true of blacksmith tools. You should experiment with different heat ranges on your tools to find the ones that best serve your needs. A difference of 50 degrees Fahrenheit makes a big difference in the hardness remaining in the tool after tempering.

Chapter 12

Making Hand-Held Tools

T ODAY THERE REALLY IS NO GENERAL BLACK-smithing of the kind common in the nine-teenth century. By 1900 the successful blacksmith shops had converted to machine shops with a full line of steam-driven power tools. Factory-made items of every variety, as well as factory-made farm machinery and builder's machinery, replaced machinery made from scratch. As a result of this mechanization, the simple blacksmith shop was reduced to a place to have a horse shod or, perhaps, to have a pick or a digging bar sharpened.

The need vanished for the kind of blacksmith knowledge that was common in the era before 1900. With this lack of need for the blacksmith came the lack of need for blacksmith's hand tools. Thus all types of traditional blacksmith tools and equipment began to disappear. Many ended up on the scrap iron pile. By 1965 there were no anvil makers in the United States; there were only a few in all of Europe. This is why you are going to have a hard time finding good used blacksmith equipment and tools. This is also why there are so few men living in the 1980s who have any personal experience in

the traditional blacksmith shop.

By 1940, for all practical purposes, the traditional blacksmith shop and its tools were obsolete. Most of the remaining tools and equipment were melted down before and during World War II. Some survived and can be found today, but good ones are rare.

With this history in mind, you can understand that you will need to make your tools. It will be hard work, but you can do it alone with very little expense. The lessons you have learned so far in this book give you a good basic knowledge to go ahead into tool making.

One very important group among these obsolete tools is the hand-held group. This terms refers to tools that have no handle. The tool is held directly in the hand, placed upon the work piece, and struck with a hammer. The chisel and the drift are among the few that have survived.

You learned in Chapter 8 to make some of these hand-held tools, hot-punches and drifts. The drift was made of automotive salvage; the hot-punch, of mild steel. Many of the tools you are about to make will be made from auto springs, axles, sway bars, torsion bars, and similar salvage steels. Some will be made of high-carbon new steel.

The following tools will be satisfactory if they are made from salvage auto parts or from carbon steel:

- Round and shaped hot-punches.
- Linch or cotter punches.
- Hot-splitters.
- Hot-cutters.
- Cold chisels.
- Hot side-cutters.
- Regular pattern fullers.
- Hot-gouges.
- Hand-sets.
- Tools of your own design for special needs.

After you have made the hand-held tools in the exercises below, you need only heat treat 1 to 2 inches of the working end. The hammer end should be left soft as it will be when it has been normalized. If you do decide to heat treat the hammer end, temper it to a dark blue or pale blue, between 570 and 610 degrees Fahrenheit.

A HOT-PUNCH FROM TOOL STEEL

This hot-punch from tool steel will be made the same way as the mild steel, round-taper punch you made in Chapter 8. This punch will be a little larger.

Stock Required

A piece of 5/8-inch round stock, 9 inches long. You may use AISI 1080 or W1 (1.0 percent) carbon steel or salvage spring steel.

Procedure

Heat one end to a yellow-orange. Draw out a round point 1 3/4 inches long to a 1/8-inch point. Make it as true as possible. When shaping is finished, heat it to a red-orange heat and set it on the back of the forge to cool slowly and normalize. Let it cool to room temperature.

When cool, file the point flat to about 3/16-inch diameter (Fig. 12-1). Heat the end of the point for

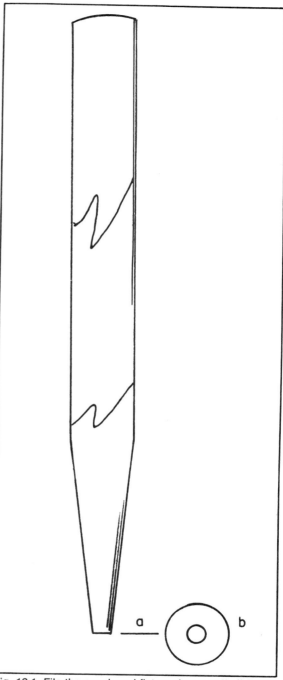

Fig. 12-1. File the punch end flat as shown at "a." Forge or grind a slight dome on the hammer end as at "b." This helps to center the hammer energy along the center of the tool.

about 3 inches until it reaches its critical heat. Remember, this is the point at which it loses magnetic pull. Be very careful not to burn the fine point.

Quench it in water at 70 to 85 degrees Fahrenheit until it reaches about 300 degrees Fahrenheit, frying pan hot. Let it cool to room temperature on the back of the forge.

Grind or file the butt end to a dome shape, which is proper for striking (Fig. 12-1). This tool does not need to be hardened. If you heat treat, quench it in oil. Draw the point to a light straw color and quench in water that is at the proper temperature.

Using and Caring
for Your Good Steel Punches

Fill an empty tin can between one-half and three-fourths full of kitchen fat.

To use the punch, mark the hole to be punched with your center-punch. Heat the work to orange. Place the work on the anvil face and center the punch on the mark. Strike easy. Lift the punch and dip it into the fat for about 1 inch. Recheck the location of the punch mark to make sure it is exactly where you want it. Place the punch on the mark and strike two hard blows quickly. Dip the punch into the fat again, repeat the striking, and dip again. When you feel the "thump," that is, you feel that the punch can go no farther, turn the work over and punch out the rosette. If the work has cooled to a low red, hit the rosette just hard enough to mark it. Reheat the work to a dark orange and finish the hole on the anvil face. Drift the hole to the required size as described in Chapter 8.

Remember that high-carbon, low-alloy steel and auto salvage steel are tough but they cannot take much heat. The maximum is 400 to 600 degrees Fahrenheit. Above this the tool begins to soften. In these temperature ranges the tool point will begin to mushroom. Cool as you go. You can dip the tool in water if necessary. I have a carbon steel punch I have used this way. It has punched more than 100 holes, and it has not yet needed to be reworked.

If you will need a hole that is smaller than you can make with the first punch, draw out a second punch that is a little finer and a little longer, perhaps with a 2 1/2-inch by 1/8-inch round point. Treat it as you did the larger one, but use it with great care because it will soak up heat very fast. Make it from the 5/8-inch round stock. The heavy stock will soak some heat out of the point.

A SQUARE HOT-PUNCH

In this exercise you will assume that you need to make a 3/8-inch square hole.

Stock Required

5/8-inch round stock, tool steel, 9 inches long.

One 3/8-inch square scrap of mild steel about 5 or 6 inches long.

Procedure

Make the punch point the same way you did for the round punch, but this time forge it square. The point should be 1 3/4 inches long by 3/16 inch square. Round off the edges a little and heat treat it.

Punch your hole the same way you did for the round hole. Don't make the hole too large.

Make a square drift from the piece of 3/8-inch scrap of mild steel. Forge a square tapered point on it. Make it so that it will enter the hole. Heat the work to an orange heat; place it over the pritchel hole or a bolster. Dip the 3/8-inch square stock in fat and drive it as you would a drift. Keep it well lubricated with fat. Work the hole from both sides until the square drift has opened the hole to size. A square slug or finish drift will serve well for this.

SLOT PUNCH,
LINCH PUNCH, AND COTTER PUNCH

The slot punch, linch punch and cotter punch are all similar in style. They work on the same principle as the round punch, but they punch out an elongated plug (Fig. 12-2). They are used like the round hot-punch. That is, you punch through the work on the anvil face until you make an elongated rosette on the other side. Then you turn the work over, punch out the plug, and shape the hole. In this case the slot punch is used to rough size the hole as well

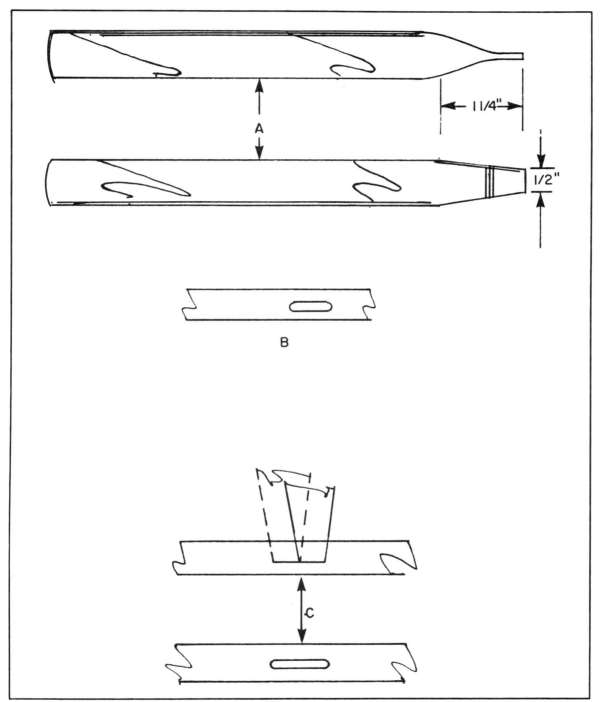

Fig. 12-2. Two views of the slot punch are shown at "A." "B" shows the type of hole made by a slot punch. "C" shows how progressive punching is used to make a long slot.

as to make it. A piece of flat stock the desired size can be worked in the hole like a drift to give the hole its final shape. A slug drift would work well here.

Stock Required

A piece of salvage or carbon steel, 5/8 inch round by 9 inches long.

Procedure

Taper the point to 1/16 inch thick and 1/2 inch wide in 1 1/4 inches.

Working over the radius of the anvil, thin the wide face down to 3/8 inch at 3/4 inch from the point. Keep the same sideways thickness of the punch. This will make a shoulder close to the cutting edge that brings the mass of the punch stock closer to the cutting edge. It also helps to soak up the heat from the point and prevents the slot from being opened too wide (Fig. 12-2).

The slot punch is used for slotting holes in round shafting for flat linch pins. A linch pin is a form of a cotter pin. The slot punch is also used as the first step in a method of opening large holes

in relatively small bar stock while still maintaining good side wall stock.

A wider slot punch with a 1/16-inch by 5/8-inch point, made from 3/4-inch or 7/8-inch stock is a handy tool for making long slots by progressive punching (Fig. 12-2).

A HOT-SPLITTER

The hand-held splitter is a useful and important tool. I prefer 7/8-inch round stock for this tool.

Stock Required

3/4-inch or 7/8-inch round stock, salvage or carbon steel, 9 inches long.

Procedure

Draw out a chisel-type point 1 1/2 inches long by 1 1/8 inches wide (Fig. 12-3). This is a flared chisel shape.

Work over the front anvil radius and *fuller* the point down 3/4 inch from the point to 3/16 inch thick. To fuller is to form an indentation during the forging process in order to move metal one way

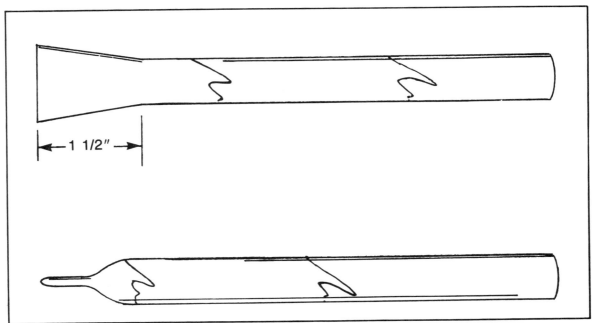

Fig. 12-3. The roughed out hot-splitter.

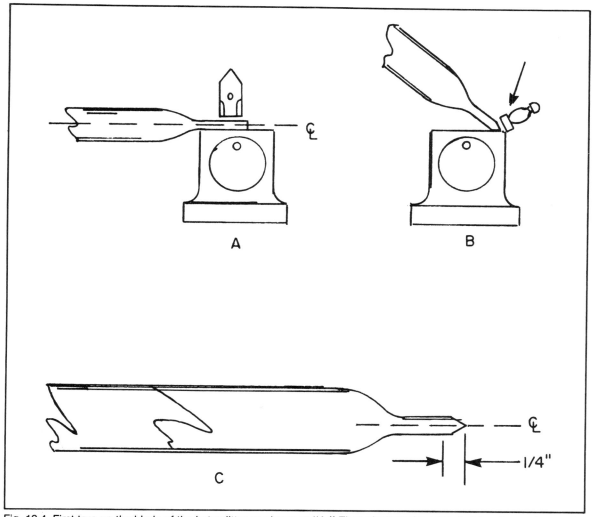

Fig. 12-4. First true up the blade of the hot-splitter as shown at "A." Then sharpen the edge, holding the work over the anvil radius as at "B." "C" shows the finished edge.

only. Maintain the original flare.

Sharpen a chisel cutting edge 1/4 inch long over the back radius of the anvil. Cool it slowly and file it to finished shape (Fig. 12-4).

Heat it to a low orange and allow it to cool slowly to room temperature on the back of the forge.

Using the Hot-Splitter

Remember that in all cases there must be a cutting plate under the work on the face of the anvil to pro-

tect it when you are using the hot-splitter. This is a sharp tool. The cutting plate should be made of fully annealed mild steel, 1/8 inch thick, 5 to 6 inches wide, and 6 inches long (Fig. 12-5). You can also use a piece of brass or bronze plate 3/16 inch thick, 4 inches wide, and 5 or 6 inches long. (See Chapter 13 for a fuller discussion of cutting plates.)

The hot-splitter is a short-bladed knife. It can be used to cut off corners or to split a piece of bar stock as needed. It can be used to split a bar endways while the bar is held in a vise.

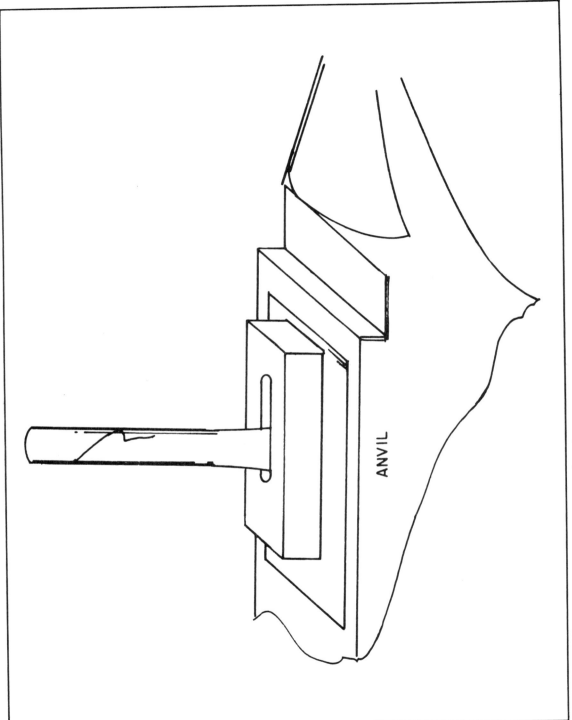

ANVIL

Fig. 12-5. Split as piece of work on a temporary cutting plate.

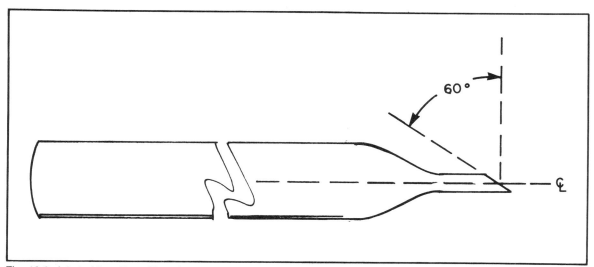

Fig. 12-6. A hot side-splitter. Note that the cutting edge is on one side. It forms a cutting edge very much like a wood chisel. The cutting angle should be about 60 degrees.

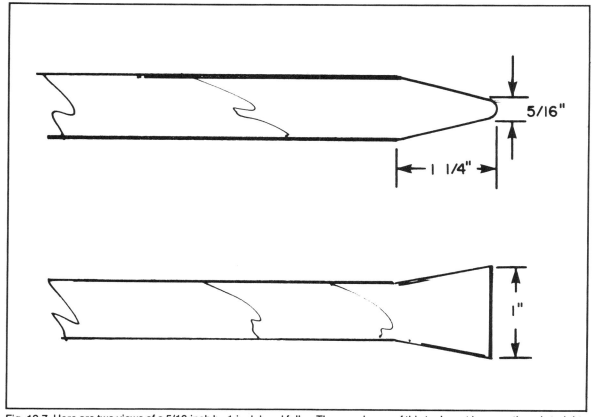

Fig. 12-7. Here are two views of a 5/16-inch by 1-inch hand fuller. The round nose of this tool must be smooth and straight.

The edge is thin and delicate. Keep it fully lubricated with fat. Work the iron in the color only. This is not a cold-cutting chisel in any sense.

A HOT SIDE-SPLITTER

The hot side-splitter is sometimes called the hot side-chisel. It is made and used just like the hot-splitter except that the final sharpening of the cutting edge is all to one side. This allows you to trim a piece off in order to leave square-cut sides or edges (Fig. 12-6). Heat treat this in the same manner as the other tools in this chapter.

A HAND FULLER

The hand fuller is used as any fuller for shouldering off a piece or rounding out a sharp inside corner in a forging (Fig. 12-7).

Stock Required

A 9-inch piece of 3/4-inch or 7/8-inch round salvage or carbon steel.

Procedure

Draw out a taper from stock size to 5/16 inch thick and as wide as it wants to go (Fig. 12-7). Normalize it.

File or grind the tapered end to a 5/32-inch radius so that when you finish, the end has a nose like one-half of a 5/16 inch bar. This bullnose must be carefully made so that no marks or creases are pressed into the hot metal under it.

You should also make a hand fuller with a bullnose having a 1/16-inch radius. This smaller fuller can be made of 5/8-inch or even of 1/2-inch salvage or carbon steel. Make it from 9 inches of stock.

Using the Hand Fuller

The fuller is used to move hot metal one way only. The action of the chisel edge spreads the metal away from the side of the chisel blade, but not away from the ends of the cutting edge. The fuller does not cut. It simply spreads the metal away from its sides, but not from its ends. To understand this process, you will make an L-shaped bracket blank with two different thicknesses (Fig. 12-9).

Stock Required

1-inch square stock, 16 inches long.

Procedure

Heat one end of the stock to a yellow-orange for about 2 inches. Place the fuller across the hot area about 1 inch from the hot end and drive it halfway through the stock as shown in Fig. 12-8. You will have a round bottom groove 1/2 inch deep.

Remove the fuller and place it crossways about 3/16 inch from the edge (Fig. 12-8). Drive it down until it is level with the first groove.

Move it back toward the center about 3/16 inch and repeat the process. As you do this, the end of the work will stretch out sideways. Continue across the end until you reach the other side. Heat as often as necessary to stay between a bright red and a yellow-orange. Work it hot.

Now go across the end again and fuller down the ridges (Fig. 12-9). Reheat if necessary.

Using your hammer only, flatten down the small ridges and square up the fullered-out end until it is 1/2 inch thick, 1 inch wide, and 2 inches long.

You will find this to be a useful forging procedure.

HOT-GOUGES

Hot-gouges are used to cut curves or carve out metal. They are useful for trimming excess metal in forgings.

Make your hot-gouge like the hot side-splitter, but curve the cutting edge. Have the bevel to the inside of the curve. For your first hot-gouge, put about 3/4-inch to 1-inch radius in the cutting edge (Fig. 12-10).

A HAND-SET OR FLATTER

The hand-set is not used much, but when you need it nothing can take its place. It is ideal for the final flatting of the mating faces of a pair of tongs or for dressing a piece tight against a shoulder.

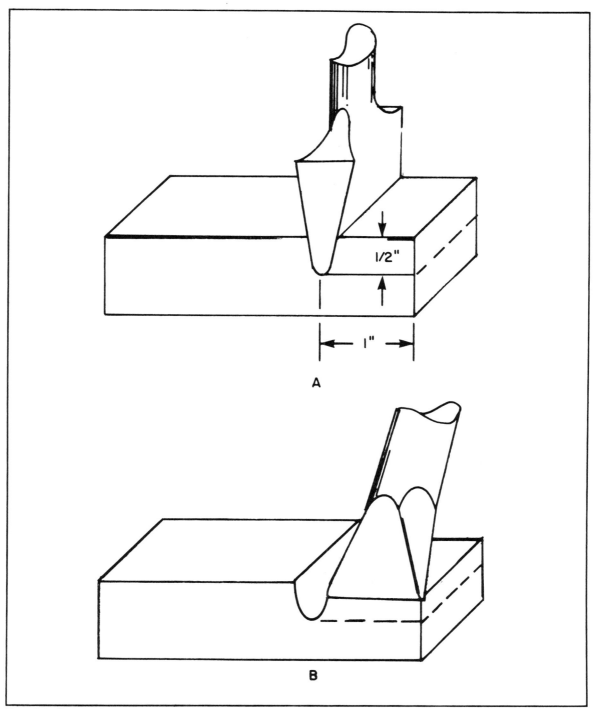

A

B

Fig. 12-8. Sink the fuller 1/2 inch into the 1-inch square bar as shown at "A." At "B" the fuller is resting sideways on the end of the bar. It is ready to fuller out the end.

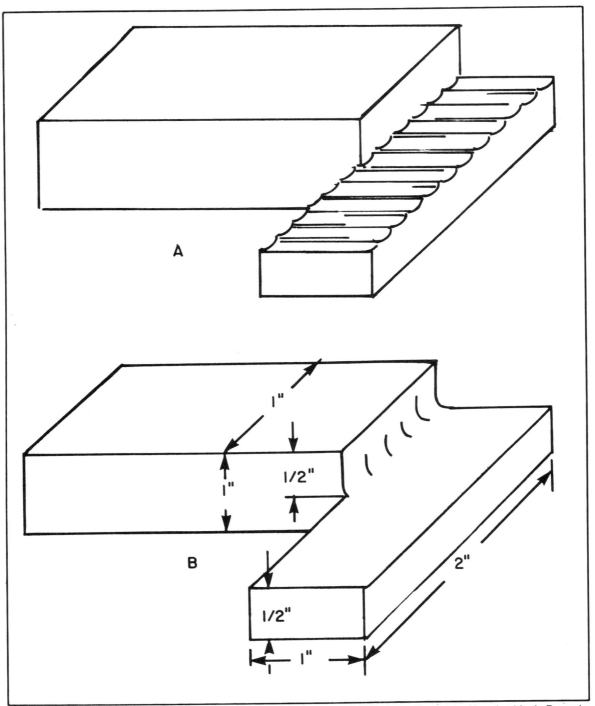

Fig. 12-9. After careful fullering the work should look like illustration ''A.'' ''B'' shows the finished bracket blank. Properly done, this makes an exceptionally strong structure.

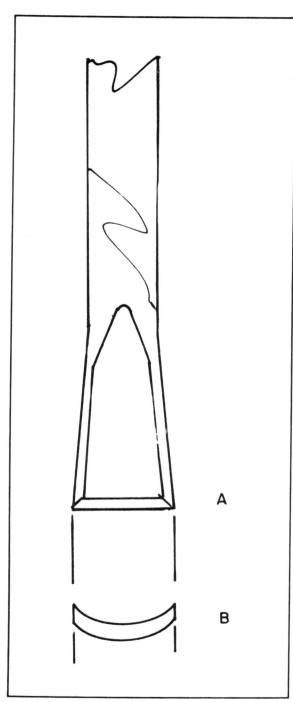

Fig. 12-10. The hot-gouge has a curved cutting edge as shown at "B," rather than the straight edge of the hot side-splitter at "A."

Stock Required

One piece of 7/8-inch round salvage or carbon steel, 10 inches long.

Procedure

Upset one end of the piece to 1 1/2 times its diameter.

Flatten the upset end so it has its face perpendicular to the axis of the bar. While you are flattening, square the upset end in sideways (Fig. 12-11). As much as possible, avoid losing cross section dimension.

Keep squaring the end until the corners at the flat face have about a 1/16-inch radius. While you are forging, hold the flat end square on the anvil face with the shaft truly vertical to the anvil face. If you are careful, very little grinding or filing will be necessary.

Normalize and heat treat as you have all the other hand-held tools.

OTHER HAND-HELD TOOLS

As you go along, you will have need for hand-held tools of various other shapes. Most of them will be made like the tools in the preceding exercises. Be careful. Some of these hand-held tools will have very hard cutting edges, corners, or ends as a result of your having heat treated them. Never use hot-cutting tools on cold steel as you may break them.

When the tools are used on hot work, they will draw heat from the work piece and soften a bit, especially along the very thin edges. If you make a habit of keeping them wet with fat and give them a chance to cool in the fat, they will hold up remarkably well. If you think you are heating a tool too much or if it will not cool fast enough in the fat, then quickly dip it in water. You have put hours of work and piles of fuel into these tools; respect them, and they will serve you well for a long time.

Many "hot working" steels can be subjected to terrific heats and pressures yet still hold their shape and sharp edges. They are the high-speed steels and high-alloy steels. They are designed for big industry and do not usually lend themselves well to the hand-powered, coal-fired blacksmith shop.

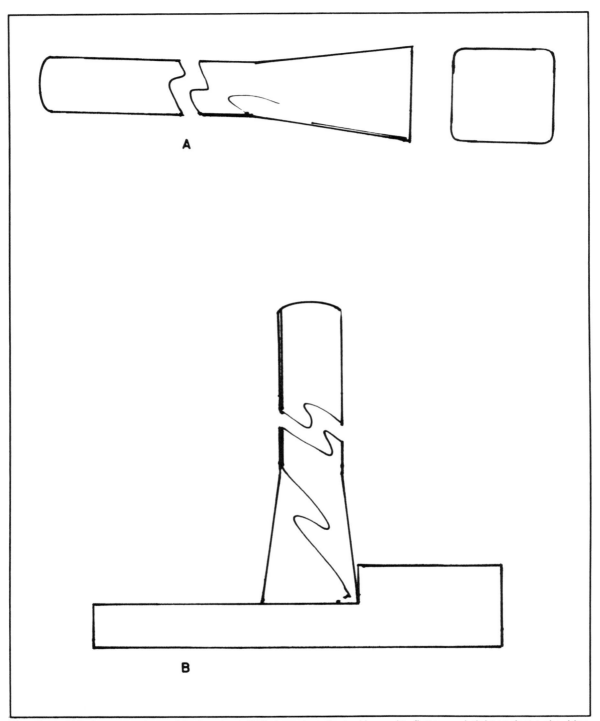

Fig. 12-11. "A" shows two views of the hand-set. "B" shows how the tool is used to flatten work tight against a shoulder.

If you are interested in these steels, consult your supplier and inquire about various "tool room" steels.

The tools made from some of these steels will be harder, and can seriously damage your anvil. The striking end of these tools are also very hard. Keep it ground with a smooth, gentle crown, or it will damage your hammer face. If this happens, your hammer will mark your work every place you hit it.

PART 3

Advanced Work

Chapter 13

Special Purpose Tools

B Y THIS TIME YOU HAVE ENCOUNTERED some problems that can be solved more easily if you have specialized tools. You will want a cutting plate to protect your anvil when you are using your punches and chisels. It should be designed to stay put while you are working. A hold-down acts as an extra hand and is very helpful. The bending fork is used to bend hot work held in the vise. A spring fuller is a real help in a one-man shop, and the cutting hardy is a real work saver. These tools will be found in any well-equipped shop.

As with the hand-held tools, you will probably find that you must make these specialized tools yourself.

HOT-CUTTING PLATES

A hot-cutting plate covers the face of your anvil and protects it and your tool when you are using cutting tools. It can be made of any soft metal that will not damage the cutting edge of the tool when it comes through the work. It must be thick enough and tough enough to prevent the cutting edge from passing through it and damaging the anvil face. The plate is shaped as shown in Fig. 13-1.

A Mild Steel Cutting Plate

A cutting plate can be made from a piece of mild steel 1/8 inch thick, between 4 and 6 inches wide. Mild steel makes a good cutting plate, and it is cheap. The plate should be cut long enough to allow a 1-inch skirt over each side of the anvil.

A Brass or Bronze Plate

Brass and bronze make good cutting plates that do not seem to skid around much on the anvil face and will not damage any blacksmith cutting edge. Brass or bronze will pick up heat fast and will retain it longer than iron or steel. It scars badly in use. Make the brass or bronze plate the same size as the mild steel plate, but make it at least 3/16 inch thick.

The Copper Cutting Plate

Copper 3/16 inch thick or thicker can be used, but

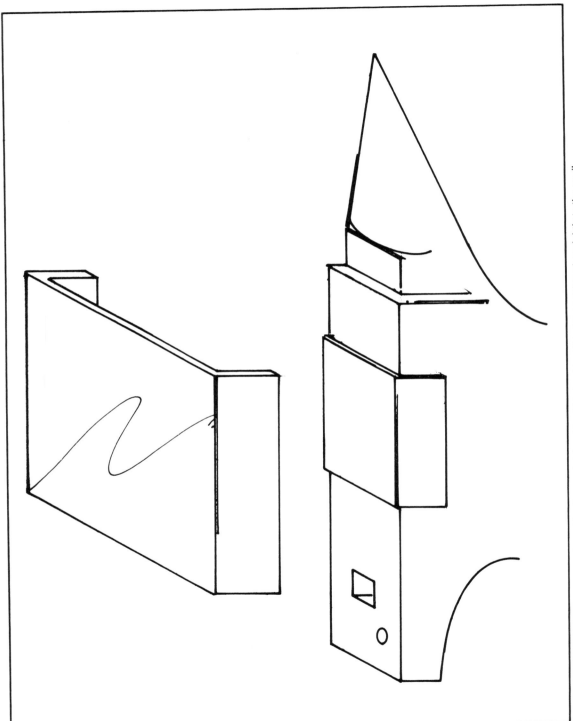

Fig. 13-1. A saddle-type cutting plate for cold or hot work. The side skirt should not bind the cutting plate tightly to the anvil.

it is quite soft and tends to squash out under the load of repeated heavy cutting. It scars badly, even worse than brass or bronze.

Use of the Cutting Plate

When you are cutting, ease up on your last blow. I consider it a foolish practice to send a hot cut-off flying around the shop. Also the last blow, the one that cuts through, marks up your cutting plate in direct proportion to the strength of the hammer blow. Marks on your cutting plate will show up on the back of your work just as marks on the face of the anvil do.

THE HOLD-DOWN

The hold-down acts as an extra hand to hold work firmly on the anvil while you are working on it. The pritchel hold-down is the handiest one I know and the simplest to make. The finished hold-down is shown in Fig. 13-5.

Stock Required

Use any 18-inch piece of round bar stock that will fit in the pritchel hole with a 1/32-inch to 1/16-inch clearance. I call this a "rattling good fit." A piece of salvage auto coil spring is just right.

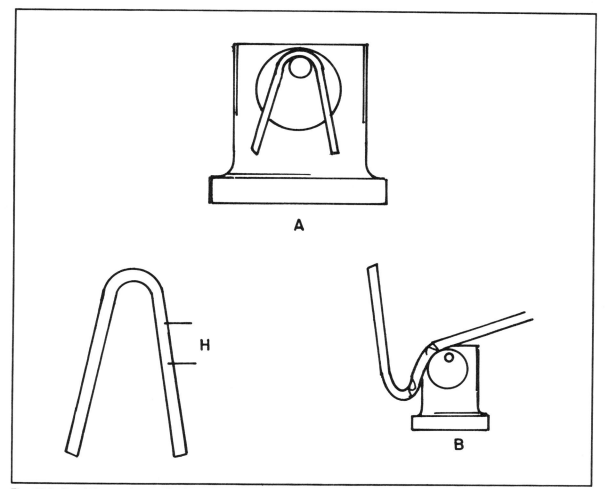

Fig. 13-2. Bend the stock over the horn as at "A." Heat the portion indicated at "H" and bend it as shown at "B."

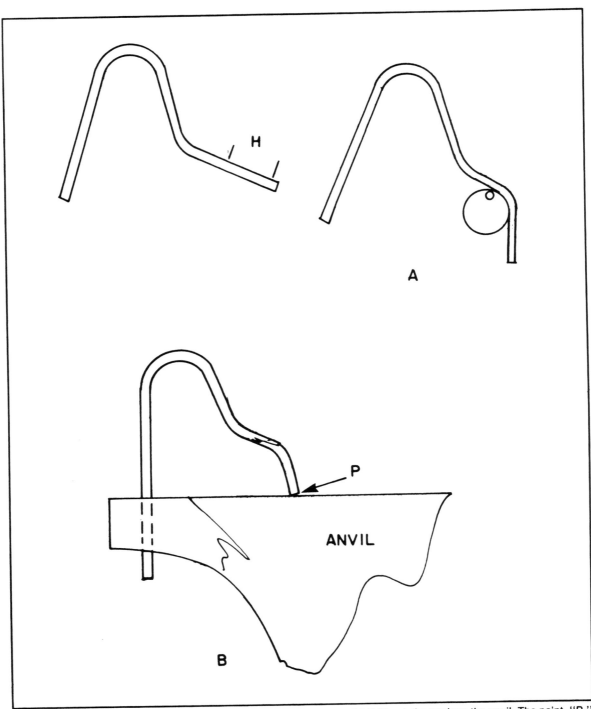

Fig. 13-3. Heat at ''H'' and bend the heated portion down as shown at ''A.'' Check the work on the anvil. The point, ''P,'' should rest on the anvil. It should look like illustration ''B.''

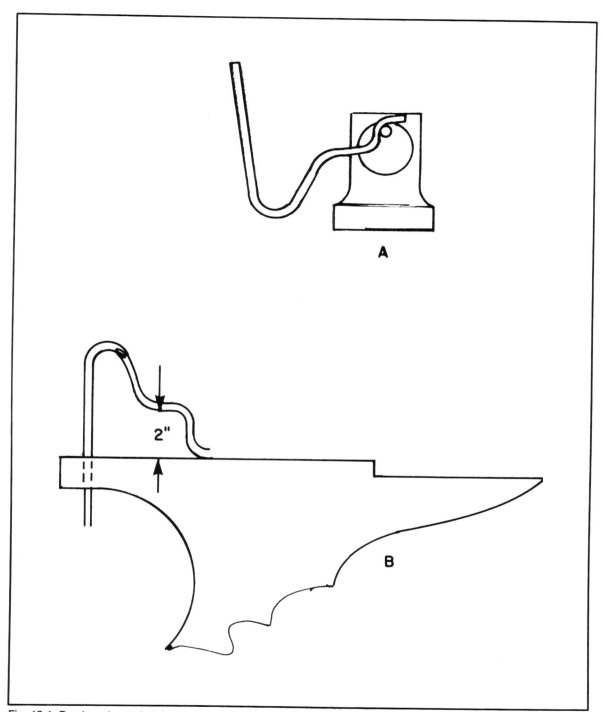

Fig. 13-4. Bend up the end of the bar, indicated by point "P" in Fig. 13-3, until it is almost perpendicular to the long straight leg as at "A." Flatten it to form a 1-inch foot. Check for a clearance of about 2 inches as indicated at "B."

Procedure

The hold-down is a particularly tricky tool to describe, so study Figs. 13-2 through 13-5 before starting.

Heat about 4 inches in the middle of the bar to a dark orange heat.

Hold both ends, lay the heated portion over the horn and bend it almost double as if you were forming part of a 2 1/2-inch ring (Fig. 13-2). Let this bend cool to loss of color.

Heat the middle of one of the legs for about 3 inches. Bend the bar the other way over the horn until this portion is not quite parallel to the long end (Fig. 13-2). Let it cool to no color.

Heat the remaining short, uncurved end up to the last curve you made; bend the last 1 1/2-inches or so in the same direction as the first bend until the leg is not quite parallel to the long arm (Fig. 13-3). Let it cool to no color.

Place the long arm in the pritchel hole. Do not force it down. Look at the contact of point "p" and the anvil face in Fig. 13-3.

Heat the end at point "p" to an orange forging heat; form a foot on the arm by flattening it to about half the stock thickness for 1 inch. Then bend the end up to form the foot (Fig. 13-4).

Put the bar back into the pritchel hole and check for contact of the foot with the anvil face (Fig. 13-5). Two inches of the bar should stick out the bottom of the pritchel hole. Don't force it. If these conditions are not met, heat the curve that needs correcting and bend it as needed. The long arm that

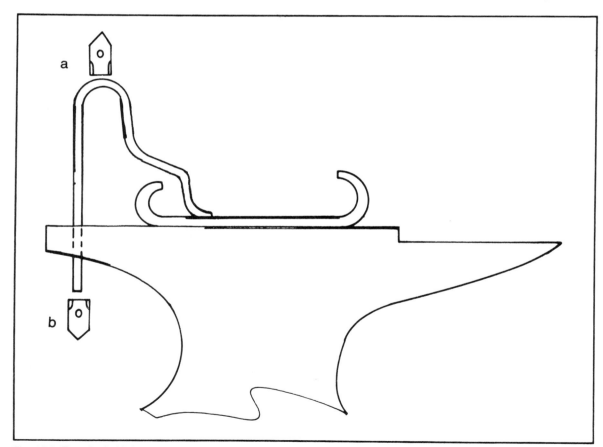

Fig. 13-5. Test the hold-down on a piece of iron. It should hold the piece firmly. To tighten the grip, hit the top as shown at "a." To release the hold-down, hit the long leg as shown at "b."

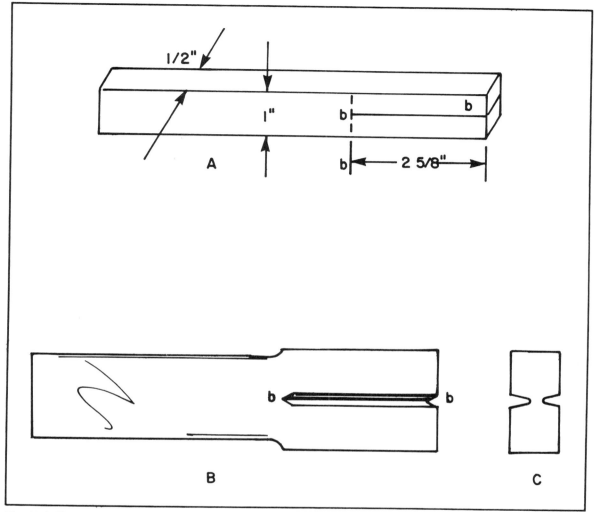

Fig. 13-6. The layout of the billet is shown at "A." At "B" the billet is cut nearly through along line "b-b." "C" shows the end view of the billet after it has been cut.

goes into the pritchel hole must be straight or slightly curved for its full length to increase the holding power.

When all is correct, no portion of the curved arm should be closer than 1 1/2-inches above the anvil face. This is to give clearance under the arm to hold down odd-shaped pieces (Fig. 13-5).

Let the work cool completely in the air as fast as it will. Do not quench it at any time. It does not need heat treating regardless of the type of steel.

When it has reached air temperature, put a

work piece on the anvil, put the hold-down in the pritchel hole with the foot on the work piece and tap it gently on the top curve. It should take a tight, clamplike hold on the work piece (Fig. 13-5).

To remove the hold-down, bump the bottom of the bar below the pritchel hole, and it will turn loose. Wire brush it and do not oil it. Oil will prevent it from working.

If the tool does not hold the work piece, check the pritchel hole to see if it has fat or oil in it. Run a piece of red hot iron through the hole to warm up whatever is in there. Wipe the hole clean with wadding made from paper toweling. Then dust the length of the hole with ash and cinders from under your forge.

To remove or adjust the tool, tap the bottom of the hold-down and lift it out or readjust as needed (Fig. 13-5).

THE BENDING FORK

A bending fork is used, as its name implies, to bend a work piece that is held in the vise.

You can get some very good training and make yourself a useful tool by forging a fork out of a solid *billet*, a piece of iron or steel not less than 1 inch in cross section and not more than 12 inches long.

Stock Required

1/2-inch by 1-inch by 7-inch stock, M.S. 1040 carbon steel will give a better product, but it is harder to work than mild steel.

One piece of 1/2-inch pipe, 14 inches long.

Procedure

Lay out one end of your bar stock as shown in Fig. 13-6. Mark the layout with a cold chisel. The mark should be deep enough so that it won't be lost in the fire. Have your can of kitchen fat and hot-splitter close at hand. Have your hot-cutting plate ready.

Heat the marked end to a yellow-orange heat. Split the piece from both sides, starting at the end. Go nearly through (Fig. 13-6).

Put the billet upright in the vise leaving all the marked-off area showing. Lubricate your splitter again and split the cut end down to the bottom of the mark. The cutting action also spreads the split ends. They will become the fingers (Fig. 13-7).

Drive your 5/16-inch hand fuller down into the split. Let it bottom out. When the work reaches a red heat, reheat it and return it to the vise.

Bend the left finger down. As you do this, keep the crotch well rounded with the fuller. Stop this process at a full red heat. Reheat and continue bending the finger down until it is at a right angle to the body of the stock (Fig. 13-7).

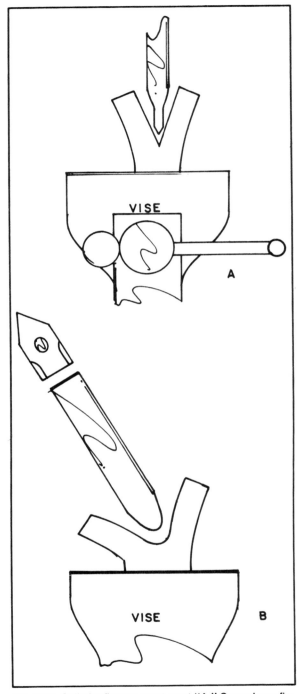

Fig. 13-7. Split the fingers apart as at "A." Spread one finger out using the hammer and fuller. The billet should look like "B" when it has been spread out.

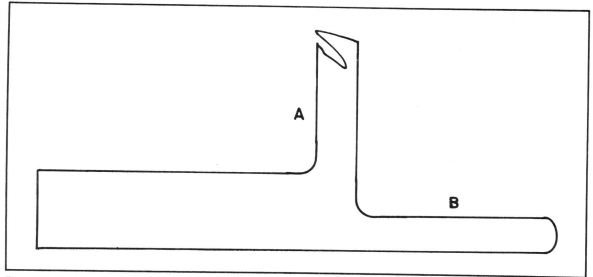

Fig. 13-8. Heat the finger "A" and forge it round. Keep it straight and at a right angle to the billet. Keep the juncture of the bends round. Heat finger "B" and forge it round; round off the end.

Heat this finger and forge it round. Keep it straight. Leave the end blunt (Fig. 13-8).

Heat the other finger and forge it round. Round off the end a little (Fig. 13-8).

Heat the body of the work yellow-orange. Hold the finger that has not been bent with your hollow-bit tongs. Draw out the body of the work into the beginning of a handle (Fig. 13-9). Forge it down to a 5/8-inch end and round the end.

You will bend the finger that has remained straight. Bend it so that it parallels the other finger. Leave about 1/2-inch clearance between the two fingers. Cut off the end of the longer finger to match the shorter one and round the end of it like the other (Fig. 13-10). True up the work and smooth the ends of the fingers with a file.

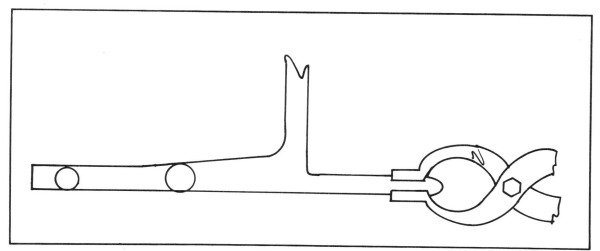

Fig. 13-9. Hold the long straight finger in the tong and start forging out the beginning of a handle. The circles in the handle indicate a cross section view.

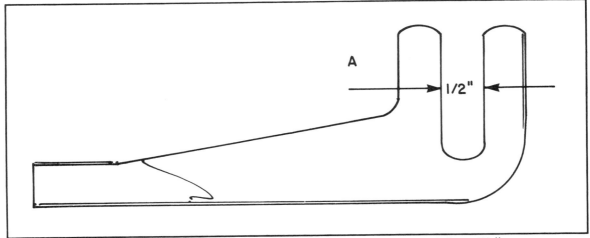

Fig. 13-10. Bend the straight-out finger to parallel finger "A"; cut and round it to match finger "A."

With a hacksaw remove the threads from the piece of 1/2-inch pipe. Remove any burrs and chips from inside the pipe.

Continue to forge the handle you started into a straight shank about 1 inch long. You want it to fit snugly into the pipe. It should require a little pressure to slide the pipe over it. Let the balance of the stock taper up as it will. Drive the pipe onto the handle portion of the fork. This provides you with a handle of usable length (Fig. 13-11).

You will find this bending fork to be a handy tool. Use it for bending hot work only.

A CUT-OFF HARDY

A cut-off hardy is, in effect, a stationary knife that is placed into the hardy hole on the end of the an-vil with the cutting edge of the blade looking up. It is probably the most useful of all the hardy tools. To finish this tool you will need to have a small amount of welding done.

The hardy should be made from the hard steels. Mild steel will not do the job here. The hardy needs strength more than any other cutting edge you will be using. Make it from an automobile axle shaft, a torsion bar, or 1040 to 1060 carbon steel. The hardy described below will be a good general purpose tool for hot and cold cutting.

Stock Required

One salvage automotive axle shaft 1/8 inch to 1/4 inch larger than the hardy hole. Measure your hardy hole from side to side, not diagonally.

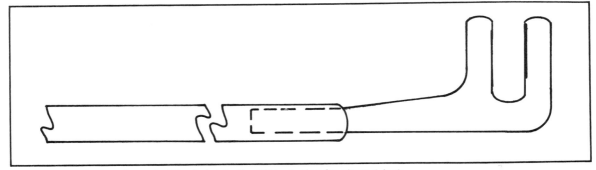

Fig. 13-11. Fit the handle end of the fork into the 1/2-inch pipe for about 1 inch.

Procedure

The front face of the hardy hole will be longer than the back face. Measure this longer side. The shank of your hardy should be at least 1 inch longer than this (Fig. 13-12).

Cut off the spline or flange of the axle squarely with a hacksaw. You will be surprised at how well this goes. Do not use a cutting torch because the burning action of the torch will ruin the steel as much as 1/4 inch deep.

Heat the cut end of the shaft to a yellow-orange and draw it to an elongated chisel edge (Fig. 13-13). Let it spread as it will. Try to maintain a 50-degree cutting angle (Fig. 13-13). Keep the side faces of the tool well formed and flat. Be sure the cutting edge is on the axial center line and square with the same line (Fig. 13-13).

Hold the cutting head 3/4 inch beyond the back edge of the anvil where the edge is sharp. You are starting a shoulder. Keep the shaft flat on the anvil face. You want no taper in this flat portion (Fig. 13-14).

Start behind the cutting head or blade of the hardy and forge a square shank with squared-off shoulders just at the round portion 3/4 inch below the bevel of the blade. Work all the way across the anvil face. Do not bend or taper the squared portion of the shaft. Use a steel square or any kind of instrument to make sure you are not forging a diamond shape (Fig. 13-14).

If your anvil has a 3-inch-long hardy hole, you will want the squared-off tang to be at least 4 inches long. Do not try to get rid of any rounded corners if this will reduce the tang to less than 1 inch between flat sides or *flats*. The flat sides themselves may be as little as 1/2 inch wide. You want to finish with a 1-inch-by-1-inch tang that is at least 1 inch longer than the long side of your hardy hole (Fig. 13-12).

Cut the hardy off at this 4-inch point with a hacksaw or a torch. Smooth the cut-off and let it cool to shop temperature. Try it in the hardy hole. If it does not go into the hole, file or grind the tang until it does.

Go to someone who has an arc welder and have a piece of 3/8-inch round mild steel welded squarely

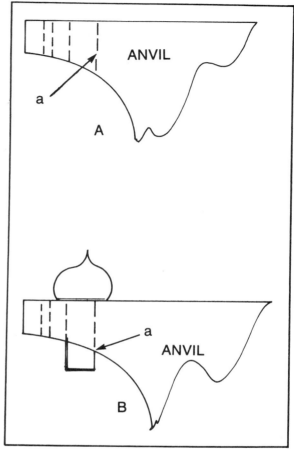

Fig. 13-12. Measure the hardy hole at the point "a" in illustration "A." When it is in place, the hardy shank will look like illustration "B."

around the 3/4-inch round portion of the hardy (Fig. 13-15). The weld should fill nicely under the 3/8-inch stock because you are building up strength above the shoulder (Fig. 13-15). Be sure the flats extend all the way up to this newly welded collar. The hardy rests on this collar when it is in the hardy hole.

Have a 14-inch or 16-inch piece of 1/2-inch bar stock-welded to the bottom of the hardy. This gives you an ideal handle to use during heat treatment of the hardy. When you are all finished with the piece, break the handle off.

The completed hardy should go freely into the hole in any one of the four possible positions. It

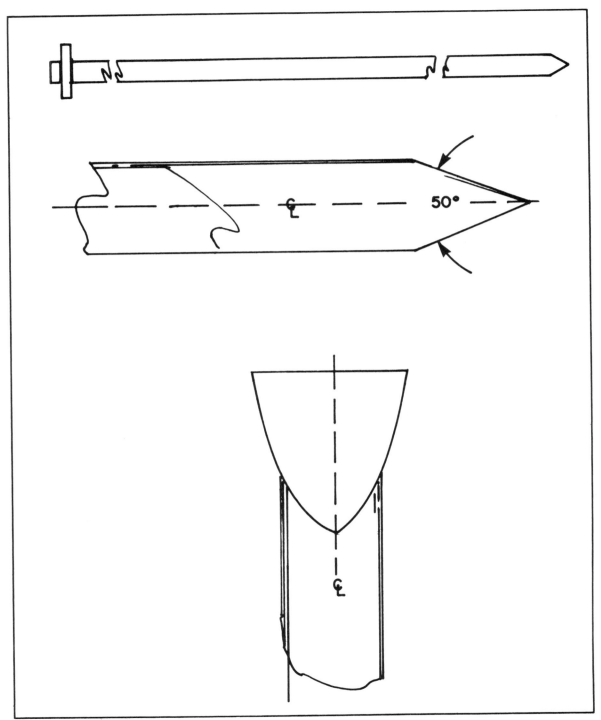

Fig. 13-13. Shape a chisel like a cutting edge as shown here.

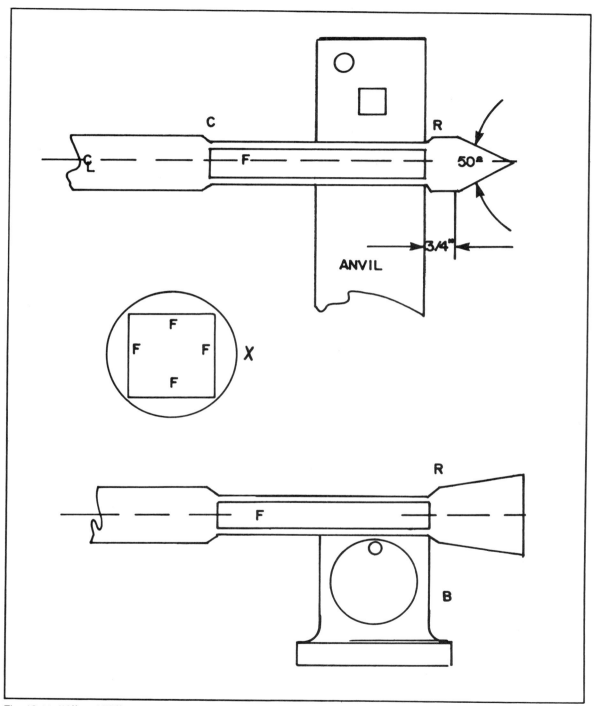

Fig. 13-14. "A" and "B" show the proper position of the axle shaft across the anvil. In both views the area at "F" shows the relative location of the flats. "R" indicates the 3/4-inch round, and "C" is the cut-off point.

187

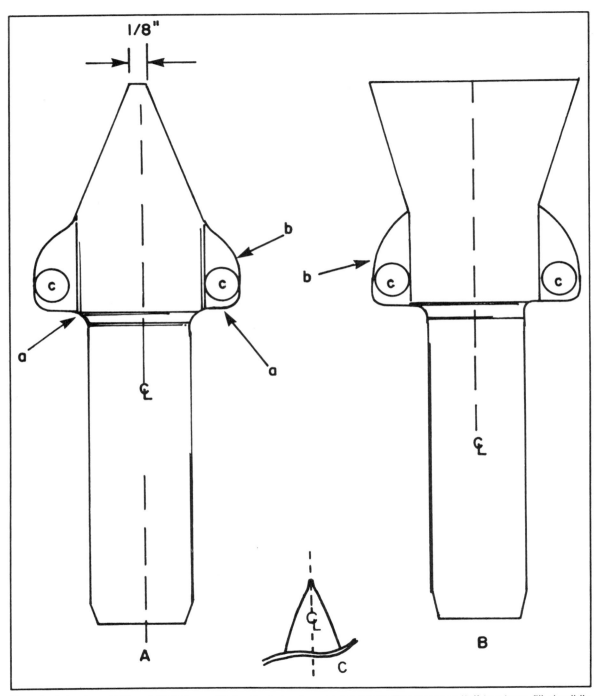

Fig. 13-15. In views "A" and "B," the welded collar is in place on the hardy. The space at "a" has been filled solidly around the rod, "c." When it is finished, it must present a flat surface to the anvil. The area at "b" is built up to add strength. View "C" shows the finished cutting edge.

should sit squarely on the anvil so that there is no rocking motion in any position. Clean the hardy with a file as necessary.

The bottom of the hardy shank should be tapered a little for about 1/4 inch all around, particularly at the corners. Form time to time you will find that you need to knock the hardy out of its hole with your hammer. If the shank is not tapered, you may find that the hammer blow will swell the shank or peen it over the edge of the shank so that you can't get the hardy out of the hole.

When all is fitted and the cutting edge has been dressed by grinding or filing to about 1/16 inch wide, no sharper, anneal the whole thing using wood ash as the cooling agent. Get a good blanket of ash all around it. Don't neglect to get plenty of ash underneath.

Hardening and Tempering the Hardy

After annealing you will harden and temper the hardy. This reheating is tricky, so follow these steps carefully.

Reduce the size of your fire.

Arrange the hardy so that the cutting edge is near the far edge of the fire (Fig. 13-16). The head and, particularly, the cutting edge must not be allowed to get hotter than the hardening heat. Go back to your notes and test pieces and refresh your memory on hardening and tempering. Use your magnet.

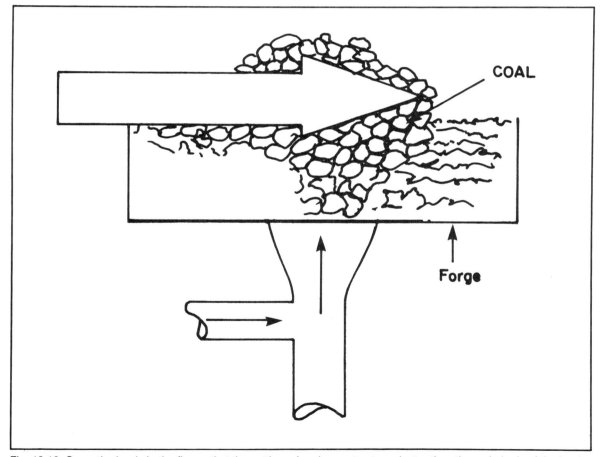

Fig. 13-16. Cover the hardy in the fire so that the cutting edge does not get any hotter than the main body of the hardy. As the whole hardy comes to heat, keep turning it over in the fire to get an even heat all the way through.

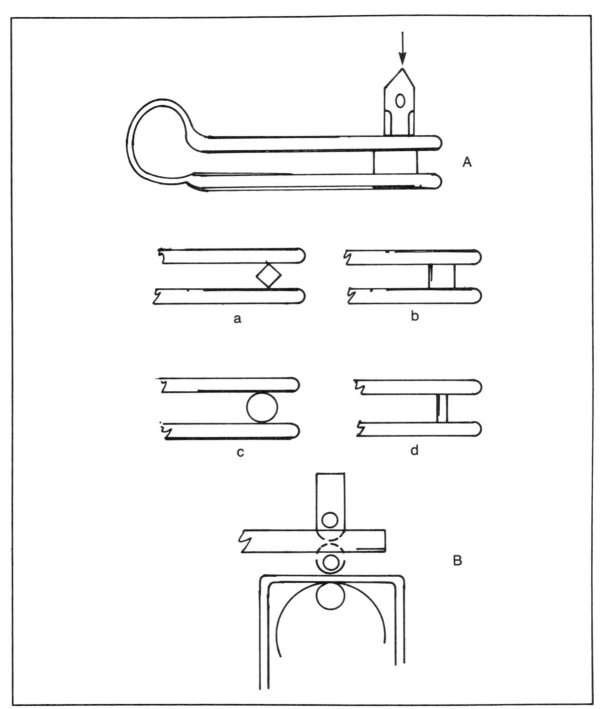

Fig. 13-17. "A" shows the spring fuller with a work piece in place. Some of the various shapes that can be worked with the spring fuller are shown at "a," "b," "c," and "d." At "B" you see an end view of the fuller with a work piece in place.

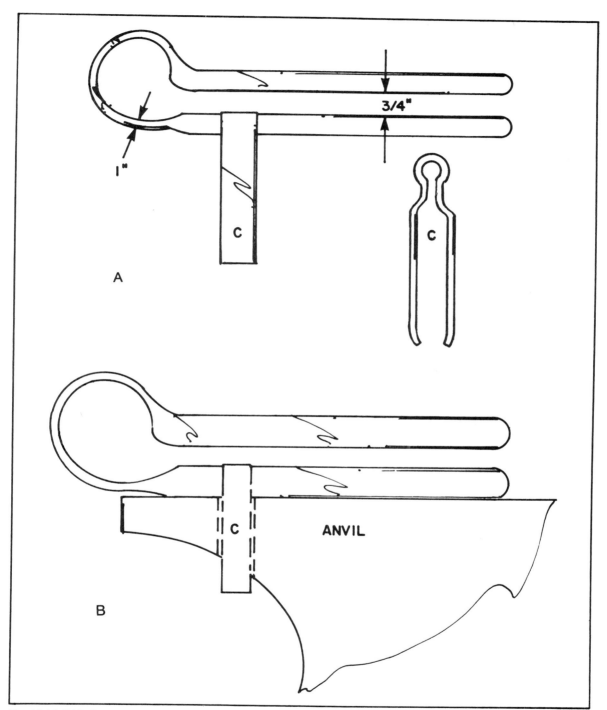

Fig. 13-18. ''A'' shows the completed fuller with its hairpin retainer. ''c'' is the hairpin retainer. The spring fuller and retainer are shown in place over the hardy hole at ''B.''

Bring the heat up very slowly. Turn the hardy over from time to time to avoid cool or overheated spots.

Bring the body and the edge to near hardening heat. When the work is nearly at hardening heat, draw the edge back toward the heart of the fire a little and let it come to full hardening heat. Odd-shaped pieces like a hardy are difficult to heat evenly.

When the hardening heat is reached, do not test or lose any time. Quench the entire hardy in water, which should be at 70 to 85 degrees Fahrenheit, until the head is cool to the touch.

Scrub one side of the cutting head clean so you can see the heat run toward the cutting edge. Then place the hardy on the resting fire so the cutting edge is beyond the fire. Don't rush the tempering heat. As the color first appears, watch closely. When the last 3/8 inch or so of the edge shows a dark gold to purple-gold color, immediately pull the hardy out and quench it. Keep it moving in the quench all the time. Give it a full 5 minutes by the clock.

When the heat treatment is finished, sharpen the cutting edge to a dull wire edge with a 60-degree included angle. Hollow out the cheek a little as shown in Fig. 13-15.

Be sure not to heat up the edge while you are hollow grinding.

Some final words of caution: an irregular mass the size of a hardy will not cool evenly. The smaller portion suffers accordingly; give it plenty of time so the stored heat will not run out to the cutting edge and soften it.

A SPRING FULLER

The spring fuller allows you to fuller both sides of a work piece at the same time.

Stock Required

A piece of round automotive coil spring stock about 18 inches long and between 1/2 inch and 5/8 inch in diameter.

Procedure

Flatten a 6-inch section in the center of the stock to 1/8 inch thick. Let the flattened section taper back to stock size in 1 inch at both ends of the section. Be sure that the round parts are straight.

Bend in the flattened part of the bar to an off-center circle as shown in Fig. 13-17. Let it cool to cold.

Normalize the bow and an inch or so to each side of the bow. After you have normalized, it requires no further heat treatment.

Make a hairpin retainer for the fuller as shown in Fig. 13-17. The stock should be 1/8 inch thick and nearly as wide as your hardy hole. The stock must fit in the hole freely. Figure 13-17 shows the complete assembly ready for use. Spread the arms of the hairpin a little to keep the fuller tight in the hardy hole.

To use the spring fuller, bring the work to forging heat. Put it between the two arms of the fuller. If the work piece is a little larger than the "at rest" opening of the two arms, stick a piece of flat stock between the arms and twist. The arms will open. When the work is in place, hold it parallel to the anvil face at all times. Strike the top arm directly over the work. This results in fullering both sides of the work piece at one time. You can fuller a piece round, square, or any shape you wish.

You can revolve the work piece for round fullering or hold it in one position for such work as starting a tongue. Keep a close watch on your work because the fuller works quickly, and you can easily fuller too deeply. There is no way to recover if this happens.

Work the stock only in the last 2 inches of the fuller arms. Don't force work into the fuller. The work must not be more than 1/4 inch larger than the relaxed opening of the fuller. The work pieces need not fill the fuller (Fig. 13-18). Any thickness up to the fuller's maximum can be worked in it.

Chapter 14

Forge Welding

T HERE ARE THREE FORMS OF WELDING. ANY one of them will do the job of bonding together two similar pieces of iron or steel.

Arc or electric welding uses heat created by an electric arc to melt the joining edges of metal together and, at the same time, from another source add the molten metal necessary to fill the weld. The state of the art today can produce very satisfactory results in keeping with the skill of the worker. Fuse welding, a method that welds without adding additional material to the weld when using the arc, is very difficult and requires great skill. In my experience it is tricky for the blacksmith to forge a previously arc-welded area into a different shape. You will seldom be successful.

Oxyacetylene or gas welding, like arc welding, is a melting process. The spread of heat from the welded area into the body of the work is much greater with gas welding than it is with electric welding; bringing the work to a full welding heat or melt is much slower. The heat of the flame is much lower than with the arc. It is quite practical for the blacksmith to hot forge an area that has been

gas welded although considerable skill and practice are needed for satisfactory results.

Forge welding or fire welding is the third process of joining similar metals. It is completely different from gas or arc welding. The areas to be welded are not brought to a melting heat. Melting heat is much too hot. If the area of the weld were at a melting heat, it could not be struck to make the joint because molten metal is a liquid and will flow. In general the forge or fire weld, section for section, might not be as strong as either gas or arc welding because of the difficulties in making a complete weld without including extraneous materials that create invisible flaws. In all cases there is no way to make a poor forge weld better. If it is bad, cut it out, bring in some new metal, and start all over again.

To ensure a clear distinction between forge or fire welding and the modern oxyacetylene and arc welding, I will use the term "forge welding" to refer to the processes used in traditional blacksmithing. Forge welding and fire welding are the same process. Flame welding refers to the process of gas welding, using some form of a blow-pipe, nozzle, or torch, which melts the weld area so that both pieces flow together and freeze or congeal into a solid mass. Additional metal is usually added to the work in either gas or arc welding.

In forge welding the two pieces of iron or steel or a mix of the two are joined by cohesion. This is a process in which the two surfaces are brought to nearly plastic heat. That is, the surface is soft enough to allow the molecules of each piece to mix and interlock with one another when they are forced together under pressure. It remains cool enough that the two pieces will retain most of their original shape if too much pressure is not applied. In practical use this would mean not hitting too hard with the hammer. No additional metal is added to the weld in forge welding.

The joining surfaces will not splash away, as they might in other types of welding, because the metal never reaches a molten state, which is to be avoided in forge welding. The best way to describe forge welding as compared to the other methods is to give an example. Slowly warm one end of each of two chocolate bars until you can shove the two warm ends together and the two bars become one. In the process, and this is my main point, the general shape of neither chocolate bar has changed. The space has vanished where the two bar ends were stuck together; no additional chocolate has been added, and you have one bar approximately as long as the combined lengths of the original two.

Remember that the larger the two pieces and the closer they are to being equal in mass, the easier the weld because the larger the mass, the slower the heat loss after the work leaves the fire. For this reason blacksmith demonstrators at blacksmith workshops and other shows always use heavy bar stock to demonstrate forge welding. Forge welding small, intricate items is an entirely different procedure. It is not usually practical at demonstrations where it is nearly impossible to provide the necessary controlled conditions for the work.

BASIC STEPS IN FORGE WELDING

In this section you will take a quick look at the forge welding sequence. When you have read through the

procedure, go on to the next section, which explains each action in detail. Study the steps carefully and practice them many times before you attempt a project.

Stock Required

Start with 1/2-inch bar stock, either round or square, M.S.

Procedure

Build your regular smithing fire. Start getting some coke into it as you learned earlier, but don't crowd it. Check your fire and remove the clinker. Blow out the loose ash with a short burst of air from the blower. Settle the coke into the center of the tuyere and pile it up. It should be about 4 inches deep to weld 3/8-inch bar stock, 5 inches to 5 1/2 inches for 1/2-inch bar stock, 6 inches deep for anything bigger. Study Fig. 14-1. The welding fire should be flat on top. Work right along because your welding fire will burn out quickly.

Lay the two ends to be welded just beyond the exact center of the fire so they are directly over the heart of the fire, close together, but not touching. Adjust them to about 1/4 inch apart and cover the work with coke. While you are waiting for the metal to reach a welding heat, make sure that your hammer is at hand on a clean anvil.

When the pieces have reached welding heat, bring them out of the fire, bump the stock (not the weld points) against the edge of the forge or anvil to knock off scale. Do not bump too hard, or you will bend the work.

Place one piece on the anvil, place the other in the joining position, grab your hammer, and strike directly over the join spot. The two pieces should be stuck. Turn them over and hit the exact join spot again, and the weld is made.

A DETAILED
DISCUSSION OF FORGE WELDING

The balance of this chapter discusses the basic steps of forge welding in detail so you understand exactly what you are doing and why each step contributes to the successful weld. When you under-

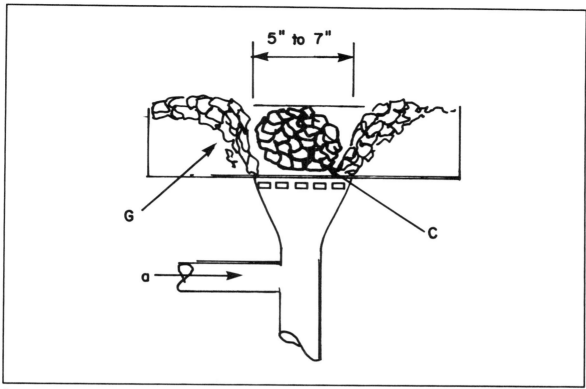

Fig. 14-1. The coke shown at "C" should be about 7 inches across. "G" shows the green or unburned coal. "a" is the incoming air.

stand the process fully, practice will make a good welder of you.

Stock Required

For your first try at welding, make up two 1/2-inch round bars of mild steel, 16 inches long. Smooth up the ends with a file. At a point about 6 inches from one end of one bar, bend the bar a few degrees (Fig. 14-2).

The Welding Fire

Go back to Chapter 5 and reread the instructions on building and maintaining a working fire. The welding fire is a development of a good forging fire. A new fire is of no use for welding. Make up the coke while you use your welding fire, but keep some well-wetted or soaked coal stacked rather high, close around the sides of the fire. When it

sticks together forming large chunks, break away large pieces, as big as your fist if you can, and set them aside. Do not put them out. Repeat the coke making. Don't turn the chunks over and try to coke both sides. It is not necessary, and you will lose a lot of good coke.

As you make the coke, you complete the work to be welded. This works out well because when you are making coke, the fire needs time to rest as the coke is cooking. During the rest periods the air blast is shut off, and the smith is at the anvil. Usually two or three heats are enough to make good coke.

Make sure that the heart of the fire is large enough to receive the entire weld area plus 1/2 inch or more each way.

Heating the Work

Place both work pieces in the fire as shown in Fig.

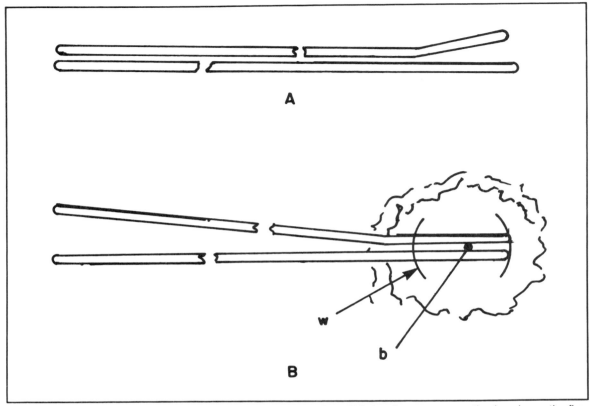

Fig. 14-2. The prepared practice pieces to be welded are at "A." At "B" the pieces are correctly placed over the fire. "b" is the heart of the fire. The area to be welded is "w."

14-2. They should be about 1/4 inch apart and parallel in the weld area. The 6-inch portion of the bars that you prepared by bending over will be in the fire (Fig. 14-2).

The handle ends of the bars may rob heat from the weld area, and the ends to be welded heat too quickly. Therefore slide the two bars, as a unit, just past the center of the fire with the ends a little closer to the far edge of the fire so they do not get the full heat of the fire. The handle ends of the weld area will be a little deeper into the fire, thus getting a little extra heat. In this way you have the best chance of bringing the entire weld area to the same heat at the same time.

After you have placed your bars, build a little igloo-type roof over the fire. This roof should house in the weld portion of the bars but should not touch it. Make the igloo out of those chunks of coke you made earlier. Place them with the best coked part toward the fire (Fig. 14-3). The space above the weld portion can be as little as 1/2 inch or as much as 1 1/2 inches. The igloo need not be stacked tightly, but should have no large openings. Try to keep the biggest opening no larger than a dime.

Start a slow air blast. The igloo cover over the weld will ignite very quickly. The space within will become extremely hot. It will be free of smoke and have no free oxygen. This is a very important point. The coke cover needs oxygen to burn. The coke must burn in order to build the top half of a welding fire. The air for this top half is coming to the fire from the atmosphere above it. Because you do not want free oxygen, there must be enough coke to consume all the free oxygen coming in from the bottom.

Keep the air blast gentle. You want enough air

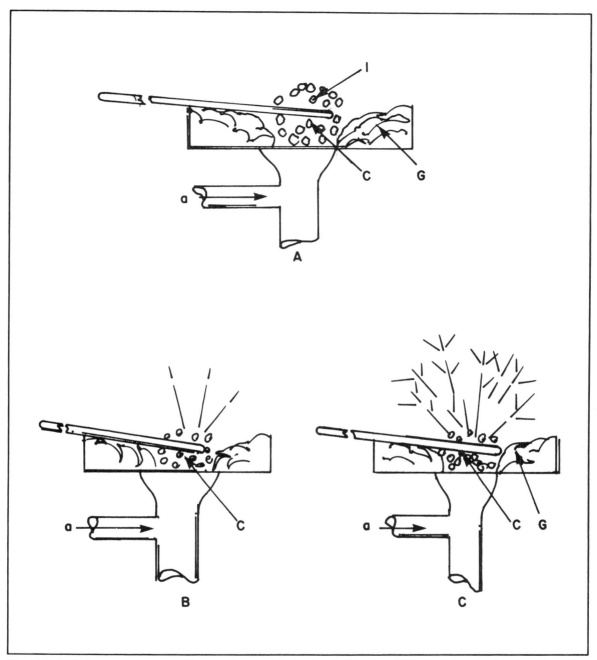

Fig. 14-3. "A" shows a side view of the practice piece in the fire. In this view "I" is the igloo of coke placed over the pieces to form an oven, "C" is the coke, and "G" the green coal. Anytime you have a fire as hot as a welding fire there will be some sparks as shown at "B." They will look like sparks from a wood fire. They are bits of trash and cinder heated to incandescence. If you have more than a few such sparks, the fire is dirty. When you see sparks that look as if they are bursting out of other sparks and the whole area looks like a Fourth of July display as at "C," your iron or steel is burning up. Pull it out of the fire immediately and quench it. The burned portion is ruined. You will have to start over.

to supply the fire without throwing cinders and trash against the work. Don't force the fire.

If any free oxygen gets to the iron it will cause scale, which is an oxide. At welding temperature, iron absorbs oxygen as fast as a sponge absorbs water, and the scale will form all over the weld area at once. It is impossible for you to make a weld if scale between the joining surfaces is present. When I cover a weld and the heat is coming up, I like to have enough coke stacked over the fire so the outer surfaces, the ones facing the atmosphere, remain black. This usually means 2 inches or more.

Recognizing Welding Heat

Assume that your fire is perfect and you are coming up to welding heat. The next question is, "What am I looking for, and how do I recognize it?" This is a most difficult question to answer when you and I are not standing together by the fire. You will begin by looking for texture on the surface of the weld area. It will appear wet, or perhaps oily. The steel will not be deformed, and it will not look as if the surface is about to drip. It will have a very clear light pinkish color. It will not be white like an electric light bulb.

When the welding heat is approached, two other things are happening that you must watch for. The first is sparks; the second is red-hot to white-hot dust particles. These might show up in the hot gasses coming up through the coke cover or igloo.

If the sparks are like the ones you see in a log fire in a fireplace, they are bits of burning fuel and impurities in the coke that have reached incandescent heat (Fig. 14-3). I call them trash and cinder sparks. Some blacksmiths call them clinker sparks. These trash sparks indicate a problem because they show that a varying amount of trash and cinder is floating around in the fire. These will hit the surface of the hot metal and stick to it. If the weld surface gets coated with this stuff, the weld will not make unless you can either knock the trash off or brush it off. When you are working small stock, you may not have time to do either because the stock loses heat too fast.

Another type of spark is the one given off by burning iron or steel. Any iron or steel with a carbon content of more than about .05 percent or "five points" as it is called, will make quite a display when it starts to burn. These sparks look like miniature sky rockets. They are sparks that burst into many smaller sparks, and in high-carbon steels there will be bursts from these secondary sparks. There is no mistaking these sparks (Fig. 14-3). They look like the beginning of a Fourth of July night display. When steel starts to burn, these sparks start to show. There is no time to delay.

If these sparks appear, jerk your metal out of the fire and quench it immediately in the water quench. It is possible that you can save the job, but in most cases when the steel within a weld area starts to burn, the job is lost, and it will be necessary to cut away the burned metal and start over again with new metal. This is true whether you are forging or welding.

Be warned to take it easy when you are coming up to welding heat. The interior as well as the surface of the metal must have a chance to come to near welding heat, or the job will be lost. Practice is very important. Complete control over all phases of the welding process is essential.

Looking at the Fire

You will need to see the exact color and surface condition of the work in order to weld it successfully, and to do this you will need to take certain precautions.

When you are watching any forge fire, don't stare at it. Look at it, then look away. Look across the shop or out the window. Look at something distant and not very bright. Don't look at white buildings that may be close by. If you stare at the fire, your eyes try to adjust to its intense light. I am speaking now from a mechanical point of view, not a medical one. If you stare at the fire, you will find that you soon have difficulty focusing on anything at arm's length. When the work comes out of the fire, it will be very bright. The time allowed between its coming out of the fire and the first three hammer blows is about 5 seconds or less. The brilliance of the metal seen against the background of the anvil, the dark shop floor, dark surroundings, and dark hammer head, creates a headlight effect.

Your eyes, as you stare at the fire, are strained to their limits just coping with an intensely bright object inside an intensely bright enclosure. Jerk the iron out of the fire, put it against a dark background, and all you can see is the headlight. You are defeated before you start. The eye cannot cope with these conditions in the time allowed. It is bad enough in ordinary forging, but in welding I think this effect accounts for 75 to 95 percent of forge welding failures. I have seen it happen many times, and occasionally I get caught, too. Take this seriously. My rule is that for each 2 seconds you spend looking at the fire, spend the next 8 seconds looking away from it, even if you are just looking at the coal alongside the fire.

Do not wear shaded lenses when working with the forge fire unless you are prepared to do so every time you look at the fire or at hot metal. I cannot overemphasize the importance of seeing the exact color and the exact surface condition of welding-hot steel. I have never known a blacksmith who could switch successfully from shaded eye covers to bare eyes or clear covers and make a weld. Develop the habit of caring for your eyes.

The Sticking Point

As your work approaches welding heat, you will begin to look for welding heat or *the stick*. The stick point is that temperature at which the two heated bars will stick together when they touch. Start gently touching the two bars together when you think the heat is nearly high enough. As you do this, carefully observe how everything looks in the fire and the changes that occur in the iron or steel.

When the bars finally stick, and they will if you have been careful up to now, it means that the surfaces of both pieces have reached a welding heat at the same time. If one surface is too hot or too cool, there will be no weld even if the other surface is just right. This testing for stick is done without removing the metal from the fire (Fig. 14-4).

If the two pieces stick together, try to separate

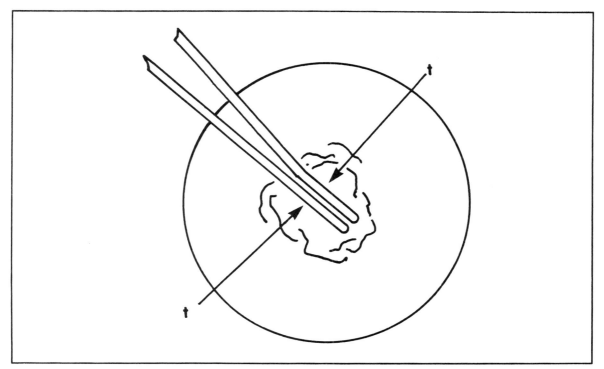

Fig. 14-4. When you think the bars have nearly reached welding heat, start gently touching them together as shown. When they stick together, they are at welding heat.

them. Keep some blower air coming because you do not want your fire to cool. Try not to tear the fire apart as you separate the two bars. Then try to stick them together with a little pressure for the full length of the weld (Fig. 14-4). If they stick, pull them out together. Quickly bump the two pieces gently against the side of the anvil or the forge on the way to the anvil face. This jars most of the trash and oxides off the weld area. It is like a dance step. Don't stop the metal on its way between the fire and the anvil face. Time lost in this important act may cause the weld to fail.

Lay the weld on the anvil with one bar above the other and hit the middle of the weld with the hammer. Use a 1- or 1 1/2-pound hammer. Don't try to crush the whole works flat. A clean, moderate blow is enough (Fig. 14-5). Quickly hit again toward the tip, and again toward the base. After these three blows, if the metal still is stuck together, congratulations, you have a weld!

Don't try to separate these two pieces. Study them and reflect on the whole procedure. You did everything just right, or you would have no weld. I know this process will work for you because ev-

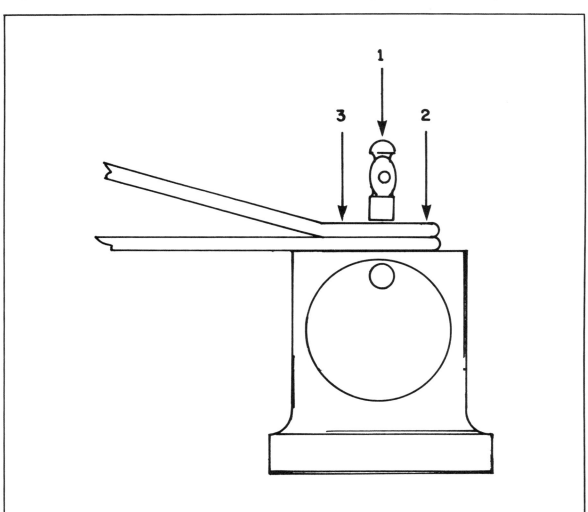

Fig. 14-5. When the practice pieces stick together, move them to the anvil and strike with moderate blows.

ery student of mine who begins the welding lessons learns to be successful at it. You now have a firm foundation for all your future welding efforts.

The Use of Flux

Flux or forge welding compounds will help you make the weld. None of them is a panacea.

One aid is flux. Flux is a material that melts and blends with the oxides on the steel to start with and with those that accumulate from small amounts of air that get to the metal. In a sense it also acts as a lubricant and solvent so when the two metal parts are driven together with the hammer blow, the mixture of flux, scale, trash, and ash splashes out in every direction for a considerable distance (Fig. 14-6). It can set your clothes and your shop on fire, so take care. If you have visitors in your shop, move them well out of range. Flux turns to a liquid a little before the steel reaches welding heat. In many cases it will make the weld area seem ready when it is not.

Flux helps because its melting and coating act as a barrier to air trying to reach the steel when it is hot. Flux should be applied at the lowest temperature that starts it melting. This is usually at a dull orange-red. You will use about a level teaspoonful of flux on your average forge weld. When the work has reached a red-orange heat, pull it out of the flame area to the side of the forge. If you leave the work in the flame, the flux will melt, and it won't stick to the work. Sprinkle the flux on the surfaces that are to be joined. If, as sometimes happens, your surfaces are wired together for easy handling, spread the flux all around the weld area and into any spaces.

In all cases the work must be hot enough to cause the flux to stick to it. Borax tends to boil severely if the metal is too hot. The commercial fluxes are more forgiving. Guard against knocking the flux off the work when you reenter the fire. After flux has been put on, handle the work as little as possible.

Starting from this point, trial and error is the best teacher. Try different heats on a test piece to find the desired heat. In all cases use plenty of flux to cover the entire weld area. In general you will

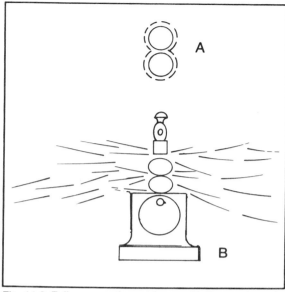

Fig. 14-6. Fully encase the weld area with flux as shown in the cross section at "A." Even after you knock the flux off, there will be splatters of sparks during the first few blows as shown at "B."

need flux to help you with every production weld.

Borax (the 20 Mule Team Borax that you find in the grocery store) is very good and cheap. Commercial welding compounds sold under various trade names are made up of powdered or shredded iron and various chemicals. They all work well, but they might leave the weld looking sloppy because the powdered iron frequently sticks to the weld area and looks bad. Sometimes it will have to be ground or filed away.

No flux will work if proper conditions for a weld are not met.

Some Ways to Prepare Your Work Pieces

There are several ways to prepare the steel for a production weld. Here are three methods that cover most of the problems you will encounter. The main point in any forge weld is to have the two mating surfaces shaped so the centers come together first. This drives out the molten flux, oxides, and trash.

Figure 14-7 shows a common lap weld used for welding in most situations. The first blow drives the center of the weld together; the second blow

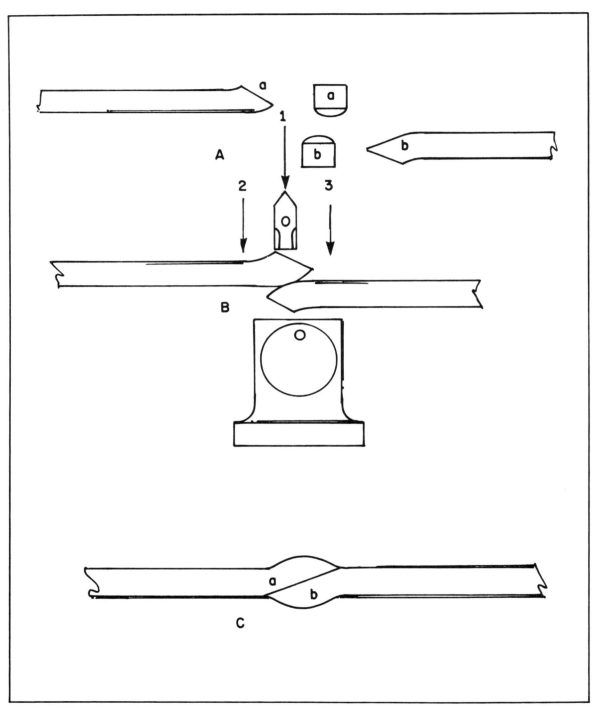

Fig. 14-7. "A" shows how the ends of a common lap weld should be prepared. "B" shows the sequence of the first welding blows. The completed weld is shown ready for dressing at "C."

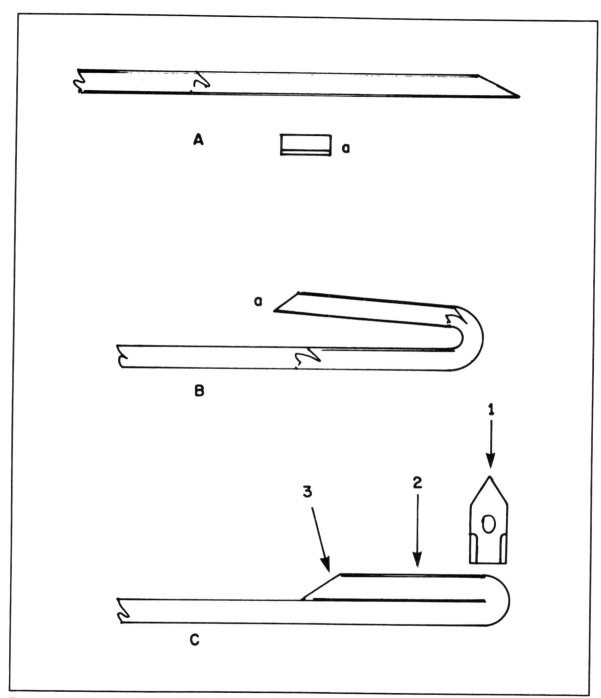

A

a

B

C

1

2

3

Fig. 14-8. In the faggot weld the end to be folded over is prepared as at "A." It is then folded as at "B." Strike the weld as shown at "C" to force the trash out from between the weld as you go. Remember to bump all welds on the way to the anvil. "C" shows the completed weld.

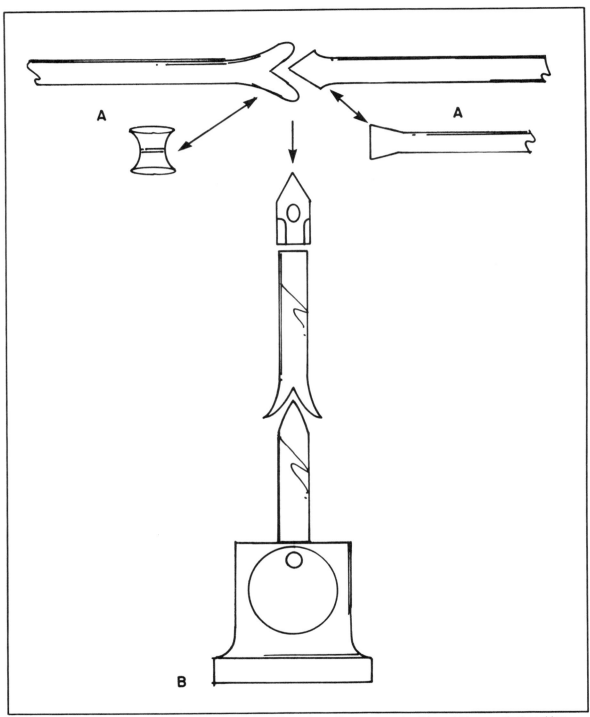

Fig. 14-9. "A" shows the two ends ready for welding. If you have the room, make this weld in a vertical position.

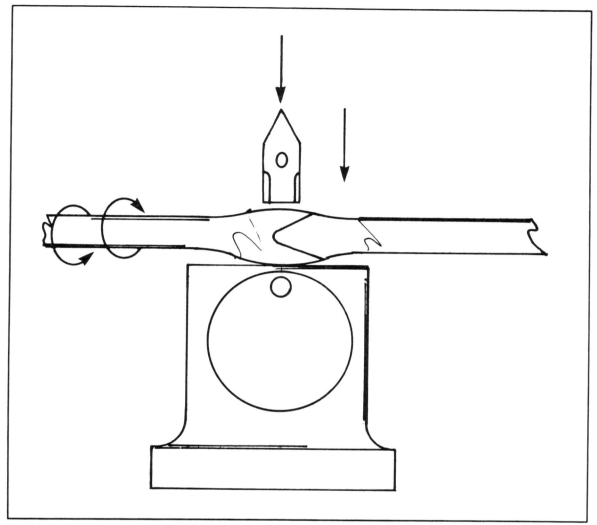

Fig. 14-10. Roll the work back and forth as you finish the piece. It may be necessary to reheat the work.

closes the end that is up; the third blow finishes the other end. If the mass of metal is quite large, you might be able to close and dress or finish the weld in one heat, but usually you will need to flux again and go back into the fire. Reheat to the same welding heat you had for the original weld and complete the weld.

Figure 14-8 shows a faggot weld that is used to build up solid bulk on the end of a bar. Here again, prepare the weld area carefully. In this weld, fold over about 2 1/2 inches of 16-inch bar. Study

the figure, noting how you will prepare the end and the fold, then make the weld.

A third method is a good one for butt welding. It uses the "V" and chisel edge principle. In effect it is a double lap weld (Fig. 14-9). You may need a helper to complete this type of weld, but it is worth developing.

The two ends to be welded should be upset. One end is split for about the diameter of the stock. The other end is shaped into a wedge that will make a sloppy fit into the split in the first end. Make this weld in a vertical position if you have the room. If you use the vertical position, place the split end with the "V" looking down so any trash will be spilled out as you work. You can also put the ends together horizontally, but you might need help for this.

When you get a good stick so the pieces can be handled as one, dress down the weld over the anvil face. Keep rolling the weld as you hammer it down (Fig. 14-10). The work is cooling, you might need to go back into the fire to finish it.

Chapter 15

Shackles, Chain, Rings, and Hooks

I N THIS CHAPTER YOU WILL LEARN HOW TO make shackles, chain, rings, and hooks. Some of these useful objects are forge welded; others are made without welding.

SHACKLES

When you make a shackle, you will start by forming a strong eye in the end of a round bar, in flat or square stock, or in the middle of either. This type of eye has other uses, but is particularly useful for making shackles. Figure 15-1 shows three basic types of weldless eyes. Each is made differently. Eye "A" is a simple hot-punched eye that can be drifted out a little to take a bolt or pin that is no greater than the stock width. It is designed primarily to take bolts, rivets, and pins, and is generally used to permanently fasten one part to another. The overall dimension of the bar around the eye is enlarged very little if at all. The process for making this eye or hole was presented in Chapter 8.

Eye "B" is a thin-walled eye that is ornamental and light weight. It is used for hanging a part

on a hook, for a bracket eye, or for a fair-lead (a fitting used to pass ropes or halyards through to prevent tangling).

The third eye in Fig. 15-1 is an upset eye. It is used for shackles, hook eyes, or any eye where strength is required. You must give considerable thought to the making of this type of eye. It may become a part of a tool for the farmer, the rancher, the contractor, the woodsman, or the blacksmith himself. The worker will use it under conditions that will demand all the strength you can build into it.

The size of a shackle is usually determined by the size of the stock in the bow. The pin is usually one size larger whether it is a straight pin, a screw pin, or a bolt and nut pin. For example, a 3/8-inch shackle will have a pin body size of 7/16 inch. A 1/2-inch shackle will have a 5/8-inch pin size.

Three distinct types of shackle are shown in Fig. 15-2. The first is an anchor shackle, the second a plow shackle, and the third is a chain shackle. Any form of shackle pin will do as long as it fits the eyes of the shackle and has a head and a wire

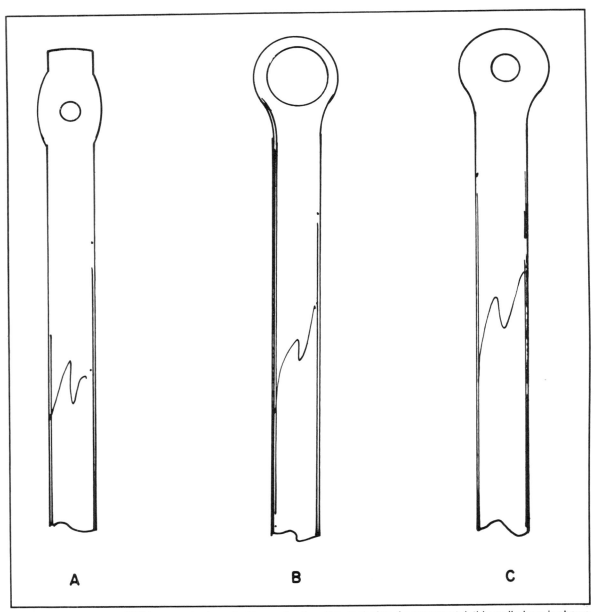

Fig. 15-1. Various eyes. "A" is a punched eye that is smaller than the stock size. An ornamental, thin-walled eye is shown at "B." "C" shows an eye punched into an upset end.

or tie hole, or a thread and nut and the same tie hole. The tie will assure that the pin will not accidentally slip out. Some shackles have one eye threaded and use a threaded shackle pin that has an eye for tying. Various types of shackle pins are shown in Fig. 15-3.

Making a 1/2-Inch Anchor Shackle

The anchor shackle is one of the most commonly used shackles.

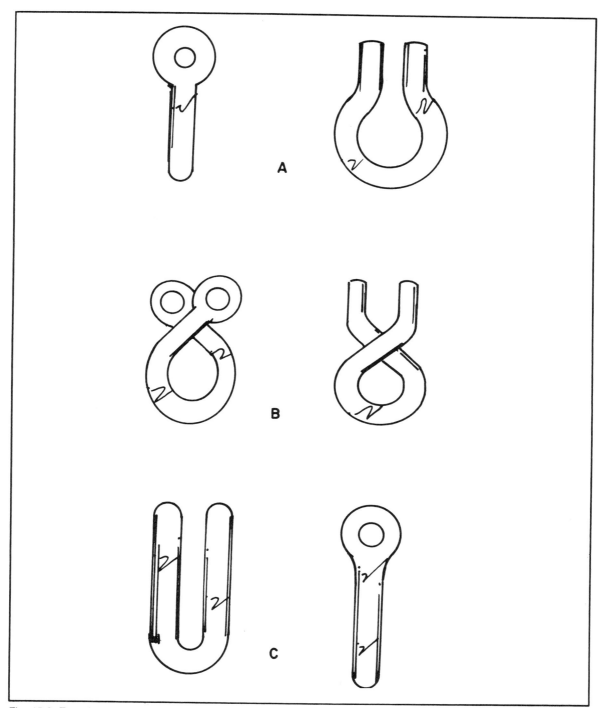

Fig. 15-2. Two views of three distinctly different shackles. "A" is an anchor shackle, "B" is a plow shackle, and "C" is a chain shackle.

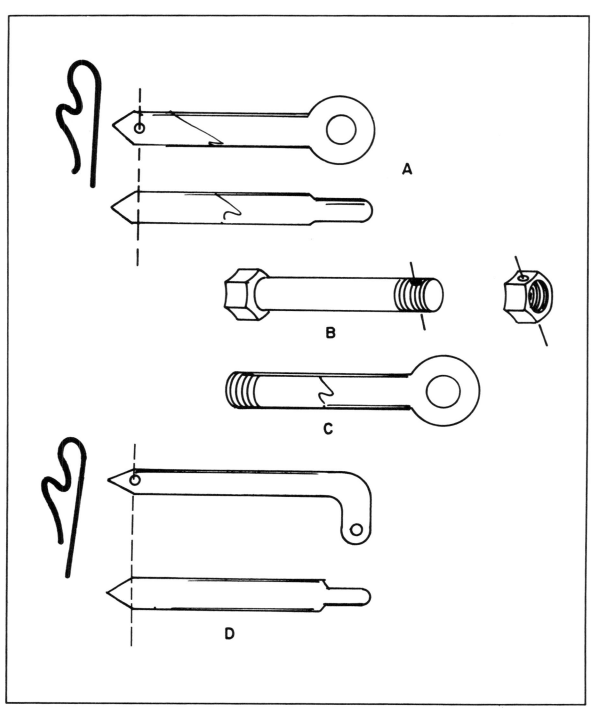

Fig. 15-3. Four common shackle pins. ''A'' and ''D'' are held in place with hairpin clips. ''B'' and ''C'' are threaded types. ''B'' uses a wire to keep the nut in place.

Stock Required

One 1/2-inch round bar of mild steel, 10 inches long.

Procedure

Round both ends of the bar. Upset at both ends to twice the stock size so that it forms a rounded knob. For this purpose the job will be much easier if you use a swage block or a 1-inch and a 1 1/2-inch bottom swage (Fig. 15-4). Both ends must be upset. You may strike the first upset while you are making the other.

Upset the bar in your 1 1/4-inch swage and continue until the knob is 1 1/8 inches in diameter.

Round the knob on the anvil face and upset a little more if needed. The knob should be shaped like a ball on the end of the bar. Flatten the knob to 1/2 inch thick (Fig. 15-5).

Mark the center line of the round at a point 5/8 inch from the end (Fig. 15-6). A little more than 1/2 inch should be between the center-punch mark and the lower edge of the eye stock as shown in the dotted lines "y" and "z" in Fig. 15-6. If there is less than 1/2 inch, move the mark until the dimensions "y" and "z" are correct. Use a 5/8-inch round hot-punch with a 3/16-inch flat point (Fig. 15-7). Keep the end wet with kitchen fat and punch a 7/16-inch wet with kitchen fat and punch a 7/16-inch hole

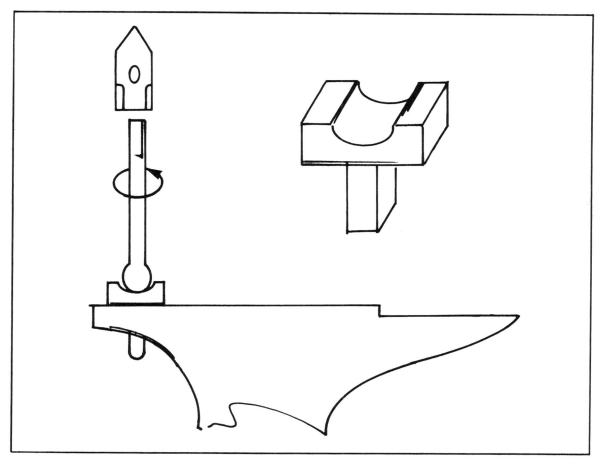

Fig. 15-4. Upsetting for an eye is done on both ends of the stock before the eye hole is located. Eyes this large can be upset directly on the anvil face, but you may find that the step on your anvil is too shallow. A bottom swage (hardy hole swage), as shown here, or a swage block will make the job much easier.

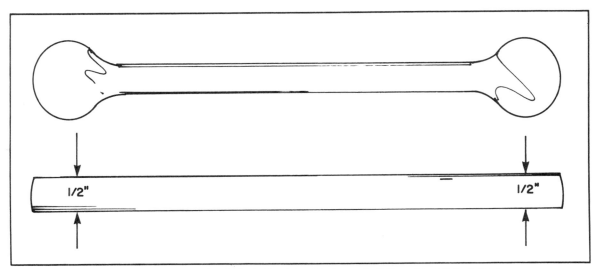

Fig. 15-5. The finished shackle blanks should look like this with the ends flattened to 1/2 inch thick.

through the stock. Cool the punch often in the fat. Keep the work hot and work both sides of the eye.

Drift the eye hole to a full 5/8-inch diameter (Fig. 15-8). Keep the eye stock thickness no less than 1/2 inch. Make sure that the drift passes squarely through the eye stock. With practice you will make this form of eye with the stock thickness and width a little greater than the pin hole size. This is the optimum size.

Now make a 5/8-inch eye hole in the other end of the bar the same way.

Study the shapes of the anchor and plow shackles in Fig. 15-2. The space between the eyes should be 1/8 inch greater than the diameter of the shackle pin. The bow for these two types of shackle should be large enough so that a round bar three times the diameter of the pin passes through it freely.

After the eyes have been shaped, bend them down 10 to 15 degrees as shown in Fig. 15-9. Install your vise jaw guards. Open the vise to 3 inches between the guards. This allows room for two thicknesses of shackle stock, the 1 1/2-inch bumping bar, and a 1/4-inch clearance. For a bumping bar you may use any piece of metal that measures close to 1 1/2 inches in diameter.

Heat the shackle between the eyes to a dark

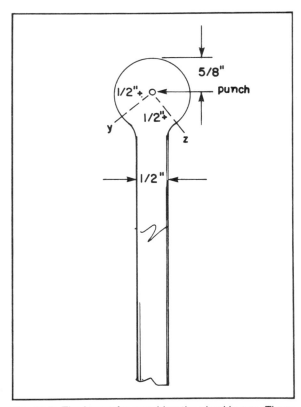

Fig. 15-6. The layout for punching the shackle eye. There should be slightly more than 1/2 inch between the center of the eye and "y" and "z."

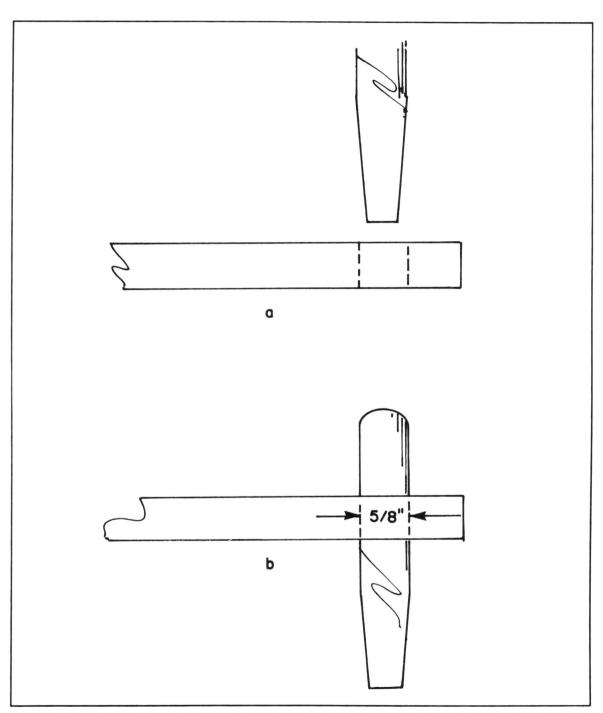

Fig. 15-7. Punch the eye hole to almost 5/8 inch as shown at "a." Then drift it out to 5/8 inch as at "b." Be sure the hole is truly square with the center line of the stock. Drift from both sides and keep the eye flat.

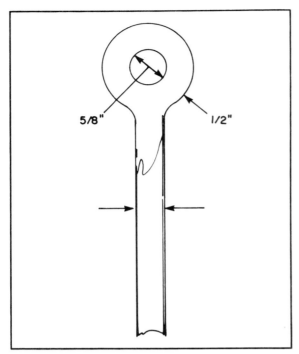

Fig. 15-8. The completed eye should look like this. Take care to have each eye true to size and square with the stock.

orange. Lay the shackle blank across the jaws, squarely, with even overhang each way. The eyes should point down. Place the bumping bar squarely across it and over the center of the jaw opening (Fig. 15-10). Firmly, but gently, bump the center of the shackle down until it folds evenly (Fig. 15-11). Hit the bumping bar with a heavy hammer.

Remove the bumping bar and the shackle from the vise. Reheat the bow up to the eyes, but do not heat the eyes or the 10-degree bend under the eyes. Place the bumping bar back in the bow and let the eyes hang down. Squeeze the eyes together in the vise until you have the desired 7/8-inch distance between them. Have a 7/8-inch spacer handy, and squeeze the eyes shut against it. A piece or two of stock will do. Let the color go out of the shackle while it is still in the vise (Fig. 15-12).

Remove the shackle and heat where needed to a dark orange. Adjust the eyes and bow as needed over the anvil horn. Adjust the holes for the pins at the same time. An old 1/2-inch bolt shank must pass through both eyes. Allow the shackle to cool until it has lost most of its heat. Cool it enough to touch without getting burned. Reheat the entire

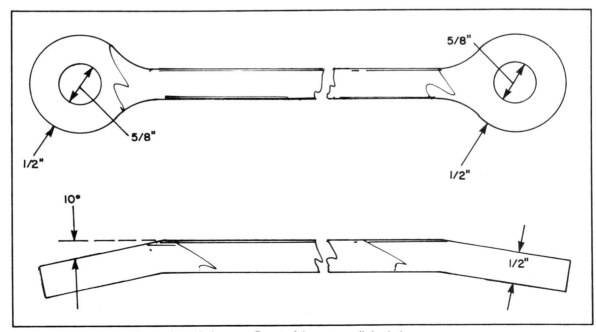

Fig. 15-9. Bend the eye down 10 to 15 degrees. Be careful not to spoil the hole.

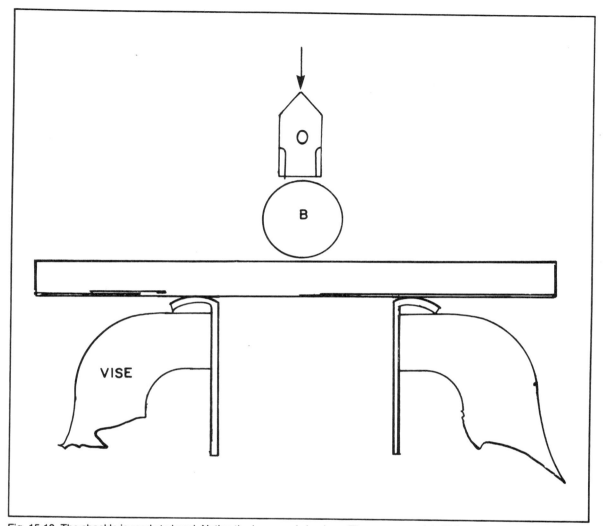

Fig. 15-10. The shackle is ready to bend. Notice the jaw guards in place. They are essential. "B" indicates the bumping bar.

shackle evenly to a dark red. To normalize it, let it cool slowly in a warm place like the back of the forge. When it is cool enough to handle with bare hands, brush it up and oil it. Although it is cold, it will, in this condition, tolerate some minor adjustments.

The Plow Shackle

The plow shackle is made just like the anchor shackle. The difference is in the 90-degree twist of the plow shackle. You will use the same bump-ing bar and the same 10- to 15-degree bend at the eyes.

Stock Required

1/2-inch round stock, 13 inches long, M.S.

Additional Material

A stack of 5/8-inch flat washers for spacers.

A 5/8-inch bolt and a nut.

A piece of 5/8-inch round stock, about 9 inches long.

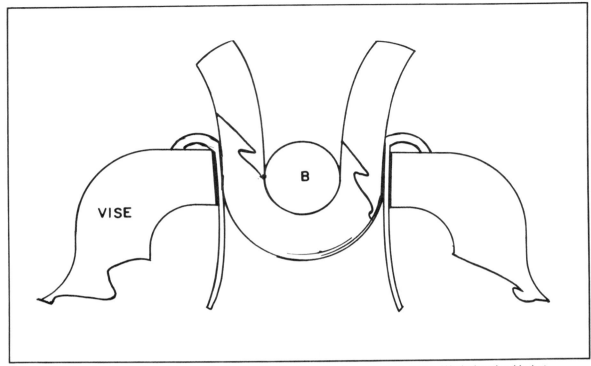

Fig. 15-11. The shackle is bent into rough shape with the bumping bar, "B," in place. Work the shackle hot.

A piece of pipe or solid shafting about 2 feet long with a diameter not more than 1 1/2 inches for a bending bar.

Procedure

Make the plow shackle like the anchor shackle. Use the same bumping bar and the same 10- to 15-degree bend at the eyes.

Make a clip shaped like a "U" bolt out of the 5/8-inch round stock (Fig. 15-13). Note how it fits under the two eyes of the shackle. Make a spacer 7/8 inch thick from a stack of 5/8-inch flat washers. It should be wide enough to fill the space between the eyes. Prepare a 5/8-inch bolt long enough to go through both eyes (Fig. 15-14).

Take two 5/8-inch flat washers and a nut. Put the 7/8-inch spacers between the eyes. Pass the bolt through both eyes and the spacers. Place a washer under the bolt head and nut. Tighten up so that the spacers will not move (Fig. 15-14). Slip the clip into place tight underneath the eye of the shackle (Fig.

15-13). Make sure that the 1 1/2-inch bending bar enters the bow of the shackle. Now adjust the vise so it is ready to take the hot work as shown in Fig. 15-15. Make a cold run on this to be sure everything is ready to go. Remove the twist bar and clip.

Be sure the bolt is set tightly. It must remain tight until the job is done. Heat the shackle as shown in Fig. 15-16, using the dribble can to keep the heat away from the eyes. Bring the bow to an orange forging heat. When it is heated, quickly slide the clip into place and lock the work in the vise. Set it up tight (Fig. 15-15). Don't crush any hot metal.

Now use the bending bar to twist the shackle a one-quarter turn to the left. This is counterclockwise when you are looking down on the bow. Adjust the twist so the bar passes through freely. A portion of the bottom of the bow, about 3/4 inch long, should be at 90 degrees to the bolt.

Allow the plow shackle to lose all color before removing it from the vise. Then place the shackle

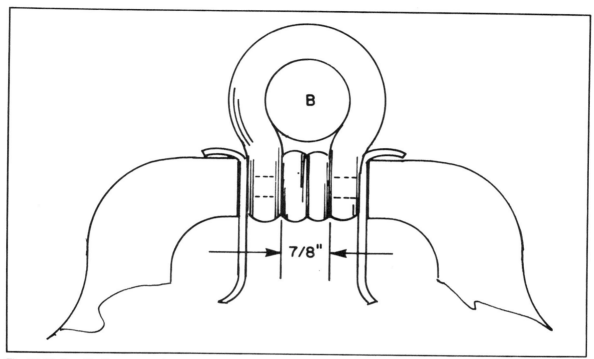

Fig. 15-12. Bend in the eyes and press them hard against a 7/8-inch spacer. The spacer may be made up of more than one piece; use as many pieces of flat stock as you need. Leave the work in the vise until it cools to a loss of color.

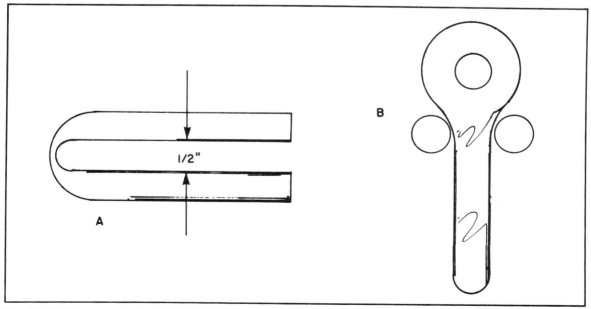

Fig. 15-13. Make up a clip shaped like a "U" bolt as shown at "A." This should fit tightly up under the eyes as shown in the end view at "B." The legs of the clip should be about 4 1/2 inches long.

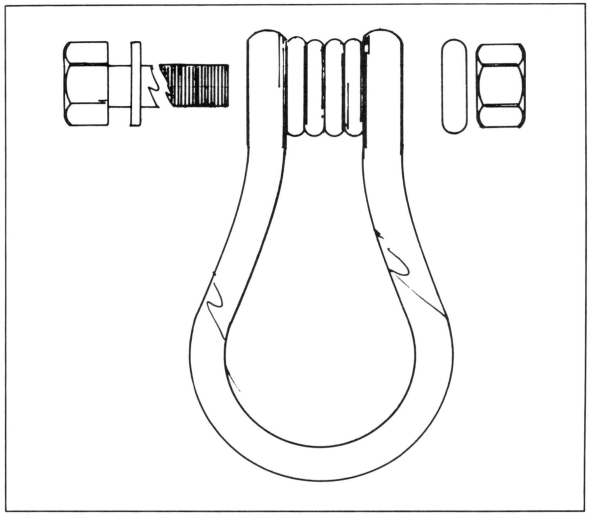

Fig. 15-14. The spacers are in place. Set the bolt up tight because it will be subjected to strain in the next process.

in the fire and bring the entire unit, with the bolt in place, to a low red hardening heat. Do not quench it. Set it aside to cool slowly. This will normalize it and is all the heat treating needed. When it is cool, remove the bolt and spacer, slip in the shackle pin or bolt, and oil it up. It should look like the bow view and pin view in Fig. 15-17.

The Chain Shackle

The chain shackle is a straight-sided shackle in which the stock is the same diameter as the pin.

The eyes are made so that the stock around the eye hole is the same size as the diameter of the pin.

Stock Required

1/2-inch by 10-inch round stock, M.S.

Procedure

As you did with the other shackles, upset both ends to twice the stock thickness to form a 1-inch round knob. Flatten the knob to 1/2 inch thick and shape it as you did for the anchor shackle (Fig. 15-15).

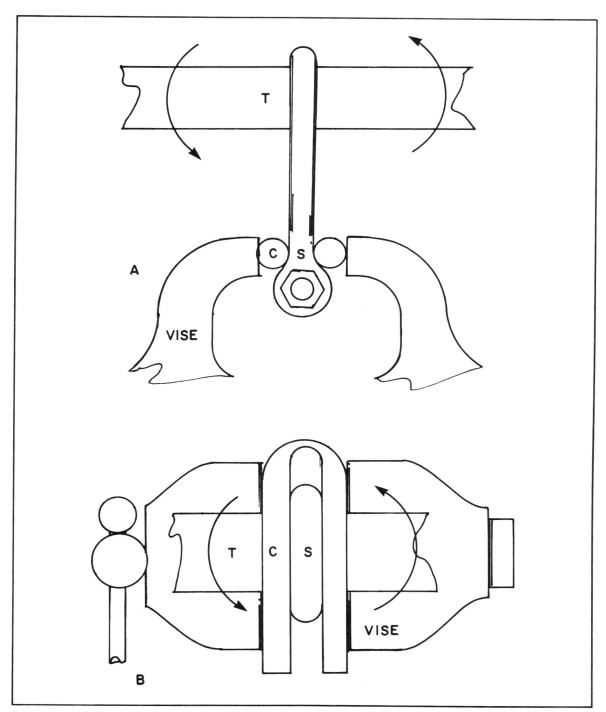

Fig. 15-15. "A" shows a side view of the plow shackle in place and ready for the twist. "B" is the view from the top. In both views "C" is the clip, "S" is the shackle, and "T" is the twisting bar. Notice that the jaw guards are not in place.

Punch mark the eye blank 9/16 inch from the end and along the stock center line. Use the 5/8-inch hot-punch that you used on the anchor shackle and follow with the 5/8-inch drift. The sides of the bow and eyes are in a straight line inside and out and are only 7/8 inch apart. Figure 15-18 shows the finished dimensions.

Form the bow as you did for the anchor

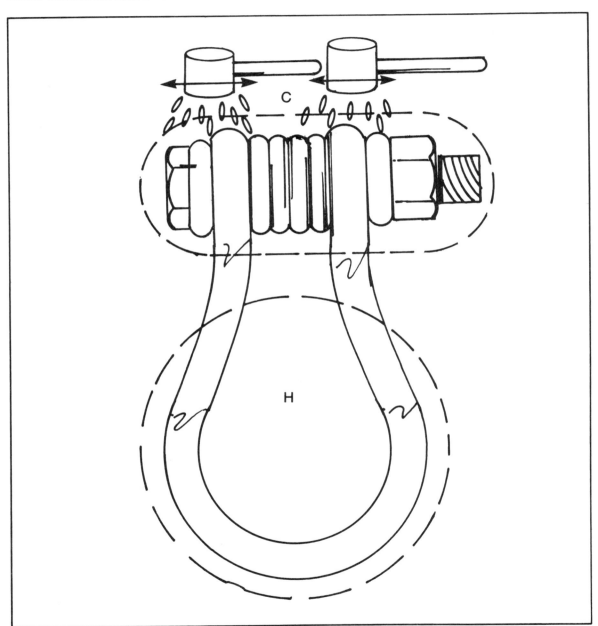

Fig. 15-16. Use the dribble can to cool the eyes of the plow shackle and the bolt assembly while you are heating the bow. Keep area "C" cool and area "H" hot.

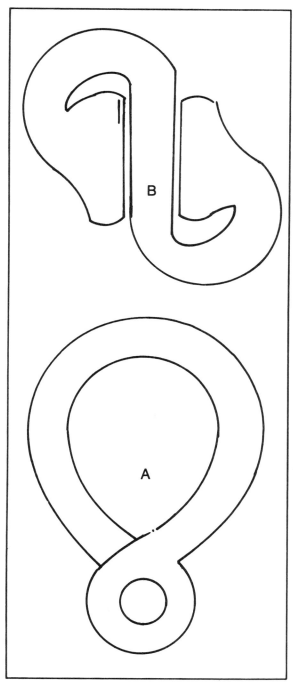

Fig. 15-17. Two views of the completed plow shackle. "B" is a view of the bow with the eyes below it. "A" is a view of the bow and the eyes. Notice that you can see through both eyes at the same time.

shackle, using a 5/8-inch bumping bar. Reduce the bar to a 7/8-inch diameter for 1 inch. A piece of 1/2-inch flat stock and a piece of 3/8-inch flat stock will make a good spacer to dress the shackle sides and square the eyes for the pin (Fig. 15-19).

When the shackle is completed, normalize it as you did the anchor shackle. Clean it up and oil it.

CHAIN AND RINGS

Chain is made of individual links or rings that pass through each other to form the chain. Links and rings are each made in the same way. The only difference in making them is in the method of determining the material required for a given size and shape. The ends of either the link or the ring can be simply butted together, or they can be welded. Welding is the process described in this chapter.

You will make a 3/8-inch passing link chain with 2-inch links. The link will have a 2-inch inside major diameter and a 1-inch inside minor diameter. It will be welded. Refer to Chapter 10, to refresh your memory on how to determine measurements for rings and links.

Stock Required

3/8-inch round stock, M.S. Cut the stock into several pieces 5 5/16 inches long. This is slightly longer than the true stock measure of 5.89 inches, but is close enough for practical purposes.

Procedure

Start with one piece of prepared stock. Upset both ends to about 7/16 inch for 1/2 inch or so.

Use a 1-inch round piece of stock for a mandrel and bend the 3/8-inch blank almost half way around the mandrel (Fig. 15-20). If you wish, you may use the 1-inch round portion of the beak of the anvil instead of the mandrel.

Heat both ends of the stock for about 1 inch and bend them toward each other over the beak of the horn until they are almost looking at each other (Fig. 15-20).

Heat the two ends to an orange heat and hammer in a short chamfer or scarf on one end. Flip it over and form a matching scarf on the other end

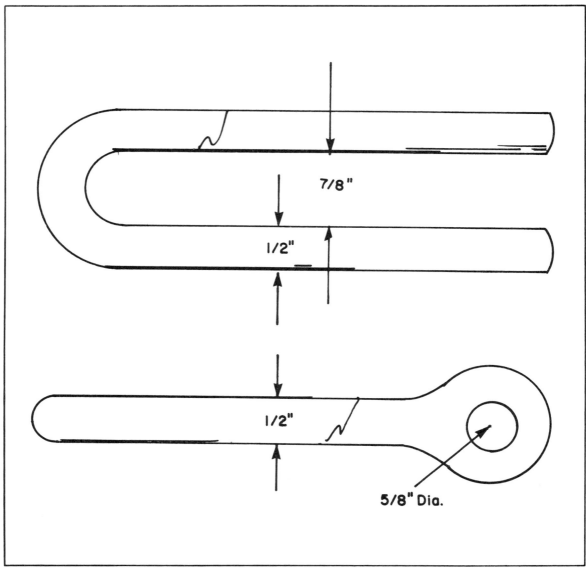

7/8"

1/2"

1/2"

5/8" Dia.

Fig. 15-18. Dimensions for the chain shackle are shown here.

(Fig. 15-21). Knock the two ends together and dress them up a little on the anvil face. They should not be scarfed to sharp edges (Fig. 15-21).

The next steps will have to do with making the weld. Before you start this portion of the work, read through all the steps and study the figures.

Check your fire to see that it is ready for welding. Place the ends of the ring or link in the fire and bring them to an orange-red heat. Remove the ring from the fire, but leave it near the fire and sprinkle welding flux (either borax or a manufactured forge welding flux) all over the weld area. It will seem to boil and fuss; then it will melt. Quickly get the weld fully covered and back into the fire. Do not knock flux off the weld while you are replacing the work into the fire.

You will use the ring tongs on the work as a handle. Squeeze the reins of the tongs fairly tight and tie them together with a wire ring (Fig. 15-22). Arrange the fire, the tongs, and the ring so the bits of the tongs never heat to color. If this happens, they will lose their holding power. The ring should be flat in the fire, not on its edge. When you think welding heat is near, carefully turn the ring over to bring both sides of the weld to the same heat. Keep the fire gentle. Don't rush this or any other weld.

Have your 1-pound hammer already in your hand. When the weld is at heat, bring it out, and bump off the scale and flux on the way to the anvil. Lay the weld flat on the anvil face (Fig. 15-23).

Hit the center of the weld with a moderate blow. Continue to use moderate blows to quickly hit over the two ends. Flip the work over and repeat on the other side. Move over to the beak of the anvil and place the weld over it so that you can rock it back and forth as you dress the weld and close it.

You might need to go back into the fire for more welding heat. If so, always flux the weld again and get back into the fire as quickly as possible. With practice you will be able to complete a weld in one heat, but this is not likely for your first several tries.

Take the wire off the long reins and cool the tongs. Let the weld cool to Crayola red. Reheat the entire ring to a yellow-orange. Gently work out the

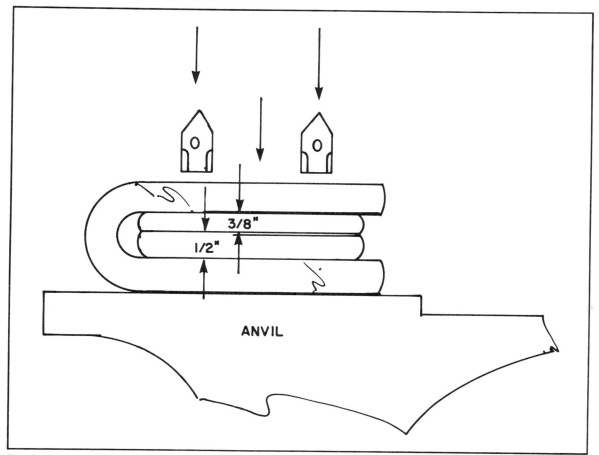

Fig. 15-19. The chain shackle with spacers in place. The final dressing of this shackle can be done on the face of the anvil. Make sure the pin will go through the eyes.

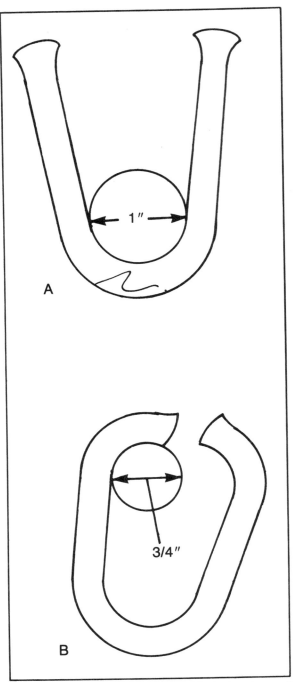

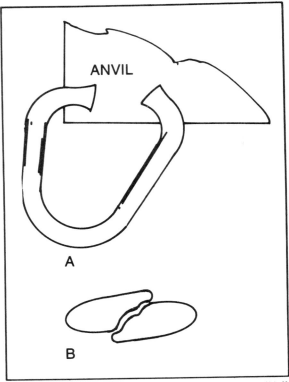

Fig. 15-21. Heat the two ends and scarf them as at "A." Bump them together until they look like "B."

shape to its proper form using your ring tongs to hold it and the light hammer to shape it. If you try to pry or twist it into shape, you might break the weld. All welds need time to cure or rest, and that is why you normalize welds and forgings when possible.

Making the Additional Links and Joining Them

Make the second link just as you did the first. Complete the weld and let it cool slowly. You now have two separate welded rings or links. Prepare the third link but don't close it up to weld yet.

Hang the other two links into the third one; then close up the third one ready for welding. This will make quite a bundle to handle at the fire and at the anvil. To manage this, take the link to be welded just a little off center as shown in Fig. 15-24, lock the tongs on it, and set the reins with a wire

Fig. 15-20. At "A," bend the 3/8-inch blank almost around a 1-inch round bar or around the 1-inch portion of the horn. At "B," bend the two ends until they nearly look at each other. Do this over the 3/4-inch round of the beak of the anvil.

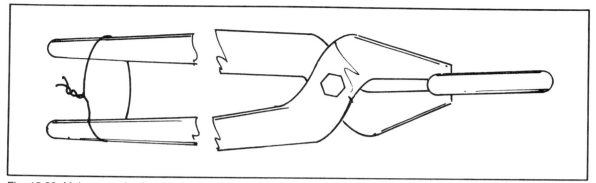

Fig. 15-22. Make up a simple wire ring to slide over the reins so that they hold the work in the fire like a handle. Keep the jaws and bits out of the fire.

tie as you did with the first two rings. Tie the finished links back alongside the jaws to hold them firmly to the tongs and out of the way of your hammer. Your tongs are now holding three links, but they are all under complete control (Fig. 15-24).

Weld the third link, treating it as you did the first two. You may not be successful in your first few tries at making chain, but keep trying. Learning to handle three links all in one bite is nearly as important as the weld itself, and it takes practice.

To continue with the chain, make another group of three links and join them with a seventh link. Here you will have two three-link chains hanging on the same tongs. Tie these back alongside the tong reins to keep them out of the way. Proceed with this process until your chain reaches the desired length.

When you use a chain made like this, notice that the links seldom bind up or kink. This is because the links are open enough that they can move freely for the full length of each other without binding against each other as they pass within a link.

HOOKS

There is a large variety of hooks. You will make three types. The first one is the punched eye slip hook. This hook is bolted or shackled to its lifting chain or cable. The second is a large eye slip hook. This type is very good for use with rope or chain. It does not bind when it is hooked over a rope or cable. The third style is a trace hook, a specialty hook for moderate loads.

Making a Punched Eye Slip Hook

The punched eye slip hook will require a 7/16-inch eye. The hook will be made on the end of a bar to avoid using tongs as long as possible.

Stock Required

5/8-inch round stock, 14 inches long. M.S.

Procedure

Prepare both ends for upsetting and upset one end to 1 1/8-inch diameter for about 1 inch. Make up a spring fuller from 7/16-inch or 1/2-inch round stock. It should have arms about 8 inches long.

Fuller all around the upset 1 1/8 inches from the end to form a neck a full even 7/16 inch in diameter (Fig. 15-25). Shape up the upset to a fat pear shape.

Flatten to 7/16 inch thickness. The two faces must be parallel (Fig. 15-25). Do not make any grooves in the neck, the fullered-down portion. Keep the whole area nicely shaped and free from nicks.

Lay off a 4 1/2-inch chalk mark on your anvil. It will be handy if you put it along the face toward the heel. Add a second mark, 1 1/4 inches long, alongside the first. These will be your gauge marks as you shape the body of the hook.

Hold the center of the neck over one end of the long gauge mark and mark the bar with chalk. Next mark off the 1 1/4-inch gauge on the bar stock (Fig. 15-26). You now have a line 5 3/4 inches long with

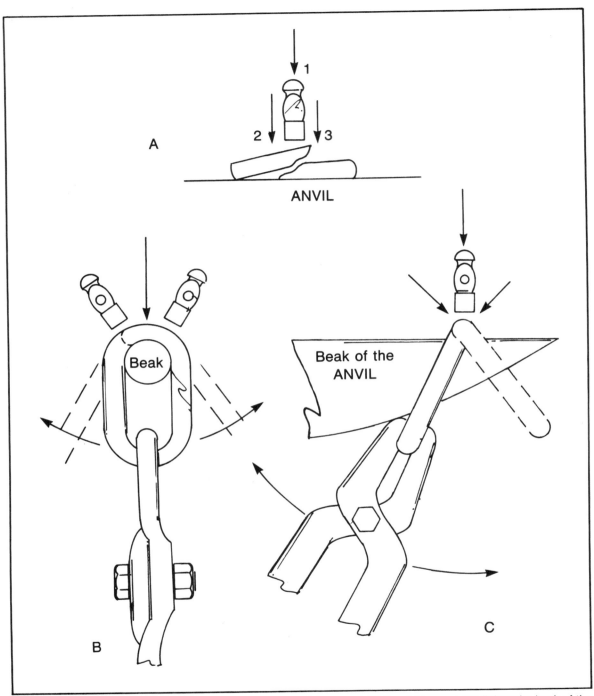

Fig. 15-23. After you have made the center weld on the anvil face as at ''A,'' quickly move the link to the beak of the horn as shown at ''B.'' As you dress the weld, swing the link back and forth and work it from side to side as at ''B'' and ''C.'' Flip it around if need be to get an even dressing.

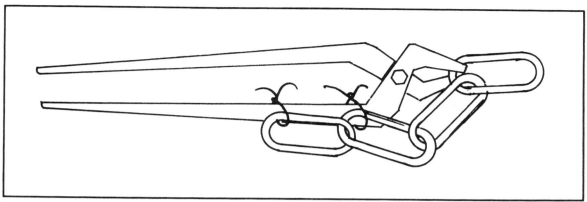

Fig. 15-24. Tie the completed links to the tongs to keep them out of the way.

a hash mark in it. Mark off 1 1/2 inches from the center of the neck and hash mark it. The 3 1/2-inch part is the main body of the hook. The last 1 1/4 inches are the tapered point of the hook. Don't wipe the measuring marks off your anvil. As you forge the balance of the hook, you must check against them to be sure there is no growth from neck to point.

Forge the point down to a 1/4-inch nose in the 1 1/4 inch length. Don't cut the work off yet. Smooth these two tapers a bit so they flow into the body, thus avoiding any hard or abrupt shouldering. The work should look like Fig. 15-27. Check your progress with the marks on the anvil to make sure that your finished work will be as designed. The point can become misshapen rather easily.

Punch the eye next. Lay out a center-punch mark for the eye hole. Draw a line crosswise through the greatest diameter. Draw another line through the center of the body of the hook and the eye blank (Fig. 15-27). Use the cross made by the lines "x" and "y" as a guide to find the spot in the eye that is the same distance from the top of the eye and from each side. This point might not be where the lines intersect, but if this happens, it is alright. The lines are there to help you judge the center of the mass of metal. When you have found the center spot, move 1/16 inch toward the neck and center punch that new spot. This is the point at which you should punch the eye. Your goal is to get the same amount of metal on the top, the two sides, and part way to the neck.

Hot-punch out the center-punch mark, dead center. Go in from each side with the hot punch until the hole is about 3/8 inch in diameter on each side. Drift it out to a neat 7/16-inch eye. If any pooching up or misshaping occurs, gently dress the sides of the eye flat and redrift. Do this until the eye looks perfect. A 7/16-inch bolt should pass through the hole freely.

Bend the hook to shape while the hook is still attached to the bar. Bend the eye to one side edgewise until the eye and one side of the body are in a straight line (Fig. 15-28). Heat the neck primarily and cool the eye so it will not be crushed. Hold the neck over the beak of the anvil. If the beak is too large, lay a piece of 1/2-inch or 5/8-inch round stock on the anvil face and bend the neck over that. When the neck bend is completed, it should look like Fig. 15-28.

Cut the hook away from the bar stock, leaving a small portion of the 1/4-inch stock so it can be dressed by forging or by filing a round nose on the end of the hook body (Fig. 15-28). The rest of the work is done over the horn. Remember you are bending the work, not crushing it, so strike accordingly with your 2 1/2-pound hammer. Wiping blows are all that you need.

Figure 15-28 is a true flat profile of this hook. For your first slip hook, I suggest that you work up a true enlargement of Fig. 15-28 to give you an actual stock dimension of 5/8 inch in the body of the hook. This serves as your pattern for the curvature of the hook. This curvature is vitally

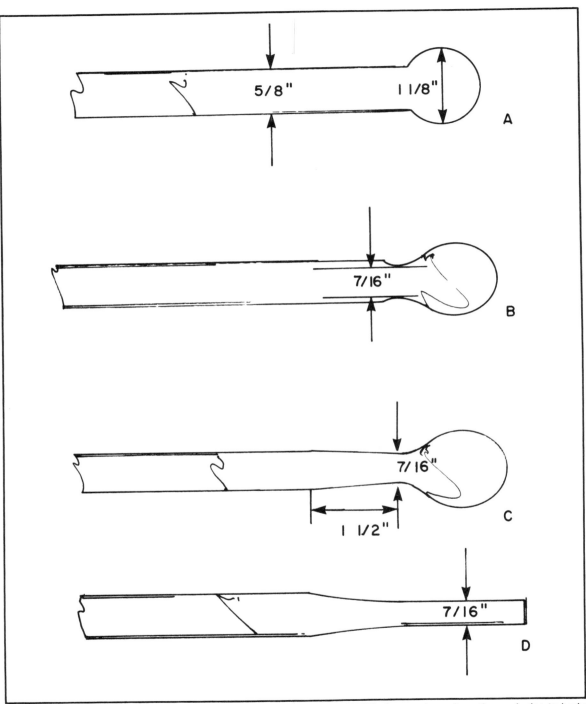

Fig. 15-25. Upset the knob, "A." Fuller down a round neck as at "B." "C" shows a taper from the neck size to body size in 1 1/2 inches. Flatten the knob to 7/16 inch thick as shown at "D."

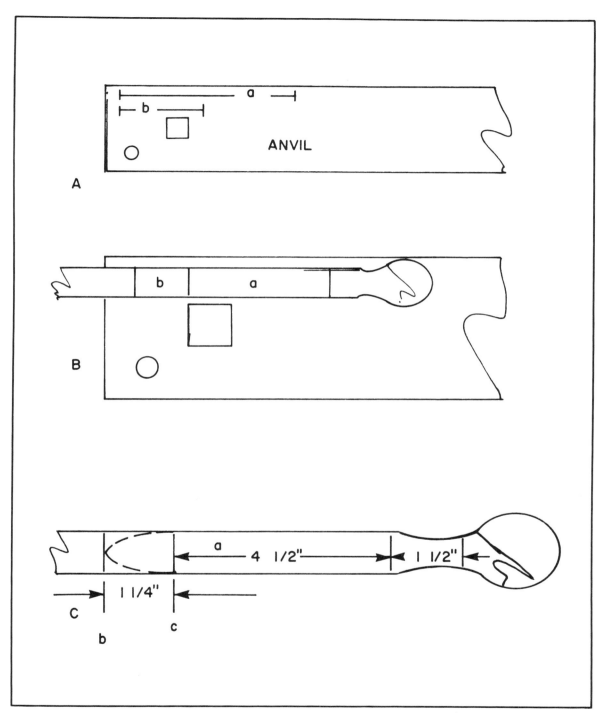

Fig. 15-26. At "A" lay off a 4 1/2-inch mark, "a," and a 1 1/4 inch mark, "b," on the face of the anvil. Transfer these marks to the work as shown at "B." At "C" you taper down from the 5/8-inch stock to 1/4 inch between "b" and "c."

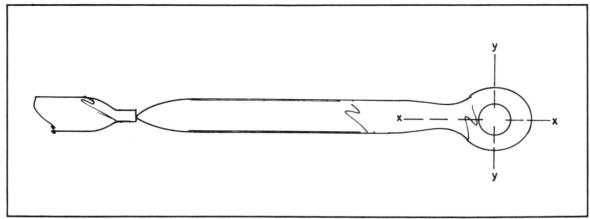

Fig. 15-27. Lay out lines "x" and "y" to assist in finding the punch mark for the eye.

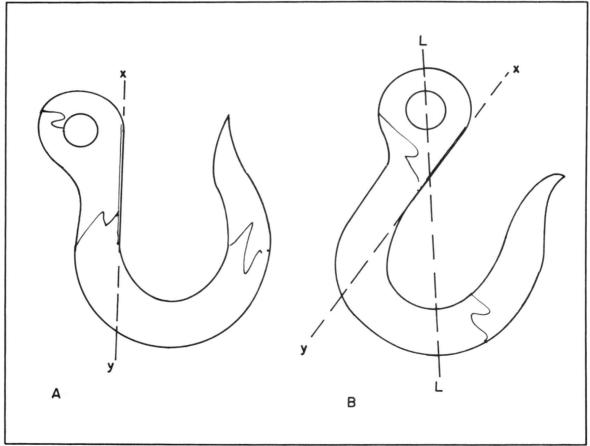

Fig. 15-28. "A" shows the eye and neck on the "x-y" line. View "A" is a flat profile. "B" shows the working profile. Line "L-L" is the load line.

important because an incorrect curvature might cause the hook to dump its load without warning. If the hook is closed up too much, it becomes awkward to handle.

When the hook is complete, let it cool to room temperature overnight. Then heat the entire hook to a deep orange-red. Give it about 5 minutes for the heat to soak through after it has reached heat. Set it aside somewhere to cool quite slowly; near the fire is good. It will be fine if it takes an hour or more to come to a finger-handling temperature.

None of it should be in a cold draft. In this cooling process you are normalizing the hook to release internal strains. After it reaches room temperature, it is ready to use. Wire brush it, clean it up, and oil it. It will receive a 3/8-inch anchor shackle.

Making a Large Eye Slip Hook

Part of a large eye slip hook is made like the small eye hook. The difference is in the eye. The hook can be started on the end of a long bar that will pro-

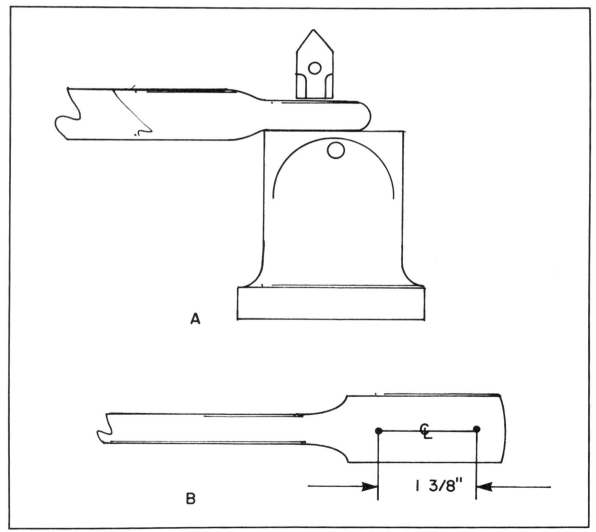

Fig. 15-29. A tongue is formed at "A." Lay out for your splitting line as shown at "B."

vide a handle, or it can be handled throughout with tongs.

Stock Required

5/8-inch square stock, 8 inches long, M.S.

Procedure

Heat one end to yellow-orange and flatten for 2 1/4 inches to 3/8 inch thick. Hold the work over the large front radius of the anvil and flip it over back and forth so the newly formed tongue is centered on the parent stock (Fig. 15-29). Let is spread sideways as it will.

Make a punch mark 9/16 inch from the end of the center line of the tongue. Make a second punch mark 1 3/8 inches closer to the shoulder (Fig. 15-29). Punch a 3/8 inch round hole at each one of these marks. Do not make these holes oversize.

Split halfway through the tongue along a center line between the holes. Flip the work over and cut through on the same center line. Keep the work hot. Be sure you have your cutting plate in place.

Bump the cutter down to the cutting plate to start the split open. Use a punch or any round taper that will enter the slot. Move the work over the pritchel hole and open the slot further (Fig. 15-30).

When the slot is open enough to go over the anvil beak, put it over. You now have a large eye started. Don't force the eye onto the horn. Forge the stock in the eye using the method shown in Fig. 16-2 for an ornamental eye.

Place the jaw guard in the vise. Have your hammer and a piece of 1/2- or 5/8-inch round stock about 10 inches long handy to the vise. Heat the work to yellow-orange around the base of the eye. Place the work in the vise with the eye up and aligned across the jaws (Fig. 15-31). Grab it below the heat and close the vise tight. Stick the end of the bar through the eye and smooth out the edge in the lower part of the eye where the 3/8-inch hole is. Do this by striking the end of the bar downward. Don't spread the eye any more than you have to (Fig. 15-31). You want the base of the eye to go over the anvil beak as soon as possible so you can work out the roughness. This eye is to become teardrop

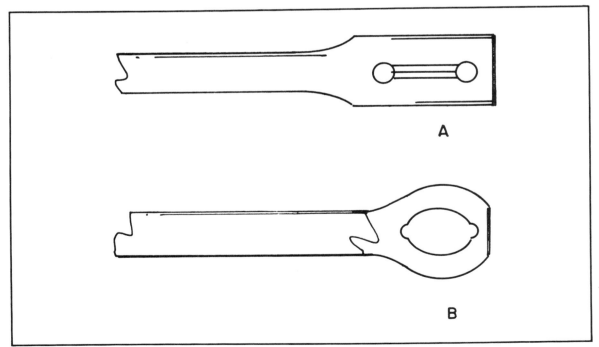

Fig. 15-30. Split between the holes as shown at "A." Open up a slot as at "B."

232

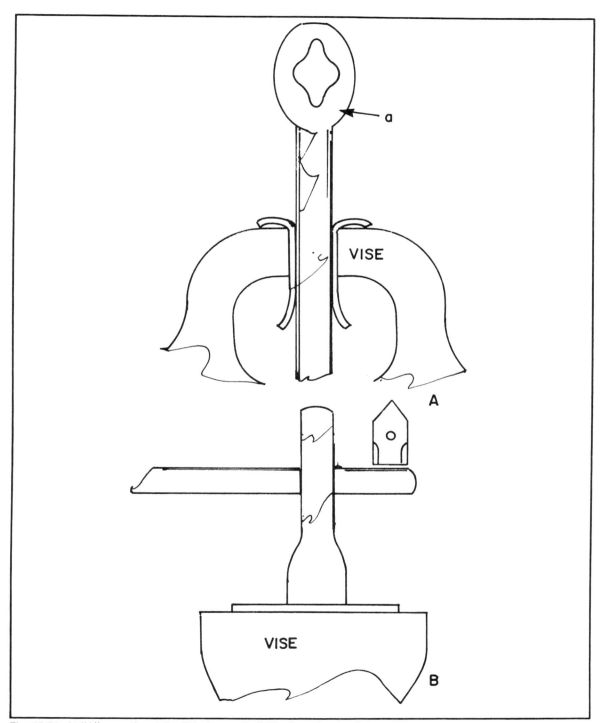

Fig. 15-31. At "A" smooth out the little bump, "a." The bumping bar is in position at "B."

shaped when it is finished, and the stock should be smooth and round so rope can be tied into it. If the eye is rough, the rope will soon wear through. Figure 5-32 shows the finished eye in its final shape. Complete this eye before you start on the hook portion.

Forge the body of the hook round. Forge a 7/16-inch neck below the eye. Taper this neck out to full rounded stock size, but don't weaken the eye (Fig. 15-32).

Draw out the 1 1/4-inch point; then shape the hook as you did with the small eye hook. They won't be the same size in every respect, but they must have the same pattern design so they work properly.

Figure 15-33 shows two views of the finished hook.

Making a Trace Hook

This trace hook is not designed to pick up heavy loads. It is used to hook harness traces to the singletrees or to the whiffletrees of a wagon. In other uses it is particularly handy for tying loads on a pickup or for tying canvas covers. Its design prevents unwanted snagging of lines or bungie cords. With some modification it makes a side hook that can be permanently installed on the side of a pickup bed or a trailer bed.

Stock Required

3/8-inch round stock, 10 inches long, M.S.

Procedure

Use tongs from the start of the heats when you make this hook.

Cold bend the bar in the middle so a 50-cent piece will fit in the bow. Don't bring the legs parallel yet (Fig. 15-34).

Bend each leg outward a small amount as shown in Fig. 15-34. All bends are in the same plane.

Close the legs together so they are parallel (Fig. 15-34). The completed bend should form a teardrop shape 3 inches long. The ends of the two legs should be even.

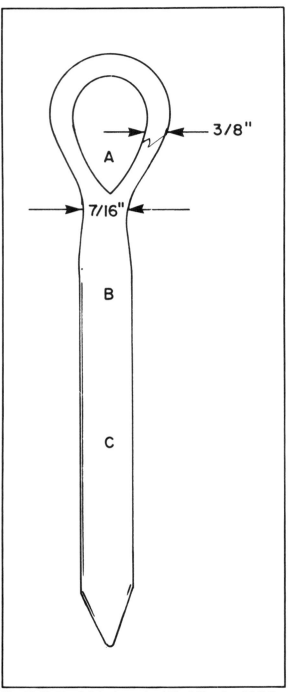

Fig. 15-32. The finished eye should look like view "A." Taper the neck and make it round as at "B." The rounded body and point look like view "C."

234

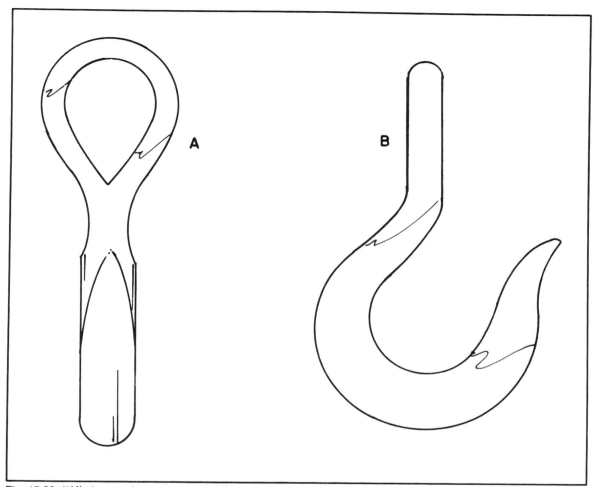

Fig. 15-33. "A" shows a front view, and "B" is a side view of the finished large eye slip hook.

Heat the full length of the two legs to an orange-red heat and flux both sides and the end to 1/2 inch from the "V" (Fig. 15-35).

Bring the entire leg length that is covered with flux to an even welding heat. When it is ready to weld, hold the work so that the legs are one over the other on the anvil; weld the entire length, starting at the ends. Work quickly and hit so that you do not push the top leg off the lower one. Strike up to the end of the flux. Reflux and go back into the fire. From this point on you will be welding and shaping at the same time.

In the next heat start at the leg ends and hit hard to flatten them to about 7/16 inch thick.

Lighten the blow as you quickly proceed toward the "V" of the legs. Work quickly and accurately. The weld should be firm now. Go back to the end and start to draw out a round taper. Keep the work hot. When it reaches orange, stop striking. Reheat to a light yellow-orange and hammer the legs into a taper with a 1/8-inch round point (Fig. 15-35). The seam between the legs should disappear in about one-half the length of the weld. The point will be ragged.

Cut off the ragged end and work the taper down to a somewhat square-sided, 1/8-inch blunt point. Figure 15-35 shows a cutaway of sections of the finished weld and point. No effort need be made to

235

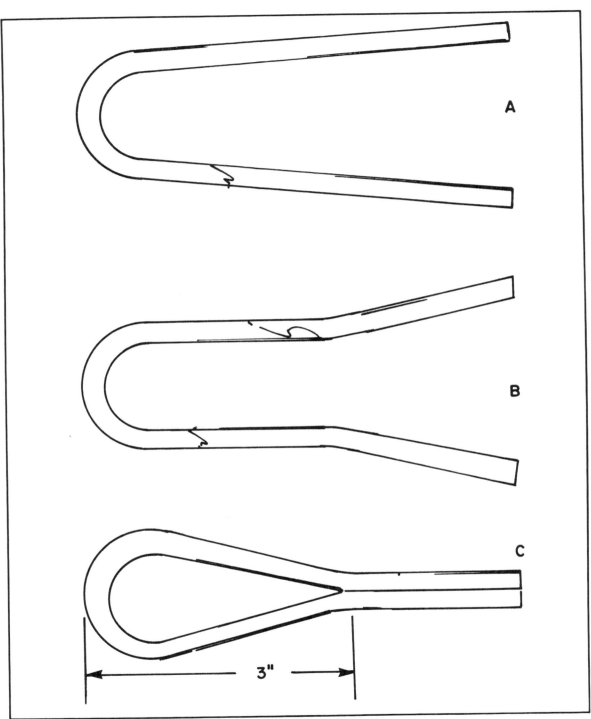

Fig. 15-34. The illustrations show the sequence of the bends needed to form the hook blank.

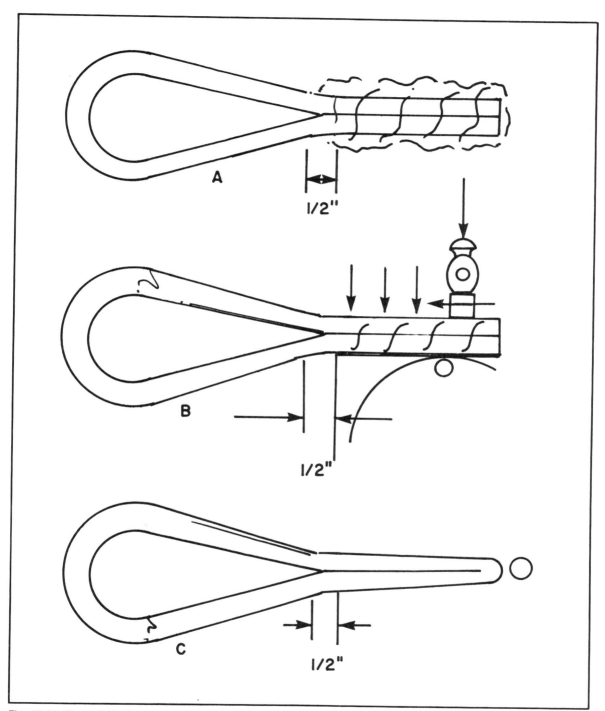

Fig. 15-35. The weld is fluxed at "A." Strike the weld first at the end and move toward the bow as shown at "B." At "C" the weld is complete.

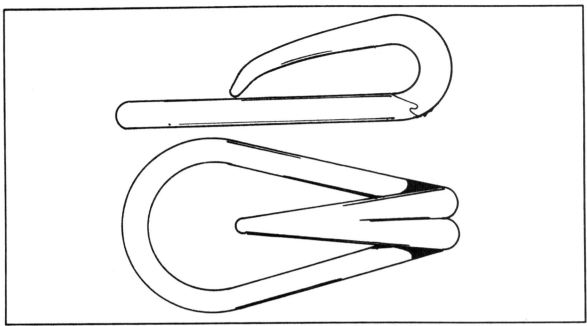

Fig. 15-36. Bend the leg area back over the teardrop.

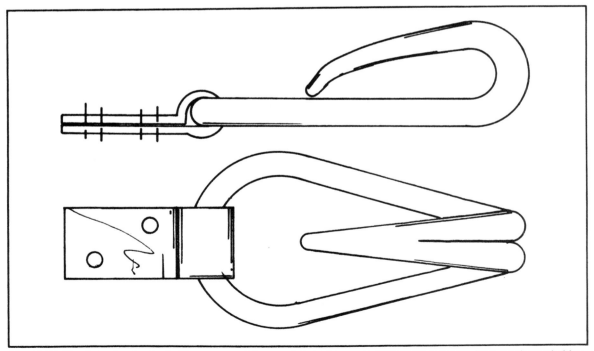

Fig. 15-37. The trace hook adapted for wagon, pickup, or tote trailer sides. This hook is not likely to catch on clothing, packages, or other items passing close by.

make any part of the weld area round.

Reheat leg and weld area to a yellow-orange heat from the "V." Bend it back over the teardrop, starting at the "V" (Fig. 15-36). This hook should be normalized throughout the welded and forged area. The cold bend need not be normalized.

This hook can be fastened to a rope, bungie cord, or end of a chain. The teardrop can be made with a flat portion. This allows a strap to pass through it so that it could be bolted to the side of a pickup bed or a tote trailer (Fig. 15-37). The idea of this design is to require that the tie line or ring be placed into the hook. It limits the size of the line or link that can enter the bowl. The point will not grab onto most items that are dragged over it.

Remember that chain, shackles, and hooks are not forgiving regardless of their shape, size, or maker. When a load comes on them, it is usually all at once, a *shock load*, and the fastenings are subject to failure without warning.

Chapter 16

Hints and Kinks: Solutions to Common Problems and Tricks of the Trade

YOU HAVE LEARNED THE GENERAL PROCESS-
es of making a piece of iron into something
useful. Only a few items cannot be made using
these basic procedures. In this chapter you will
learn a few new processes, some ways to approach
a project, and some odds and ends of advice.

A LEATHER APRON

Your best bet for getting a good leather shop apron
is to make it yourself. This can be done with a little money and a little effort. The best place to buy
leather in my region is in small towns. The leather
outlets sometimes handle seconds and large scraps.
Cowhide will make a good apron at a reasonable
cost. Buy "dry tanned" leather in a garment thickness. This will be a thin, flexible skin that has been
split down to about 1/16 inch thick.

Before you buy your leather, find an old bed-
sheet or other discarded fabric or buy new muslin
from a fabric store to make a pattern of the apron
you want. Cut and adjust your fabric so that it hangs
right and covers you thoroughly (Fig. 16-1). Leather
is sold by the square foot, but it comes in irregular

shapes. You will need to transfer your cloth pattern to paper to take with you when you go
shopping.

Glue newspapers together to make a piece
large enough to cover the pattern. Lay the paper
on the floor, lay the pattern over it, and trace
around the cloth pattern with a marking pen. Cut
out on the lines, and you have a paper pattern that
can be toted from store to store.

When you are considering a piece of leather,
lay the paper pattern out on it so that you can tell
if there is enough leather and little waste. Sometimes you can find two or three pieces, enough to
complete the apron, that can be sewn together and
that will be cheaper than a single large piece. Don't
forget that you will need leather for the shoulder
straps.

Talk to the storekeeper about how to go about
doing the leather work. He can give you good suggestions and explain methods of working.

HOW TO TREAT A NEW ANVIL

If you buy a new anvil, you will want to grind some

of the edges to provide small radii for some of your work. Do not grind or file any edge until you have tried to shape a few pieces on it. Before you make any changes to an edge, set the anvil up with the horn to your right for a while; then try it with the horn to your left. Bend some hot scrap iron on the horn each way to get the feel. You will find that one direction is more comfortable for you than the

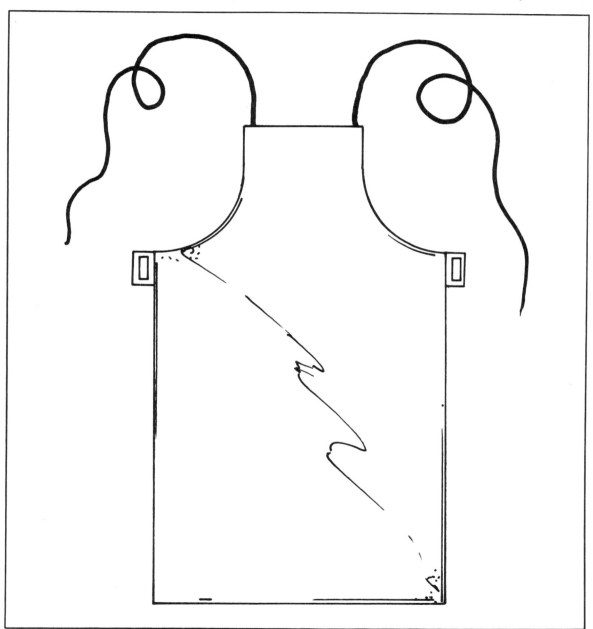

Fig. 16-1. You can make a good blacksmith's apron. To protect you adequately, it should reach from above your shirt pocket to well below your knees. It should wrap around your body.

other. Start with it in the more comfortable position. You can always change it later if you want.

After you have used your new anvil for a few days, you will learn what a sharp edge does when you try to make a bend over it. It tends to cut your work, but that very feature of a sharp or abrupt edge on the anvil face is a great asset when you learn to take advantage of it.

A very small radius along a portion of the face is almost necessary for working up bends that have a small inside radius and for other types of work. You will want to file a portion of the sharp edge to produce this radius. For starters make any radius small when you are working it up. Start with a 1/8-inch radius at the step and continue this back about 4 inches; fade it out in the next inch so that the total change in the edge is not more than 5 inches long. Do this to both sides so they will match up straight across the face from each other. Use the anvil for a long time before you change it any more.

Usually the point of the horn will serve for most radii or close bent work when the 1/8-inch radius is not large enough. Most new anvils will have the edges of the face softened a little so they don't chip or break. Thus they can be filed. Use a large, sharp mill file. Use heavy pressure and move the file slowly, letting it get a bite. To judge how much metal to remove, guide your eye with this thought: a 1/16-inch radius will give the appearance of the round or "roll" of a 16-penny nail or the shank of a number 10 wood screw. A 1/8-inch radius will give the appearance of the roll of a 1/4-inch bolt shank.

DESIGNING YOUR PROJECT

Before you make an object, you first see it in your mind's eye, but usually in an incomplete form. Get in the habit of drawing on paper or on a blackboard the parts and pieces of your project. Lines are easy to erase and change, and no waste of material or fuel is involved. It might be a good idea to review a book on perspective drawing.

Sketching your project has several advantages. You will complete the picture that is in your mind's eye and produce a permanent record to which you can refer. Because you have this permanent picture, your mind is more free to work out the problems of actually shaping the hot iron. By studying your sketches and drawings, you will be better able to work out the sequence of events to be followed in making the object.

THE PROPER SEQUENCE

Getting things in the proper sequence can be a real problem. It is very easy to "lock yourself out." That is, you may perform a portion of the forging process too soon or too late and prevent yourself from going any farther on that piece of iron. If this happens, you start over. This is a heartbreaker, but it happens to all of us now and then.

Sketches and drawings will help you get your steps in the proper sequence. Think a job through before you begin; blacksmithing is a thinking trade. You are creating something from an idea; be patient with yourself. Be willing to experiment and practice, and you will find that you avoid most of the traps and disappointments.

USING THE HORN OF THE ANVIL

As you learned earlier, no rule says the horn must be to your left or to your right. Try it both ways and set up your anvil the way it suits you.

The Horn as a Bottom Fuller

One very good use for your horn is as a variable bottom fuller. You made and used a hand-held fuller in Chapter 12. You can also use the anvil horn as a fuller. Suppose that your project calls for an eye or a loop with a hole in it that is bigger than the stock. Also suppose that it must have a thin wall that is too delicate or otherwise impractical to weld. As an example assume that you will be making a 1-inch round eye on the end of a 1/4-inch by 3/4-inch bar. The process is one of punching and drawing.

You first punch a 1/4-inch hole, 3/4 inch from the end of the bar. Carefully drift the hole out to 3/8 inch or even to 1/2 inch so that it will just start over the point or beak of the horn (Fig. 16-2). Note the angle of the eye over the horn.

Draw down the excess. This adds length to the

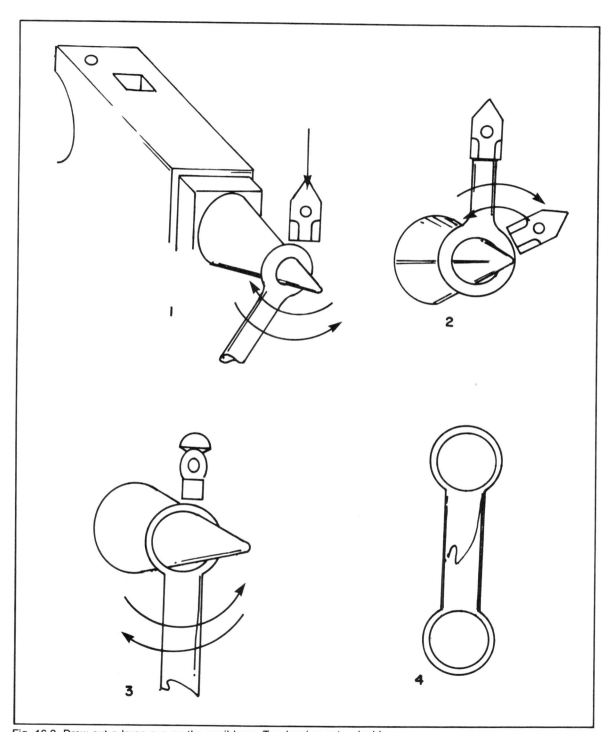

Fig. 16-2. Draw out a large eye on the anvil horn. Try drawing out a double.

stock around the eye. Keep your metal hot. Do not work it below a red. As the extra metal is drawn out, it will widen. Flatten it back to size frequently to avoid cold shuts, crimps, that cannot be removed. As the eye expands, keep rocking the bar back and forth under the beak. Keep turning it over to keep the lengthening process even. In this type of forging, finish up the work as you go along; there is no going back. Stop when you have what you want.

The Profile of the Horn

Take a fresh look at the anvil horn. From the top view it has a triangular profile. Therefore, when you are working on the horn, hold your work across the desired profile rather than across the axis, or your work will be moving faster on one side than on the other (Fig. 16-3).

When you are about to make hooks, rings, or any bend over the horn, first ask yourself, "Do I want to fuller this work? Draw it out? Just bend it?" If the answer is to just bend it, then use a wiping blow. Don't crush the metal, or it will lengthen. Visualize your anvil as standing on its heel. The horn would then become a cone over which you could work a stretching action. You can work this same stretching action by using your hammer horizontally when the anvil is in its normal position.

Do not scar the horn. It is as important as the anvil face and much softer. If it were as hard as the face, it would break off easily.

To widen a piece, lay it the long way on the anvil horn and work near the point, but not over the point. This would make ridges in your work. This is another method of fullering your work. When you work on the horn, aim the hammer at a single point on the horn and pass the work back and forth under it (Fig. 16-4).

CARE OF YOUR POST VISE

When you hold a piece in one end of the jaws of your vise, you spring and bind the vise pivot or hinge. The racking caused by the off-center grip can spring the jaws out of line easily and permanently.

To avoid this, place a scrap of metal the same size as your work in the other end of the jaws. If the scrap is 5/16 inch or less, simply grab it with a wooden spring clothespin. Lay the clothespin across the jaw and let the scrap dangle down into the bite. The spacer will hang there while you adjust your work (Fig. 16-5).

If the spacer has to be larger than 5/16 inch, use a suitable scrap about 4 inches long and split it lengthwise for about 3/4 inch and form a "T."

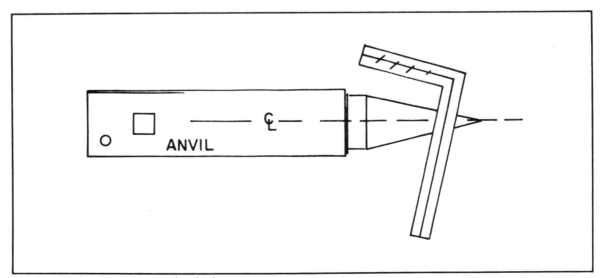

Fig. 16-3. Notice the various angles the horn presents.

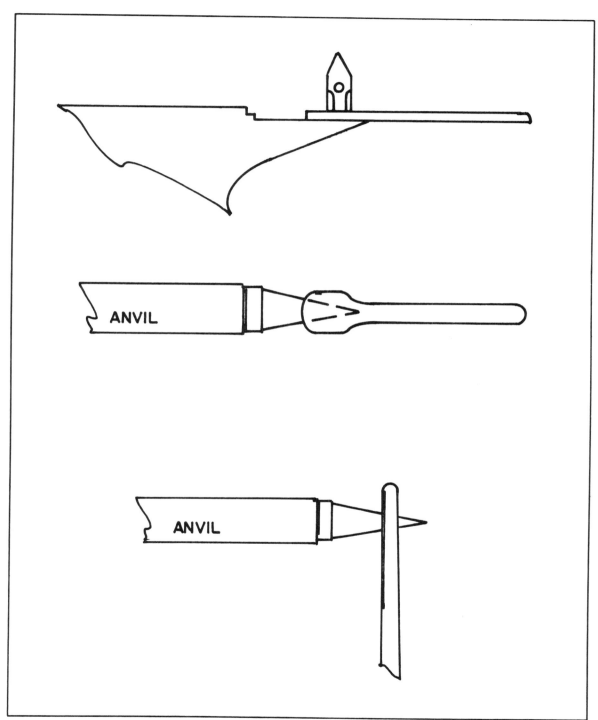

Fig. 16-4. Use the horn to widen a piece or to lengthen it.

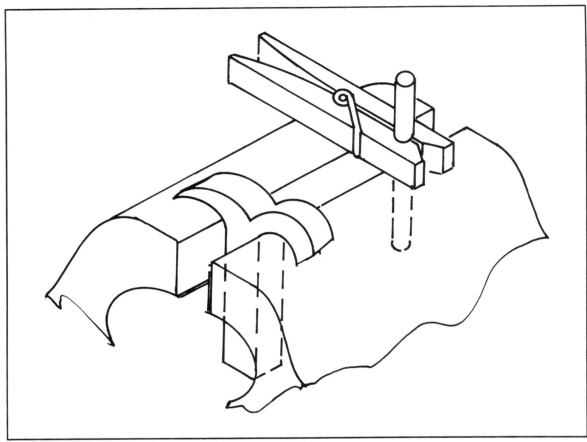

Fig. 16-5. Protect the vise from springing by using a spacer.

To make this, either cut it with a hacksaw and then heat and bend the ears out, or heat the scrap and hot-cut it; then bend the ears out.

LOCAL COOLING

Local cooling is the process of quickly cooling a small portion of work within a heat. This process allows you to control the limits of a bend or to hold a forging heat within definite limits. Local cooling can be done by putting water on a given area with the dribble can or by quenching a portion of the work. This trick is particularly useful when you are upsetting.

JAW GUARDS FOR THE VISE

Jaw guards protect hot or delicate work when it is held in the vise. Make them from pieces of 14- to 18-gauge steel sheet metal. They should be as wide as your vise jaws are long. Allow enough top flap so that they can hang on the vise jaws without falling off when the vise is open. The bend is not made sharp so when hot or delicate work is held in the vise, the rounded or softened bend protects the work from marks made by the sharp top edge of the vise jaw and from any marks or imperfections on the face of the jaw. Jaw guards are illustrated in use in Chapter 15, Figs. 15-10 through 15-12.

A HANDY RIVET-CUTTING JIG

A rivet-cutting jig makes it simple to cut many rivets of a given size to the same length. It is held in the vise.

Stock Required

A piece of mild steel 1/2 inch square and about 3 inches long.

Procedure

Drill a 3/16-inch hole through the center line of one side of the bar, 3/8 inch from one end.

Lock the bar in the vise with the drilled end straight up and about 5/8 inch above the jaws. Arrange the bar so the drilled hole is perpendicular to the vise screw.

Lay out a line on top of the bar, perpendicular to the hole and 3/8 inch from one side (Fig. 16-6).

Use an 18-tooth hacksaw to split the bar down, edgewise, to just below the hole. Be sure that the cut is to the side of the line so that 3/8 inch of solid stock remains (Fig. 16-6).

File away about 1/16 inch of the bar from the top down to the top of the hole. Do this on the outer face of the 3/8-inch portion. This creates a little space between the head of the rivet and the top of the jig and will allow any suitable device, such as the back of an old hacksaw blade, to be used as an extractor.

Put your 3/16-inch by 5/8-inch rivet into the hole from the 3/8-inch side. Hold it in tightly with your thumb so it will not revolve with the motion of the saw.

Use a 24- or 32-point hacksaw. Carry most of the saw's weight and saw the rivet in two in the slot (Fig. 16-6).

Pry out the rivet and put in a new one. It will punch out the cut-off piece of the preceding one. The rivet will be 3/8 inch long. This type of jig can be made up for any size rivet.

MEASURING ON YOUR ANVIL

It is convenient when you are working hot iron to

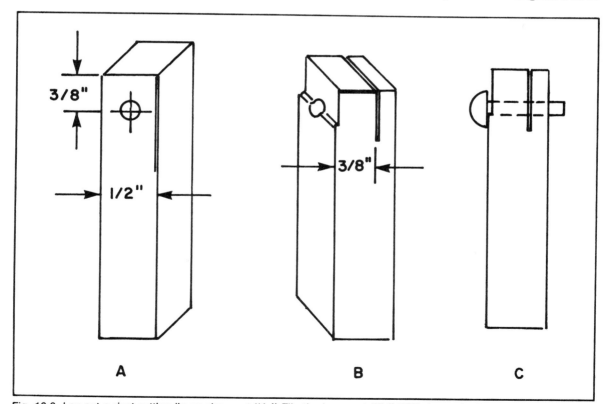

Fig. 16-6. Lay out a rivet-cutting jig as shown at "A." File the bar as at "B." "C" shows the jig in use.

measurements to lay out some chalk marks on the face or side of the anvil. Let each mark be a desired length. Then all you need to do is hold the piece of work up to the mark to check it out. This is much faster than using a tape measure or ruler and does not require putting down the work or your hammer (Fig. 16-7).

When you are finished with the marks, rub them out. When you are bending small eyes or return bends, lay out their measurements on the anvil face or side in chalk marks.

SOME NOTES ON COAL

All coal is made up of carbon, volatile matter, water, ash, various gasses, dirt, and rocks in varying amounts. When coal is burning it breaks down into its components. What is left, after the carbon, volatiles, and water vapor are gone, is the ash, dirt, and rock. The ash is anything in the coal that was not burned in the forge. These noncombustibles get so hot that a quantity of material melts and flows to the bottom of the fire and forms a rather flat blob over the grate. This blob is called a *clinker*. If it is not removed from time to time, it will nearly shut off the air blast at the grate.

To get rid of the clinker, let the fire rest for a few minutes. The clinker will cool and harden somewhat. Slide the blade of your lance poker down along the edge of the fire to the grate, then along the grate under the clinker. Tip the handle of the poker up to about 30 degrees and slip the shovel under the whole works. Pull the poker out. Slide it into the fire on top of the clinker to hold the clinker onto the shovel as you tip the clinker over and dump the fire back onto the grate. After the clinker is out, reorganize your fire and proceed as usual. Don't forget to open the ash door at the bottom of the tuyere.

Sometimes enough ash and trash will collect in the tube below the grate to shut off the air flow. Check your air pipe from time to time to be sure it is open.

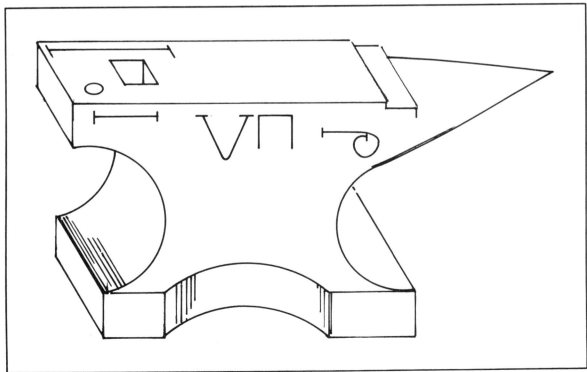

Fig. 16-7. Chalk marks on the face or side of the anvil will give you a quick check on measurements.

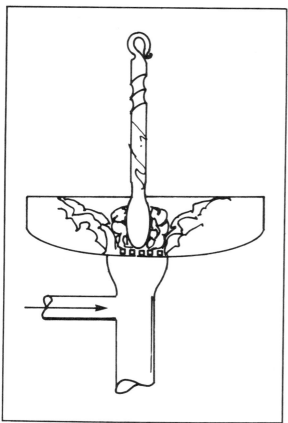

Fig. 16-8. You can punch a hole in the clinker with your lance poker if time does not permit you to remove the clinker.

If you have a clinker but need only one or two more heats, put your lance poker straight through the center of the fire and dig a hole in the clinker. Then proceed as usual (Fig. 16-8).

The dark gray dust that collects in the chimney and all around the forge and on top of things in the shop is the same material as the clinker. The tiny particles, *fly ash*, blow out of the fire with the air blast. I mention this from time to time as trash from the fire. It sticks to your hot iron and makes up part of the scale every time the metal is heated to a full forging heat.

COMPANIONSHIP

Blacksmiths, like other specialists, like to get together from time to time to share experiences, watch other blacksmiths give demonstrations, and make friends within the trade. At least 22 regional organizations hold meetings and publish newsletters. Many more smaller groups operate at a local level. Often the local groups are branches of a regional group.

The national association is called Artist Blacksmith Association of North America or ABANA. If you write ABANA, they will send you the address of your regional group. They all operate on a volunteer basis, so their mailing addresses change from time to time. To find a current address for ABANA, find a blacksmith in your town who might know or write to one of the commercial publications listed in Appendix A of this book.

I recommend that you join at least one of the groups. It will give you someone to turn to when you run into snags; the newsletters and meetings will give you new ideas and new ways to approach problems; the get-togethers are helpful and fun.

A FINAL REMINDER

You now have a good grasp of the fundamental processes of blacksmithing. From this point you can develop your skills along whatever path your interests take you.

Always remember to think things out, to keep records, and to maintain safety habits. Be creative and experiment with expressing modern shapes and ideas in this traditional medium. Above all, enjoy your work.

Appendices

Appendix A
Publications

BELOW ARE NAMES AND CURRENT ADDRESS-es of publications directed to blacksmiths and/or farriers. Many blacksmiths' associations publish magazines or newsletters, but I have not included their addresses. Because they are usually edited by volunteers, the addresses change as new people assume the duties of editor.

Anvil
P.O. Box 774387
Steam Springs, CO 84077

American Farrier's Journal
P.O. Box 700
Ayer, MA 01432

Fabricator
29996 Grandview Avenue, N.E., Suite 109
Atlanta, GA 30305

The Blacksmith's Gazette
P.O. 1268
Mount Vernon, WA 98273

The Hammer
c/o The Flax Company
180 North Wabash Avenue
Chicago, IL 60601

Appendix B

Finished Projects

THE FOLLOWING PHOTOGRAPHS SHOW THE kinds of ironwork that can be made by someone who has mastered the techniques presented in this book. Other designs are limited only by a smith's imagination and willingness to practice.

All the ironwork was forged by Jim Converse, Pat Converse took the photographs.

A three-piece fireplace set with stand. The handles have animal heads. The set stands 32 1/2 inches high. It was made from various sizes of square stock. Techniques used include splitting, twisting, and forge welding. No modern techniques were used.

This barbecue-fork-and-spoon set is 22 inches high. The bowl of the spoon is made of heavy sheet metal shaped on the anvil and swage block. The entire fork and the handle of the spoon are made from one piece of 1/8-inch-by-3/4-inch flat bar stock.

The trammel is 21 inches long in a closed position and 31 inches long when open. Trammels were used by colonial housewives to adjust the height of a pot over the fire in the fireplace. (The copper kettle shown was commercially made in Portugal.) The main body of the trammel is made from two pieces of 1/8-inch-by-3/4-inch flat stock.

I built this chest out of wood and riveted the forged iron work to it. The chest is 15 inches long, 12 inches wide, and 12 1/2 inches high. I use it to hold supplies for my muzzle-loading rifle. It is often fun to combine forged iron with wood.

258

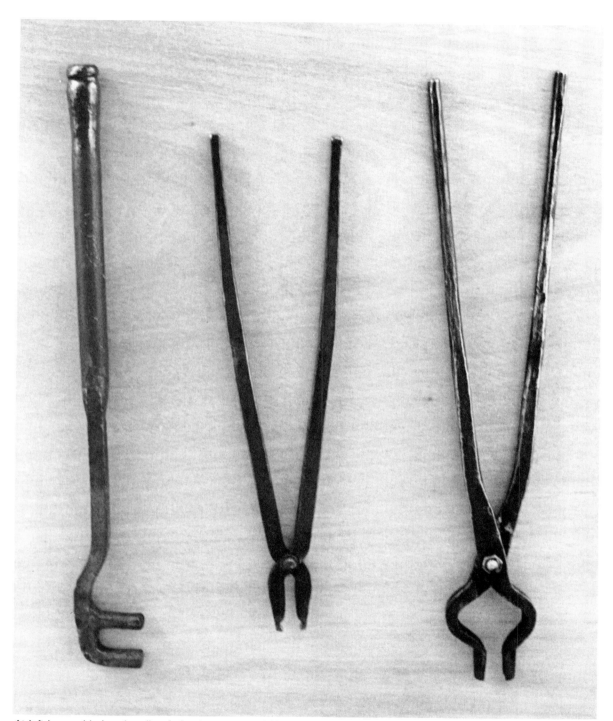

At left is a welded up bending fork, at center a quickie ring tong, and at the right is a hollow bit bolt tong. These are similar to work pieces described in the text.

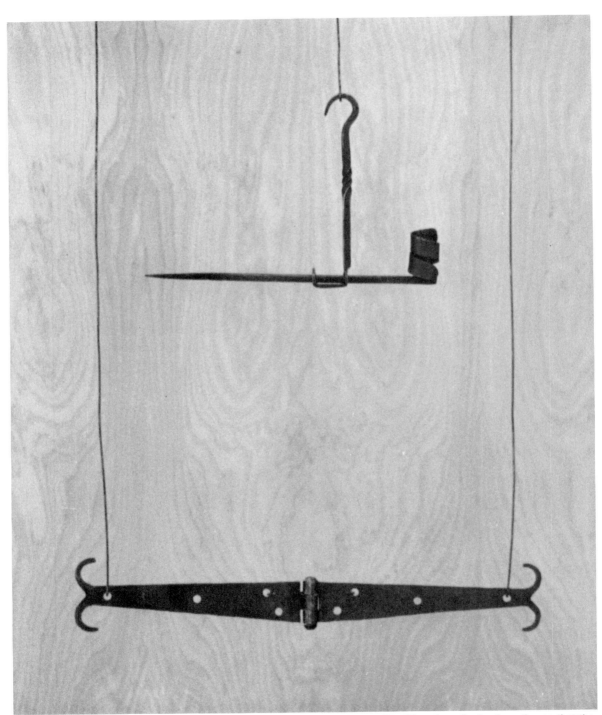

The miner's candle holder (top) is 9 inches long. The piece holding the candle slides along the hook portion so that the candle can be balanced according to its weight. The colonial style strap hinge (bottom) is 15 inches long when open.

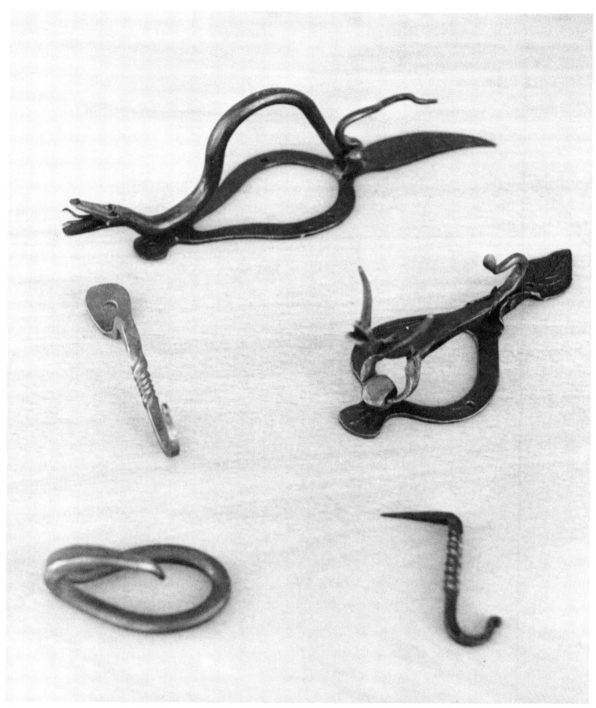

Clockwise from the top are a snake door knocker, a horned dragon knocker (the dragon carries a rock to knock with), a drive hook, a trace hook, and a pad eye hanger.

These are hearth tools similar to the ones described in Chapter 6.

This dragon door pull is 15 1/2 inches high. The back plate is made from 3/16-inch plate. The dragon is forged from 3/4-inch solid, square stock.

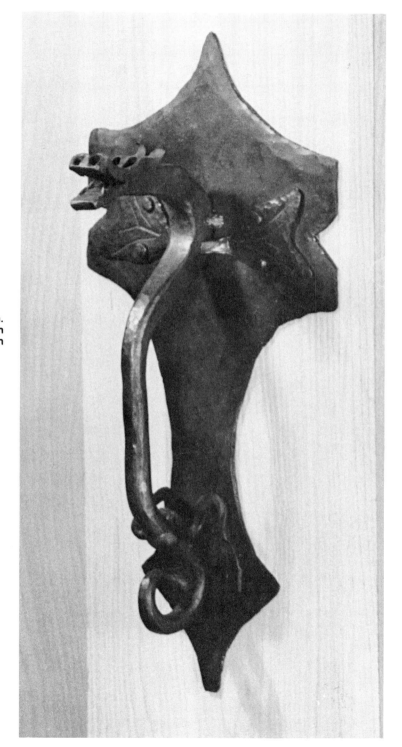

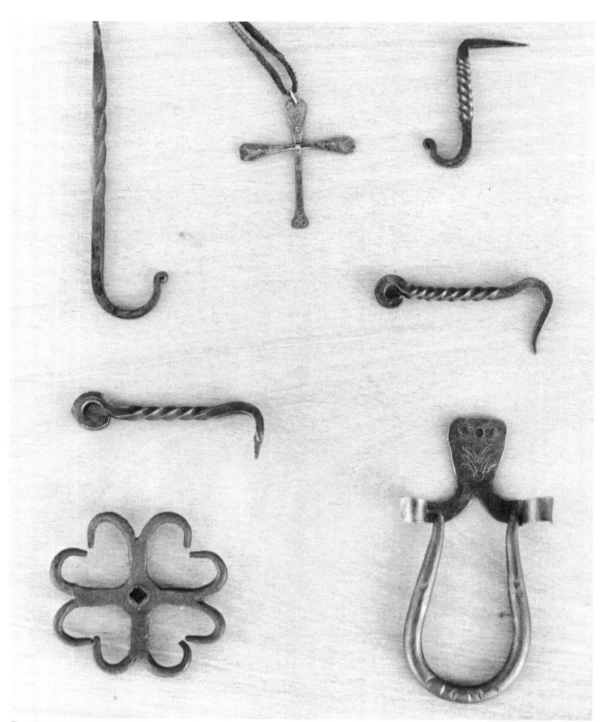

Reading clockwise from the top are a decorative cross, a drive hook, a gate hook, a door knocker, a flower pattern water faucet handle, another style gate hook, and a flush wall hanger.

Glossary

Glossary

I N THIS GLOSSARY WORDS ARE DEFINED AS they apply to traditional blacksmithing and as they are used in this book.

ABANA—Artist Blacksmith Association of North America.

AISI—American Iron and Steel Institute.

alloy steel—Iron and various elements mixed to give the iron permanent characteristic changes. Carbon content or heat treating qualities will vary according to the mix.

anneal—The process of using suitable temperatures and cooling to produce the softest state possible in metal and to reduce as much internal stress as possible in any given piece of iron or steel.

anvil tool—Any tool that is installed on, or inserted into, an anvil to perform special services that are not practical if performed on the anvil alone, a tool that can be held in or on the anvil instead of in the blacksmith's hand.

bar stock—See stock.

billet—Any piece of iron or steel that is round or square in cross section and is not less than 1 inch in cross section and not more than 12 inches long.

bite—The amount of the opening and the shape of that portion of the jaws of a tong that actually holds the piece to be worked on. For example, the tongs may have a long bite, a short bite, sharp bite, shaped bite, or a good bite.

blade—The cutting portion of any tool such as a knife, a shovel, or a garden hoe.

blank—Any piece of metal or part thereof that is ready, without further treatment, to be shaped into a final product.

bolster—A piece of steel that is to be placed on the anvil or held in the vise and that contains one or more holes of a specified size and shape. It may be used to finish the shaping of a tenon by driving the tenon into the hole or holes.

bow—In tongs this is the circular shaped portion

of the jaws of the tongs between the bite and the hinge. This is usually built in to increase springiness or to provide for extra capacity behind the bite. In shackles this is the circular shaped portion of the shackle between the eyes.

bump—To bend or reshape a whole product without disfiguring any specific portion of it by using a hammer, considerably heavier than usual, in a gentle manner.

caking quality—A quality of powdered or finely ground coal that causes it to stick or cake together and hold its shape. This quality is very helpful in making coke.

carbon steel—Steel that contains carbon added to increase its hardening ability. In general the American Society for Metals considers steel with less than 0.30 percent carbon to be low carbon; 0.30 percent to 0.50 percent carbon is high carbon.

carbon-alloy steel—A combination of carbon and any of various alloy components in the steel.

choke—To grip a hammer handle close to the hammerhead or to grip the reins of tongs close to the hinge.

circumference—The distance around any circle.

clinker—Noncombustible, nongaseous material in the coal that has melted down and formed a doughlike mass over the grate of the tuyere. When a clinker cools below a molten state, it becomes a brittle solid mass.

coke—A brittle, lightweight material, nearly pure carbon, that remains after the volatiles and most of the noncombustibles have been removed from coal. You make coke in your forge as you burn green coal.

cold-cut—A hardy or chisel made for cutting cold iron or steel.

crimp—A bend in metal, so sharp at the apex that it cannot successfully be forged out. It may be large or small and is to be avoided in all blacksmith work.

critical point temperature—That temperature at which iron and steels lose their magnetic attraction. This is a very important temperature used in heat treating of iron and steels. It lies within a very narrow temperature range.

cutting plate—A large, flat piece of metal, made of iron, steel, or nonferrous metal, that is placed on top of the anvil face to protect the anvil from injury when hot or cold cutting is done.

cut washer—A flat washer left in the raw state after it has been punched out of the parent sheet stock. It is usually oversized to allow for variation in stock size of bolts and rivets.

diameter—The distance across the exact center of a circle.

draw down—To reduce diameter or thickness.

draw out a point—To forge a point on the end of a rod or a bar.

draw the temper—To temper to a desired hardness or to reduce hardness.

dress—To smooth and refine the work.

dribble can—A small tin can nailed to a wooden handle. The can has one 8-penny nail hole in the left edge. It is used to dribble water on unwanted hot spots on the iron while the iron is in the fire.

endo—To move something endways only. To strike one end of a bar while the other end is resting on the anvil to cause all energy to travel the length of the bar only.

eyeball—To look something over, usually to estimate its size or shape.

fly ash—The dusty particles of ash, cinder, and dirt that go into the air from the forge.

fuller—The process of forming an indentation during the forging process in order to move metal one way only. A tool for performing the fullering process.

hand hammer—Any hammer with a head weight of 4 pounds or less, designed to be held in one hand.

hand tool—Any tool held in the hand.

hardy tool—Any tool held in the hardy hole of the anvil.

header—A tool designed to receive the shank of a rivet or nail so that a head can be hammered onto the rivet.

heat—That portion of metal that is to be heated

or is already heated to forging temperatures. "To make a heat" means to heat a work piece to forging temperature.

holding hand—The hand that the smith uses to hold his work piece or tongs while he is working at the anvil or at the fire.

iron—In this book, iron means any iron or steel.

kitchen fat—The fat drippings from meat or fowl that has been strained and is free of water.

linchpin—A form of cotter pin, usually made of flat stock and usually several times as wide as it is thick. It is designed to be used repeatedly.

linchpunch—A hot-punch shaped with an elongated flat nose or point. It is designed to punch narrow elongated holes in round stock to receive a linchpin.

mild steel—See steel.

normalize—To allow a piece of steel or iron to cool slowly from forging heat to room temperature in the atmosphere. This process relieves internal stresses caused by forging. It is not the same as annealing.

quench—To immerse hot iron in a liquid, usually water. The water or oil used as a coolant.

radius—One half the diameter of a circle, the distance from the center of any circle to its edge. "The radius" is the name given to the rounded edge of an anvil. The anvil is ground or filed to the smith's need. The radius avoids producing anvil scars or cuts on the inside of an over-the-edge bend.

rein—A somewhat archaic name for the handles of blacksmith's tongs or pliers.

S.A.E.—Society of Automotive Engineers

slug drift—A drift of a specified accurate size with a short, slight entrance taper on each end. It is used for dressing holes to an exact size.

soak—To soak a piece in the fire means holding it at a given temperature for an extended length of time to allow the heat to become the same internally and externally.

sprinkle can—A tin can with about five or six holes punched in the bottom. It is attached to a handle and is used to sprinkle down the fire.

steel—Any of the purified iron and iron alloys available today.

stock—The metal from which an object will be made.

swage—A tool used for working metal, hot or cold. The metal may be hammered into the swage or hammered down to fit over it.

swage block—A perforated cast iron or steel block with grooved sides. It is used in heading bolts and rivets and for shaping bars or flat metal by hand work.

tang—The nail-shaped end of a chisel, file, or other tool. The tang is usually driven into a wooden handle.

tongue—A flattened projection thinner than the main stock.

tool steel—Any combination of carbon and alloy components. The combination will depend on the requirements for the tool.

vapor blanket—The steam or gas or both created around a piece of hot metal when the metal is dipped in water or oil.

vise tool—Any tool that is held in the vise while it is being used.

Index

Index

Other Bestsellers From TAB

Other Bestsellers From TAB

☐ **66 FAMILY HANDYMAN® WOOD PROJECTS**

Here are 66 practical, imaginative, and decorative projects . . . literally something for every home and every woodworking skill level from novice to advanced cabinet-maker: room dividers, a free-standing corner bench, china/book cabinet, coffee table, desk and storage units, a built-in sewing center, even your own Shaker furniture reproductions! 210 pp., 306 illus. 7″ × 10″.

Paper $14.95 **Hard $21.95**
Book No. 2632

☐ **CABINETS AND VANITIES—A BUILDER'S HANDBOOK—Godley**

Here in easy-to-follow, step-by-step detail is everything you need to know to design, build, and install your own cus-tomized kitchen cabinets and bathroom vanities and cabi-nets for a fraction of the price charged by professional cabinetmakers or kitchen remodelers . . . and for less than a third of what you'd spend for the most cheaply made ready-made cabinets and vanities! 142 pp., 126 illus. 7″ × 10″.

Paper $12.95 **Hard $19.95**
Book No. 1982

☐ **BUILDING OUTDOOR PLAYTHINGS FOR KIDS, WITH PROJECT PLANS—Barnes**

Imagine the delight of your youngsters—children or grandchildren—when you build them their own special back-yard play area complete with swings, climbing bars, sand-boxes, even an A-frame playhouse their own size or a treehouse where they can indulge in their own imaginary adventures. Best of all, discover how you can make excit-ing, custom-designed play equipment at a fraction of the cost of ordinary, ready-made swing sets or sandbox units! It's all here in this practical, step-by-step guide to planning and building safe, sturdy outdoor play equipment. 240 pp., 213 illus. 7″ × 10″.

Paper $12.95 **Hard $21.95**
Book No. 1971

☐ **RAISING CHICKENS—Haynes**

Now veteran chicken handler and hatchery owner Cyn-thia Haynes puts you in touch with the realities, the rewards, and the potential hazards of raising your own chickens . . . and gives you the kind of practical, "voice of experience" advice and guidance that just isn't available from any other source. From choosing the chicken breed for your particu-lar needs to finding a source for chicks or brood hens, you'll find it here! 272 pp., 274 illus. 7″ × 10″.

Paper $12.95 **Hard $21.95**
Book No. 1963

☐ **UPHOLSTERY TECHNIQUES ILLUSTRATED—Gheen**

Here's an easy-to-follow, step-by-step guide to modern upholstery techniques that covers everything from stripping off old covers and padding to restoring and installing new foundations, stuffing, cushions, and covers. All the most up-to-date pro techniques are included along with lots of time- and money-saving "tricks-of-the-trade" not usually shared by professional upholsterers. 352 pp., 549 illus. 7″ × 10″.

Paper $16.95 **Hard $27.95**
Book No. 2602

☐ **HOW TO TROUBLESHOOT AND REPAIR ANY SMALL GAS ENGINE—Dempsey**

Here's time-, money-, and aggravation-saving source-book that covers the full range of two- and four-cycle gas engines from just about every major American manufacturer—from Briggs & Stratton, to West Bend, and others! With the expert advice and step-by-step instructions provided by master mechanic Dempsey, you'll be amazed at how easily you can solve almost any engine problem. 272 pp., 228 illus.

Paper $10.95 **Hard $21.95**
Book No. 1967

☐ **THE WOODTURNER'S BIBLE—2ND EDITION—Blandford**

If you've admired fine, hand-turned wooden candle-sticks, kitchenware, jewelry, or children's toys that sell for high prices in exclusive shops and gift catalogs . . . here's your chance to make your own at a fraction of the cost for your own enjoyment, as gifts, even to sell! If you've tried unsuccessfully to find custom-made architectural woodwork like new posts or stair rails . . . now, you'll be able to make them yourself, easily and inexpensively. And if you're an an-tique collector or refinisher, this book gives you the know-how you need to produce authentic replacement parts from missing drawer pulls to replacement chair rungs or spindles. 400 pp., 332 illus. Large, Easy-To-Use Shop Format, 7″ × 10″.

Paper $16.95 **Hard $24.95**
Book No. 1954

☐ **MAKING KNIVES AND TOOLS—2ND EDITION—Blandford**

Here is the completely revised and expanded new sec-ond edition of a guidebook that has become the "bible" in its field. Written by a highly respected metalwork-ing/woodworking craftsman, it shows you how you can make almost any type of edged tool or knife, at amazingly afford-able cost! You'll learn how to make pro-quality knives and tools from plain kitchen knives to shaping tools. 256 pp., 187 illus.

Paper $12.95 **Hard $18.95**
Book No. 1944

Other Bestsellers From TAB